APOCRYPHA

An Introduction to Extra-Biblical Literature

V. REV. DR. STEPHEN DE YOUNG

ANCIENT FAITH PUBLISHING
CHESTERTON, INDIANA

Cover Photo: ©Shaiith-Shutterstock
Cover engraving: ClipArt ETC
Back Cover Image: © Sergey Panyche-Shutterstock

Published by:
  Ancient Faith Publishing
  A Division of Ancient Faith Ministries
  1050 Broadway, Suite 14
  Chesterton, IN 46304

ISBN: 978-1-955890-36-6

Library of Congress Control Number: 2023933057

Contents

Extra-Biblical Literature and the Orthodox Church

Understanding Canonicity

MODERN WESTERN CULTURE, both within and outside the Church, is deeply influenced by Protestantism and, in particular, puritan Protestantism. This means that regarding ancient religious literature from the Jewish and Christian traditions, our views have been shaped by a particular form of the belief in *sola scriptura,* or "scripture alone." This understanding of the Scriptures, simply put, divides such ancient religious literature into two categories: what is included in the Bible and what is not. What is included is considered to be of ultimate value. What is *not* included is seen to have no value or is even pejoratively labeled as heretical or filled with false teaching. Even Protestantism's most frequent debate partner, Roman Catholicism, has come to debate only what should be included in the Bible rather than questioning this understanding of canonicity as such.

The binary understanding of canonicity brings with it a number of mostly unexamined presuppositions. It assumes, for example, that at some point in time, a particular group decided on the contents of the Scriptures. If the self-proclaimed defenders of canonicity do not use the word "decided," then they will say that the canon had been "recognized." Yet they still understand this recognition of the canon as something that happened at some specific point in the history of the early Church. Whoever the involved parties were, the assumption is that they saw some problems with any and all of the noncanonical texts, leading to their exclusion. According to this reasoning, these non-biblical texts are, at best, irrelevant to Christian theology, if not outright harmful to Christians.

The Christian East, however, has not understood canonicity and the exact table of contents of the Scriptures in this binary manner. First, while all Eastern churches ultimately have accepted the same twenty-seven texts as the New Testament, this acceptance took place over several centuries. The Revelation of St. John did not begin to gain widespread recognition until the sixth century and still did not enjoy full acceptance as late as the ninth. Additionally, the exact contents of the Old Testament vary between Eastern churches: the Coptic, Ethiopian, Slavic, and Greek churches have received different books. These churches recognize the reality that the canons of both testaments were never established by an authoritative act. This state of affairs is acceptable in the East because the East has traditionally taken a view of canonicity that includes three categories.

Three Types of Canonicity
The first category is what could be called "canon" proper: the texts that are read authoritatively in the worship of the Church. The second category consists of books not read in the Church

but considered beneficial for Christians to read in the home. The third category consists of books not to be read at all—books that are deemed to be harmful or heretical. Disagreements, then, between Eastern churches about whether or not a book belongs to the Old Testament are not arguments about whether a book is heretical or its theology is false. Rather, they are disagreements as to whether that text should be read liturgically in the Church or whether it is merely helpful to Christians for reading in the home and in educational settings. Within the first few centuries of the Church, both East and West shared broad agreement about the contents of the third, harmful category. The precise borders of the first two categories, however, differ from church to church. But that difference is of such a nature that the diversity is easily tolerated.

At the beginning of the ninth century AD, St. Nikephoros, then Patriarch of Constantinople, published a text called the *Chronography*, which recorded history from the creation of the world up until his day. Appended to the end of this text is a record, up to that point, of what books belonged to those first two categories. As books of the first category to be read liturgically in the Church, St. Nikephoros lists the shorter, Hebrew canon of the Old Testament and all the books of the New Testament except for the Revelation of St. John.

The patriarch then lists books of each Testament that are accepted by some churches and not others. For the Old Testament, he lists the books of the longer Latin and Greek Old Testaments as well as the Odes of Solomon. For the New Testament, he lists the Revelation of St. John as well as the Revelation of St. Peter, the Epistle of Barnabas, and the Gospel of the Hebrews.

Saint Nikephoros then lists the books considered "apocrypha," not read in churches but useful for Christian education.[1]

For the Old Testament apocrypha, he lists a number of Jewish texts of the Second Temple period. For the New Testament, he lists a number of noncanonical acts of various apostles, gospels, and texts that we now know as the Apostolic Fathers. Saint Nikephoros's attitude toward these works is not an exception; it was the general rule within the Byzantine Church. The comprehensive nature of his list of texts, however, is uniquely helpful in letting us know exactly what the Christian Church in the East considered valuable among all the literature that survived from those early centuries. We find the works from Nikephoros's list preserved at ancient Orthodox monastic settlements and elsewhere, bearing witness that the list represented the general opinion in the Church.

Introducing Worthwhile Texts to Orthodox Christians

The goal of this book is to serve as an introduction to this body of literature for contemporary Orthodox Christian readers. That said, we will not address many other ancient works, such as the six particular books known as "the apocrypha" in Western discussions of the Old Testament canon. We also will not discuss many of the texts from the early Church regarding martyrs, or various epistles; they are the subject of a great deal of scholarship available elsewhere.

---

1   In modern Western discussions, "the apocrypha" refers to a particular set of texts accepted as canonical within Roman Catholicism and not within Protestantism. Saint Nikephoros uses the term in a more general sense that we will explore further in this book.

Further, it lies beyond the scope of this book to discuss the vast number of texts from the early Church that were deemed heretical at various times and in various places. Since the discovery of the Nag Hammadi library in 1945, a number of books associated with ancient forms of Gnosticism have become available in English. Many of these, such as the Gospel of Mary and the Gospel of Truth, have become well known in modern media circles and are the subject of other books as well. They belong to the third category, books not to be read, which we will not cover here.

The Hellenization of the Christian Faith?

The two most important categories of extra-biblical literature are Second Temple Jewish literature and early Christian writings, such as the works of the Apostolic Fathers. Second Temple Jewish literature reveals to us the religious world and mindset of the first century AD, from which Christianity emerged. It shows us the theological lens through which the apostles viewed the revelation that came in the Person of Jesus Christ. The Apostolic Fathers and the Fathers of the second and third centuries show us the continuity with and transformation of Second Temple Judaism, which came to constitute the Christian religion. Not only is the New Testament rife with allusions and, in a few cases, direct references and quotations from Second Temple Jewish literature, so are the early Fathers. They understand the Scriptures, both the Old and the New Testament, through that same religious grid.[2]

This is not to say that the later Fathers moved away from this

---

2   The Second Temple Jewish worldview is the subject of my book *The Religion of the Apostles*, also from Ancient Faith Publishing (2021).

understanding or replaced it with another. It has become a commonplace to argue that at some point—though this point differs in the telling—Christianity in the East moved away from its Jewish roots to replace them with Greek philosophy, hellenizing the religion. This view is more related to a way of reading certain later Fathers than to the words of the Fathers themselves or their mindset. As the Fathers brought in new Greek terminology, some critics assume that these words bring with them meanings from other philosophical systems, usually Platonism. Instead, the Fathers use Greek language from the philosophical and, in some cases, religious worlds to describe Christian concepts that emerged from Second Temple Judaism. Philosophical and religious Greek terminology is best suited to conveying these ideas.

When reading the words of the Fathers in light of Second Temple and early Christian texts, particularly in the Greek or in Greek translation, it becomes apparent throughout Orthodox history that the Fathers, Orthodox iconography, and Orthodox hymnography are filled with references to this extra-biblical literature and its interpretation of the scriptural text.

The greatest demonstration of this reality is that the vast majority of the Second Temple Jewish literature still available in the world has been preserved to the present day by the Orthodox Church. While finds such as the Dead Sea Scrolls include many of these works, the primary texts of importance were already known before the Dead Sea Scrolls were discovered in the middle of the twentieth century. These perspectives and religious understandings were handed down not just in oral teaching but also in writing. Readers should not underestimate the importance of this handing down—this "traditioning." Manuscript copies did not simply continue to exist in an Orthodox library; a deposit of Orthodox literature did not just happen to survive for two millennia or more. Instead, Orthodox Christian monastics actively copied these texts over and over again, for centuries. Reading, studying, and copying these works was an expensive and time-consuming exercise. Monastics harbored no ambiguity regarding their extra-biblical nature—the texts are not included in lectionaries or biblical codices. Yet generations of Orthodox Christian faithful considered their preservation to be vitally important for the theological understanding they impart.

Lost to History

That said, not all the texts that appear in St. Nikephoros's list have made their way down from the ninth century to today. Several of them have since been lost to history. Some of them, such as Eldad and Modad and the Prayer of Joseph, have not survived but appear to have been very significant in the Church of the first millennium. Saint Nikephoros records that the Book of Eldad and Modad, for example, consisted of eleven hundred lines. A single four-word quotation of the text in the Shepherd of Hermas is all that has survived, along with a handful of general references to the text from various Fathers. The Prayer of Joseph, likewise, is known only in three quotations in different patristic works.

It is important to remember that the preservation of these works is not merely happenstance. It is not the product of the will of humans, either. Ultimately, as Orthodox Christians who believe in Holy Tradition, we must accept both that the preservation of these texts in the Church reflects their importance and that the loss of certain texts is likewise no accident. Additionally, it is always possible as the life of the Church unfolds upon earth that some of them may again appear and play a part in the Christian life once more.

The texts discussed in this book represent many of the significant examples of Second Temple Jewish literature that have been preserved within the Orthodox Church because of their relevance to understanding the Christian Faith and the Scriptures. Indeed, among educated, literate Orthodox Christians, only recent generations are unfamiliar with these works, as is clear from their transmission and copying history and their presence in all the surviving ancient Orthodox libraries. Likely many more works, and more complete and better manuscripts, were present in the great monastic foundations of Constantinople before its fall.

While most contemporary Orthodox Christians are aware of the importance of the Church's liturgical traditions, its iconographic traditions, and the writings of the Church Fathers to interpreting and understanding Scripture, many—perhaps even most—are unaware that this tradition of extra-biblical texts even exists. Though not Holy Scripture, they represent an important and too-long-neglected element of that tradition that our forefathers in the Faith have handed down to us.

Pseudepigrapha and "Real" Authors

Finally, a note is needed on the subject of pseudepigraphy. Many of the texts discussed here are categorized as *pseudepigrapha*—literally, "false writing." This means that the work was not actually written by the person who it claims, or who others believed, wrote it. In the case of literature that does not name a particular author, it seems odd to discredit a text based on someone having guessed its author at some point in history and guessed wrong. However, in cases in which a text clearly claims to have been written by an Old Testament personage, an apostle, or a leader of the early Church but was not, the issue is more complicated. Modern scholars and laypeople alike take for granted that if a text claims to be written by someone who did not, in fact, write it, the text is lying and therefore ought to be completely disregarded; at the very least, it should be viewed with suspicion.

The ideas that literature derives its authority from the reputation of its author, that it is improper to write under an assumed name, or that historical fiction cannot have any serious function are not self-evident. For many of the books of Scripture considered canonical uncontroversially by all Christians, we do not even know the identity of the author. Other authors are known solely for the work they composed, as, for example, St. Jude in the New Testament. A text with a relatively or even completely unknown author can still have authority. To place the authority in the author causes an entire cascade of problems. For example, if archaeologists uncovered works written by biblical authors but not heretofore included in the Scriptures, would they need to be added to the Bible because of their automatic authority? Does any note or list written by an apostle or other author of Scripture bear apostolic authority de facto? Certainly such a text might be considered a relic and an important part of tradition, but the authority of a work within the Church has never derived directly from the preexisting authority of its author.

Likewise, the legacy of the apostles is a good example of the continuity of authority within the Church through time. At church councils, for example, bishops seen as successors of individual apostles were said to have spoken with the voice of the apostle himself. Why could a bishop not communicate in writing using the same idiom? Further, the tradition of taking the name of a martyr or other saint at baptism is an ancient one dating back to the apostolic era. Part of this patronage relationship with a departed saint is that the living Christian works, strives, and accomplishes the Christian life in the name of his or her patron. Why then would it be a lie to present one's literary efforts in the name of that saint as a way of ascribing any honor or praise to the saint rather than to oneself?

Again, we moderns have the genre of historical fiction. While historical fiction is, at the end of the day, fiction, the adjective "historical" is not meaningless. A work of historical fiction may convey a wealth of accurate information and understanding of the way of life and experience of people in another time and place. Such a work can convey biographical information about historical figures who appear as characters within it. Additionally, it can reveal the way in which a later generation interprets and understands past events and people. In many cases, however, historical fiction does not spell out the fact that it was not really written by the central character who speaks in the first person. Such a book does not necessarily have a disclaimer or explanation that it is a product of a much later era. But someone from another culture, time, or place who finds such a work and decides it is worthless because it contains fictional elements would be reacting ignorantly.

All these responses to pseudepigraphy are ultimately examples of "presentism." Presentism is the error of reading present-day cultural values, ways of thinking, and presuppositions back into the past. It assumes that these texts somehow tricked or deceived everyone in the past, but we as moderns are savvier than they and will not be so fooled. Such hubris fails to understand that past generations, even ancient ones, were populated by people capable of as much nuance or subtlety as any contemporary person.

Ancient people's literary conventions, ways of approaching a text, and understanding of the authority—or lack thereof—of its contents were, in some cases, quite different from ours. To understand the written works that were important to previous generations of Orthodox Christians, we have to learn how those fathers and mothers in the Faith read and understood them. Only when we understand their importance to our forebears can we properly interpret these ancient texts and apply them to our own lives in Christ.

A Word about Translations

As in my previous books, all translations of the Scriptures and other ancient sources are my own. That said, no translation is ever perfect, and that includes the ones I present. Translation is more an art than a science, especially when working with ancient languages that are constructed very differently from the English language. Sometimes, in making a particular point or argument, a translation may need to be very precise about a certain word or explain that the same word is used in two places. For a variety of reasons, however, a standard English translation may lack that precision. For all these reasons it seems best to translate afresh for significant quotations.

Old Testament Scripture references are given according to both the Hebrew tradition (which most English Bibles are based on) and the Greek tradition (on which the *Orthodox Study Bible* and certain other translations are based). When these two systems differ from one another (for example, when the Hebrew tradition numbers a psalm differently from the Greek), the Hebrew reference precedes the Greek, and a slash (/) separates them.

How to Use This Book

Readers can approach this book in multiple ways. One way is to use each of the chapters as an individual introduction to the texts it describes. Depending on the length of the work in question, in many cases the chapters in this book are summaries— meaning that they are not a good substitute for reading the text itself. Rather, they are intended to help regular people read and understand these works by pointing out important elements and connections to the Orthodox Christian tradition.

Or readers can simply read this book from front to back. Over the course of examining this variety of texts, certain themes emerge. Important among them is an understanding of how the Church has made use of this type of literature, which is neither part of the Scriptures nor objectionable. How the Church reads these texts has important implications for how we read, for example, the Church Fathers.

At the end of this book are a number of helpful tools. The

back matter includes a glossary (Appendix B), a list of books for further reading (Appendix C), and an index. The list of St. Nikephoros, which greatly informed the choice of texts to cover in this book, is also included in Appendix A.

Finally, the purpose of this book is to give lay readers access to part of the richness of the Orthodox Christian tradition. The literature discussed here forms a part of that tradition that has been sorely neglected in our modern age. Often, these books are missing puzzle pieces connecting elements of Liturgy, Scripture, and patristic writings. Familiarity with these works will fill out readers' understanding of the breadth and depth of the Orthodox Christian Faith.

PART I

Old Testament and Second Temple Literature

CHAPTER ONE

The Edge of the Old Testament Canon
4 EZRA AND 4 MACCABEES

What Is the Old Testament Canon?

WHILE ANY NUMBER of urban legends exist regarding the formation or declaration of the canon of Scripture, in reality, the Orthodox Church has never decreed an official canon. Rather, the content of the Holy Scriptures has been the subject of varying degrees of agreement between local Orthodox churches. This consensus is relatively clear in regard to the twenty-seven books of the New Testament, yet the Revelation of St. John is read publicly only in very few places. Saint Nikephoros of Constantinople bears witness to the fact that even in the ninth century, disagreements continued regarding Revelation's recognition in some Eastern churches.

Regarding the Old Testament, agreement is much less clear. The Church shares universal agreement as to the authority of the Torah and the Prophets, the first two major divisions of the Hebrew Bible and the Old Testament. But the third category, the writings, shows much more variation. For example, many of the texts discussed in this book are part of the canon of the

Ethiopian and Coptic churches. Ethiopian and Egyptian Jewish communities delivered their canons to these churches, and thus they remain the same as they were before the Council of Chalcedon. And in the West, St. Jerome did not fully embrace the seven additional books of the Latin canon, and the debate over their status continued until the time of the Protestant Reformation. At that time, the Council of Trent officially accepted those seven books[3] for Rome while, for the most part, Protestant communities treated them as deuterocanonical at best. All seven of these books have been accepted consistently in the Christian East, with the possible exception of certain early Syriac communities.

Defining the Old Testament's exact limits within the Orthodox Church's many language traditions remains difficult. Though there is explicit agreement on a particular set of books and their authority across all Orthodox traditions, the exact list of books found in a published Orthodox Bible will primarily be a function of the language tradition from which that Bible comes. Also, many of the Old Testament books that are authoritative within all the local churches are not read publicly in our present liturgical life, which further complicates the issue of the canonicity of some of these books.

This chapter deals with two books that are contained in the Slavonic Old Testaments but not the Greek within Orthodox Christian communities. Fourth Ezra, or 2 Esdras, and

---

3   These are the books of 1 and 2 Maccabees, Tobit, Judith, Wisdom of Solomon, Wisdom of Sirach, and Baruch. Additionally, the Greek and later Latin texts of Esther and Daniel are significantly longer than the Hebrew/Aramaic versions.

4 Maccabees are commonly placed in an appendix in Slavonic Bibles. Rather than resolving this difference, their placement in an appendix merely begs the question as to these books' canonical status. An appendix implies that they hold a different status from the books that make up the main body of the Old Testament. It also, however, implies that they hold a different status from the vast number of texts that are not included in appendices.

4 EZRA (2 ESDRAS)

Popularity in the Church

One of the books viewed as authoritative yet not read publicly today is 4 Ezra, also sometimes known as 2 Esdras. Though scholars agree that its central portion was initially written in Hebrew and then translated into Greek, neither the Hebrew nor the Greek is extant today. It is not included in the Greek tradition of the Old Testament. However, this text enjoyed widespread acceptance in the early Church and was cited by a wide range of Church Fathers, usually as "the prophecy of Ezra" or "the apocalypse of Ezra." Saint Ambrose of Milan cited it with particular frequency.[4] Such was its popularity that St. Jerome translated it as part of the Old Testament of the Vulgate, though he placed it in an appendix with other popular texts that he did not consider authoritative, such as the six contested books already mentioned.

Fourth Ezra was well known in the West in its Latin form

---

4   In his Letter to Anicius, c. AD 383, St. Ambrose refers to the central narrative of 4 Ezra as historical fact.

until the time of the Protestant Reformation. Christopher Columbus cited 4 Ezra 6:2[5] as one of his proofs of the world's composition in his appeal to the Catholic monarchs for funding. Likewise, the book is found in Ethiopian and Armenian Old Testaments and, importantly for the Orthodox Church, in the Georgian, through which the book found its way into the Slavonic biblical tradition. It has been included in every approved Slavonic and Russian printed Bible. Fourth Ezra is, therefore, a text at the fringe of the Old Testament tradition, either just in or just out, depending on the Orthodox linguistic tradition.

Textual History

Regarding the title of the book, the various texts associated with the Prophet Ezra were arranged and numbered in Second Temple Judaism and the ancient Church in various ways. In most English Bibles, one will find the Books of Ezra and Nehemiah representing this material in the Old Testament. Originally, the texts now known as Ezra and Nehemiah were contained and preserved in one scroll. These were later divided into 1 and 2 Ezra, with the latter later being renamed Nehemiah.

Within the Greek Old Testament tradition, another text, 1 Esdras, represents an earlier stage in the development of the Ezra-Nehemiah book. First Esdras in the Greek tradition reproduces the last two chapters of 2 Chronicles, followed by the majority of Ezra's text, though in a different order. In the

---

5   The second chapter of 4 Ezra describes the creation of the world and indicates that the earth is six parts land and one part water. Taking this literally, Columbus did the math and estimated that Japan was roughly 2,400 miles from Portugal. In reality, the two countries are 6,790 miles apart.

traditional Greek numbering, then, 1 Ezra is this composite book, 2 Ezra is what we now call Ezra, 3 Ezra is what we now call Nehemiah, and 4 Ezra is the text that we are now preparing to discuss. In the Latin numbering, St. Jerome translated Ezra-Nehemiah as one book, entitled 1 Esdras, and the book we now prepare to discuss he entitled 2 Esdras. To minimize confusion, the remainder of this chapter will use the title 4 Ezra.

Background

At the fringes of the Christian canon, the Church has preserved for us many Second Temple Jewish texts in Christian recensions, or versions, edited by the Christian community from a Hebrew original. In the case of 4 Ezra, the editing is fairly obvious. The first two and last two chapters are found only in the Latin version—in none of the Eastern versions—and contain explicitly Christian material. The first two chapters, sometimes separated by scholars and referred to as 5 Ezra, are a Christian interpretation of some of the apocalyptic material in the original book. This material centers specifically on prophecies in 4 Ezra concerning the destruction of the temple in Jerusalem, the concurrent judgment of Judea's people, and the calling of the Gentiles. These chapters describe the fulfillment of these prophecies in the first century and point forward to Christ's Return. The last two chapters, 15 and 16, are likewise clearly Christian, echoing New Testament and other early descriptions of Christ's Return in the form of Ezra's prophecies. Scholars sometimes refer to these final chapters as 6 Ezra.

Fourth Ezra proper, then, is made up of chapters 3–14 of the Latin text, or 1–12 in Eastern-language editions. Scholars generally agree 4 Ezra was produced within Jewish communities in the early first to mid-first century AD. Many have argued, however, that certain elements, prophecies, and imagery within the book date to previous centuries before their compilation into this text. Fourth Ezra is structured around a series of revelatory visions that Ezra received during his earthly life in the fifth century BC, and several textual features connect it to other Second Temple Jewish literature of the last few centuries before Christ. One prominent example is the appearance of Uriel, the fourth of the seven archangels, as Ezra's mediator and guide through many of his visions. While St. Gabriel and St. Michael are mentioned throughout Scripture, and St. Raphael appears in the Book of Tobit, St. Uriel appears throughout Jewish and Christian traditions and literature but is not named in the more broadly recognized Scriptures.

The Archangel Uriel appears as the angel who rescues St. John the Forerunner from Herod's massacre of newborn children and leads him to the desert.[6] Saint Uriel is also the angel who accompanied the infant Christ, the Theotokos, and St. Joseph the Betrothed in their escape to Egypt.[7] His name in Hebrew means "the fire of God," and he is identified in Jewish tradition as the angel with a flaming sword who guards the gate of Paradise. Additionally, the Apocalypse of Peter presents St. Uriel as the angel who judges repentance. Both St. Dionysius

---

6   Uriel's involvement with St. John the Baptist is found in a number of apocryphal gospels and fragments from late antiquity and the medieval period. Likely the most famous memorial of this tradition is the appearance of Uriel in Leonardo da Vinci's *Virgin of the Rocks*.

7   These traditions are preserved in several places by the Coptic Church and in the apocryphal Gospel of Pseudo-Matthew.

the Areopagite and St. Gregory the Dialogist name him among the archangels. In Orthodox iconography, St. Uriel is often identified by name in the Synaxis of the Holy Archangels.

The Seven Visions of 4 Ezra

Seven visions comprise the text of 4 Ezra, with St. Uriel serving as a guide in much the same way that St. Gabriel does in Daniel. Ezra receives the first three visions in response to his questions. First, he asks how God can be just when Israel was left in the misery of exile. Despite returning to the land, the nation remained under foreign rule. Second, he asks why Israel was sent into exile in the first place. Third, he asks why a pagan empire and not Israel is the power that controls the known world. In all three cases, language reminiscent of the Book of Job explains that humans cannot understand God's ways; however, all the pain, turmoil, and suffering to which Ezra points is temporary, as the Day of Judgment is coming. On that day, justice will be established for all, the righteous will be vindicated, and the unrighteous will be punished for their sins. Judgment here comes as a promise, not a threat, to a suffering people.

The second set of three visions concerns the coming of the Messiah. The fourth vision involves a bridegroom who dies on the threshold of the bridal chamber before the wedding can be consummated. The bridegroom's mother mourns his death, and in the vision she becomes a city identified with Zion itself. This mourning then turns to rejoicing in the following days. Ezra's vision is redolent of much of the imagery of the New Testament concerning Christ as the Bridegroom, and it becomes the source for a considerable amount of the hymnography of Holy

Week and Pascha in the Orthodox Church. The connection can be seen in the Bridegroom Matins services and especially in the Theotokion of Pascha, where the hymns draw together the imagery of the Theotokos, the city, and Zion in celebration of the Resurrection of Christ.[8]

The fifth vision is that of a three-headed eagle with two sets of twelve and eight wings respectively, which is identified with the fourth kingdom of Daniel's vision and therefore with Rome. A lion representing the Messiah, the Lion of the tribe of Judah, defeats this beast and burns it alive. In the sixth vision, the Messiah Himself is attacked by an angry mob whom he consumes with fire. He then leaves them for another group of people who become His disciples. This vision is interpreted in the later Christian additions as referring to the judgment of the Judean people and the turn of the gospel to the Gentiles.

The seventh and final vision serves as a sort of capstone to the text and reflects a version of a Jewish tradition involving the loss of the Old Testament Scriptures. This tradition was carried over into many early Christian communities in multiple versions, not only in 4 Ezra but also in texts such as the Epistle of Barnabas and others. The Fathers reference this story occasionally; St. Jerome at one point refers to the specific form of the tradition in 4 Ezra. The varying traditions hold that at some point

---

8 The Theotokion of Pascha: "The angel cried to the Lady full of grace: Rejoice, rejoice, O pure Virgin! Again, I say: rejoice! Your Son is risen from His three days in the Tomb. With Himself He has raised all the dead. Rejoice, rejoice, O ye people! Shine, shine! Shine, O new Jerusalem! The glory of the Lord has shone on you. Exult now, exult, and be glad, O Zion! Be radiant, O pure Theotokos, in the Resurrection, the Resurrection of your Son!"

in Israelite history, all the books that we now call the Hebrew Bible were lost. Most commonly, this was thought to have happened at the destruction of Solomon's temple and the Babylonian exile. Other traditions, such as that of Barnabas, however, place this loss as early as the Israelites' sin with the golden calf, shortly after the Torah was given.

In the seventh vision of 4 Ezra, Ezra remedies this problem by mystically receiving these texts again and writing them in a sort of spiritual stupor, reproducing them word for word. He writes out the twenty-four books (the ancient numbering of the thirty-nine books of the Hebrew Bible), and the voice of God tells him that these books are to be made available to everyone. The same voice then enables Ezra to reproduce "the seventy," which are to be entrusted only to the wise. While some scholars have suggested that these seventy books belonged to some sect or other, no known sect of Judaism or Christianity possessed a canon of that size, and no other books somehow related to 4 Ezra make likely candidates for inclusion. It is much more likely, then, that this is a reference to the Septuagint, the work of the Seventy, reflecting the special status the Greek translation of the Hebrew Scriptures still held within first-century Judaism. The faithful considered the Greek text of these books to be of the same origin as the Hebrew text.

Significance to the Church
The Book of 4 Ezra has two major foci that the later Christian additions emphasize. The first is the powerful moment of the grieving mother who becomes the city, which has been translated in Orthodox worship as a dramatic and transformative

liturgical moment at Pascha. The figure of the Christ, the Messiah, is in the text a pivot point in history, from one age to another, rather than its final end. The specific pivot point occurs in the events immediately after His death and in the movement from mourning to rejoicing. Because of this change and the coming of the messianic age, humanity from all nations must prepare for the coming judgment.

> Therefore, I say to you, O nations that hear and understand, "Await your shepherd; he will give you everlasting rest, because he who will come at the end of the age is close at hand. Be ready for the rewards of the kingdom, because the eternal light will shine upon you forever." (4 Ezra 2:34–35 Vulg.)

4 MACCABEES

Textual History

As with 4 Ezra, 4 Maccabees is a biblical text that lies at the very edges of the Old Testament canon in the Orthodox Church. In later Greek manuscripts, the book is included in an appendix. In older Greek manuscripts, no such distinction is made, though 4 Maccabees, instead of following 3 Maccabees, is often found at the end of these texts along with Psalm 151 and the Prayer of Manasseh—two liturgical fragments. The book is present in Old Georgian Old Testaments and for a time was included in the Romanian Old Testament. Because of their relegation to the "apocrypha" in most English Bibles, 1 and 2 Maccabees are not well known to most English readers; 4 Maccabees is therefore even less so.

Review of 1, 2, and 3 Maccabees

The four books of the Maccabees differ in genre, type, and content, though they stem from events in the same general era. Following the death of Alexander the Great, his successors, known in Greek as the *diadochoi*, went to war to carve up his empire among themselves. The Greek imperial powers who therefore ruled portions of the world were by nature hostile to the Judeans, later abbreviated as "Jews." At this point in history, the third through first centuries BC, significant Jewish populations resided in Judea, Alexandria in Egypt, Antioch in Syria, Mesopotamia, and smaller communities scattered throughout the known world. Because the Jews refused to worship the gods of the Greeks, the Greeks saw them as traitors. The sacrificial rituals of the Greeks were civic acts in which the entire *polis* participated. They bound the community together and bound them all together with their gods. When misfortune befell a pagan Greek community, therefore, and the people intuited that they had earned the gods' disfavor, those who refused to perform the proper religious rites were an obvious target for blame. The books of the Maccabees describe this persecution and its results.

Third Maccabees is the odd man out among these books because it is set in Egypt under the Ptolemaic dynasty, the Greek dynasty that ruled Egypt until Cleopatra. The text describes faithful Jews facing persecution while living in Egypt, particularly in and around Alexandria, during the late third century BC. These events take place a few decades before the events of the other books of the Maccabees. The texts of 1, 2, and 4 Maccabees all deal with the Seleucid dynasty's oppression of Judea itself in the early second century BC. This Greek dynasty ruled from their newly established capital, Antioch on the Orontes in Syria.

Following a disastrous battle against the Ptolemies in an attempt to expand his empire to the south and west, Antiochus IV Epiphanes returned to Jerusalem. He blamed his military defeat on the failure of the Jews to honor the gods and so entered the temple in Jerusalem, rebuilt after the return from exile, and sacrificed a pig there to Zeus. The Jews referred to this act as "the abomination that causes desolation," and it is mentioned and alluded to frequently in the latter parts of the Old Testament and in the New Testament (e.g., Dan. 12:11; Matt. 24:15–16; Mark 13:14; Luke 21:20–21). This pagan sacrifice defiled the temple and made it unfit for its intended use in worshipping Yahweh, the God of Israel. The Jewish people had already endured incredible pressure to conform to Greek culture and religion, and many of them had given in. After the desecration of the temple, this persecution intensified at the hands of Antiochus.

First Maccabees describes, in a straightforward historical account, the revolution that proceeded to unfold. Judas Maccabeus, which means "Judah the Hammer," and his brothers took the atrocity in the temple as the last straw and raised up a revolutionary army to overthrow the Greeks. They were successful and established an independent Judea, making treaties with Sparta and Rome for its defense to prevent the Seleucids' potential counterattack. Judah and his brothers established a new monarchy, the Hasmonean dynasty, with a family member also being made high priest. The Sadducean high priestly families encountered in the Gospels are descendants of these men and not of Zadok, despite the origin of their name.

After their victory at the Battle of Emmaus, the temple was rededicated and brought back into service. The anniversary of that rededication became an annual feast, now celebrated as Hanukkah by Jewish communities. Second Maccabees covers the same time period but gives a more personal portrait of individuals who suffered for their faith at the hands of the Seleucids. The most celebrated of these, whose story is told in some detail in 2 Maccabees, are the seven Maccabean martyrs, their mother, and their teacher, St. Eleazar. These martyred saints are celebrated in the Orthodox Church on August 1.[9]

4 Maccabees: A Treatise in Two Parts

Fourth Maccabees is another genre entirely, following the form of a philosophical treatise or Old Testament wisdom literature. In reality, it is most likely a melding of the two, written by a Jewish person of Hellenistic background at the end of the first century AD. The text also has features of a homily or oration, focusing on the lessons in virtue to be learned from the example of the Maccabean martyrs. As can be ascertained by some of the details contained within the book and the traditions reflected there, it was likely written in the city of Antioch in Syria. The relics of the Maccabean martyrs were kept in a shrine, first Jewish and later Christian, in the city of Antioch from the time of their deaths until the collapse of the ancient city at the turn of the fifteenth century.

---

9   Kontakion of the Seven Holy Maccabee Martyrs: "Seven pillars of the Wisdom of God and seven lampstands of the divine Light, all-wise Maccabees, greatest of the martyrs before the time of the martyrs, with them ask the God of all to save those who honor you."

Before their commemoration as Christian saints, these martyrs were remembered in Jewish synagogues with a day of fasting on the ninth of Av (roughly in July or August). The composition of 4 Maccabees was likely related to the prominence of
these martyrs in the Jewish community of Antioch in the first
century. For a considerable period, sources attributed 4 Maccabees to Josephus, the Jewish historian. In fact, during the
period in which 4 Maccabees was included in Romanian Bibles,
it appeared there under his name. However, scholars have thor-
oughly disproven that the works of Josephus and this text were
written by the same author, as evidenced not only by discrepan-
cies in grammar, style, and vocabulary, but also by conceptual
contradictions.

PART 1

The Book of 4 Maccabees can be roughly divided into two
halves. The first half takes the form of a treatise on reason, or
wisdom. This introductory portion's central theme is the supe-
riority of reason (*logos* or *logismos*) over the passions (*pathe*).[10]
Reason exists as an overarching category and is a power of the
soul that allows it to resist, overcome, and tame the passions,
which express themselves through particular desires. The Torah
describes reason, and it has a real presence in the world.

Within the lives of individuals, reason takes the form of wisdom, which produces virtues. Desires, which ultimately stem

---

10 The author of 4 Maccabees describes his project in this way: "I could
prove to you from many and various examples that reason is dominant over the emotions, but I can demonstrate it best from the noble
bravery of those who died for the sake of virtue, Eleazar and the seven
brothers and their mother" (4 Macc. 1:7–8).

from the passions, continually assail these virtues. The author gives many Old Testament examples throughout this portion of the text, such as Joseph's flight from Potiphar's wife. For the author of 4 Maccabees, wisdom and understanding of the creation in which we live and the creation that we are reinforce the truth of what the Torah communicates; they produce the virtues that allow people to resist temptations and overcome the passions.

PART 2

The second major section of 4 Maccabees is an extended meditation on these themes from the example of Eleazar, the seven Maccabean martyrs, and their mother. In praise of these martyrs, the author of 4 Maccabees retells the story told in 2 Maccabees, but in a dramatized form. The Seleucids tortured Eleazar to death in an attempt to get him to violate the Torah, specifically by eating pork. Pork was a major staple of the Greek diet, and pigs were also the animals most commonly sacrificed to the Greek gods. The pork being offered here had presumably also been offered to idols, adding the sin of idolatry to ritual uncleanness. After Eleazar's death by torture, the Seleucids then torture the seven martyrs to death in turn in front of their mother, both to try to get them to reject the Torah and to induce their mother to do the same. She, however, encourages them on to bravery, and after her sons, she also dies by torture.

Martyrdom in Second Temple Judaism and the Early Church

This narrative in 4 Maccabees reflects the Second Temple Jewish understanding of martyrdom in its fullest form. All the elements that will come to characterize the literature of early Christian martyrology at the beginning of the second century are present here, revealing another point of continuity: the heroic resistance of the martyrs to denying their faith, the characterization of their tortures as a contest in which they are victorious by their willingness to go to their deaths, and the urging of close family members and friends not to save themselves but to endure even unto death.

However, even more importantly, within the Second Temple Jewish understanding of martyrdom as expressed in 4 Maccabees, we gain important information about how first-century Jewish believers viewed a sacrificial death. While human sacrifice was always expressly forbidden as an abomination, within Second Temple Judaism the idea developed—largely concerning the martyrs of the Maccabean era—that one could, through a faithful death, offer one's own life as a sacrifice to the God of Israel. In 4 Maccabees 6:27–29, Eleazar prays as he dies, "You know, O God, that though I might have saved myself, I am dying in burning torments for the sake of the Torah. Be merciful to Your people, and let our righteousness suffice for them. Make my blood their purification, and take my life in exchange for theirs." Both the element of sin offerings in the Old Testament—sacrifice offered as a ransom for the offerer's life—and atonement—purification from and the wiping away of sin— are present in this understanding of St. Eleazar's death. When

Jewish believers of this period learned of the sacrificial death of the Messiah, 4 Maccabees describes for us the lens through which they would have understood this.

Significance to the Early Church

Readers can find clear and direct lines of continuity from the first portion of 4 Maccabees to Orthodox monastic literature. The understanding of sin as passions, and of passions expressing themselves as desires that give rise to temptations, is present in both. The text describes the necessity of cultivating virtues through the keeping of commandments, which are themselves reinforced by spiritual benefits. The author discusses the need to sift one's thoughts: we cannot prevent thoughts from entering the mind, but we can cut them off before they are able to take root. Here also is found the beginning, in the understanding of the *logos*, of the connective tissue between the Word of God in the Old and New Testaments and the understanding of the *Logos* and the *logia* in St. Maximus the Confessor. Fourth Maccabees, therefore, represents an important link in the chain connecting the wisdom literature of the Old Testament to the monastic wisdom that has come to characterize the mind of the Orthodox Church.

Additionally, the way this story is told in 4 Maccabees also helps us understand St. Paul's vehemence before his experience on the road to Damascus, as well as the opposition he himself faced afterward, regarding the provisions of the Torah down to the level of what should and should not be eaten. Within the living memory of the people to whom St. Paul was preaching, their forefathers and heroes in the Faith had been willing to lay down their lives over these very issues.

CHAPTER TWO

The Book of Enoch (1 Enoch)

INTRODUCTION: ENOCHIC LITERATURE

WITHIN THE VARIED LITERATURE of the Second Temple period, easily the best-known subset is the Enochic literature. Likewise, within the Enochic works, the Book of Enoch or 1 Enoch is by far the best known in terms of awareness of—though not necessarily actual familiarity with—its contents. The Enochic literature is made up of a number of texts. Sometimes these are numbered, that is, 1, 2, and 3 Enoch. At other times the Church names them according to the language of the preserved text, as in Slavonic Enoch. Some texts, such as Jubilees, do not actually have Enoch's name in the title but nonetheless reflect the same apocalyptic traditions. The commonality among the various texts is that Enochic literature presents a set of religious beliefs and practices that anticipate Christianity and that would, for at least a century, rival the early Christian movement. A prime example is the Qumran community, who produced the Dead Sea Scrolls. While much debate has surrounded their identity—in particular, their identity as

Essenes—even casual cataloging of their library clearly shows they represent a community formed around Enochic literature and traditions.

Textual History of 1 Enoch

The Book of Enoch, or 1 Enoch, is the largest and historically central element of this literature. Though commonly referred to as a single book, it is actually a composite of several texts composed over a period of time and reflecting development in religious experience:

The Book of the Watchers: chapters 1–36, the earliest portion of the text (third century BC)

The Book of Parables or Similitudes: chapters 37–71, likely the latest portion (late second or early first century BC)

The Book of Luminaries: chapters 72–82, dealing with astrological observations and the calendar

The Book of Dreams: chapters 83–90

The Epistle of Enoch: chapters 91–108

These titles are not merely subheadings, as should be clear from the dating of the earliest and latest sections and their respective arrangement. Rather, they are separate works compiled over several centuries.

Throughout the Second Temple period, the Enochic tradition represented a powerful rival to Pharisaism. But the triumph of Pharisaism and its transformation in late antiquity into Rabbinic Judaism have skewed historical recollection of the actual religious state of affairs during the pre-Christian era. Enochic

Judaism is sometimes categorized by scholars as a "non-Torah-based" Judaism—an idea that may seem a contradiction to modern ears. On a multitude of counts, however, 1 Enoch not only departs from but argues against the Pharisaic consensus. In Jubilees, the giving of the Torah is subsumed into larger spiritual warfare traditions, but 1 Enoch never even mentions specific commandments and laws—even those as significant as circumcision. The book rejects the second temple itself as outright idolatry. While Pharisaic Judaism, as recorded in the Gospels, was ascendant in the first century AD within Palestinian Judaism, the Enochic tradition deeply formed significant portions of Egyptian (including Alexandrian) Judaism and all Ethiopian Judaism. To this day, Ethiopian Judaism remains in the Enochic tradition.

Contents

Obviously, the central figure of 1 Enoch and of the majority of the related literature is Enoch himself, who is the subject of only four verses in the Book of Genesis:

> When Enoch lived sixty-five years, he begat Methuselah. Enoch walked with God after he begat Methuselah three hundred years, and he begat sons and daughters. Thus, all the days of Enoch were 365 years. So, Enoch walked with God, and he was not because God took him. (Gen. 5:21–24)

Enoch is the seventh figure mentioned in the genealogy from Adam to Noah. While the Hebrew in Genesis often translated as "he was not" is open to a variety of interpretations, it was firmly established by the third century BC that this wording meant that God chose Enoch, based on his way of life, to be taken to His presence. The rendering of the Septuagint reflects this understanding by using the Greek verb *metatithemi*, a verb literally meaning "to take something from one place and put it in another."

A century later, Sirach refers to Enoch as having "pleased God and [been] translated (*metatethe*) into Paradise so that he might give repentance to the nations" (W. Sir. 44:16). The reference here to "the nations" is especially significant, as there was no distinction of Jew and Gentile in the antediluvian era. Sirach, then, is attributing some sort of heavenly role to Enoch in the post-Sinai period. This evidence from Hellenistic Judaism shows that the traditions that came to be written in 1 Enoch already held wide currency by the third century BC, as 1 Enoch purports to be the record, written by Enoch himself, of this journey to the heavens and his reception of a new role from the Lord of Spirits.

In his journey through the heavens, Enoch receives visions of the spiritual reality underlying his own era, the era of the genealogies of Cain and Seth that precedes Noah's Flood. He sees the coming of Noah and the Flood and interprets these visions as an initial fulfillment leading to greater future fulfillment in the coming of the Messiah. As we will see in the discussions of the other parts of 1 Enoch, important scriptural themes crystallize within the book. These include the origin of evil in rebellious spiritual powers, the association of the Son of Man—the second Power in heaven and the second hypostasis of Yahweh, the God of Israel—with the coming Messiah, and even anticipations of the Christian reappropriation of the Jewish festal calendar.

New Testament References

The New Testament authors refer to these concepts in a way that assumes them as the majority position of the Jewish faithful in the first century AD. The authors do not argue for or demonstrate these ideas; they merely allude to and reference them. The New Testament mentions Enoch three times: The first is a brief reference in St. Luke's genealogy of Christ from Adam, as would be expected (Luke 3:37). The second occurs in Hebrews 11:5 in the listing of faithful figures and their legacy, where the author uses the same terminology as the Greek Genesis and Wisdom of Sirach to state that Enoch had been translated from this world. The emphasis of Hebrews is clearly on the fact that Enoch, unlike all other figures in the genealogies of Cain and Seth, does not die.

The third mention of Enoch comes in Jude 14–15 and is especially significant because it includes a quotation ascribed to him, from 1 Enoch 1:9. In these two verses, St. Jude is clearly drawing deeply from Enochic traditions. First, he identifies Enoch as "the seventh from Adam." Though this is apparent from counting generations in the Genesis genealogy, its ascription as a title occurs in 1 Enoch 60:8. This title has a particular relationship to Enoch as the origin of the Enochic calendar, which we will discuss later under the Book of Luminaries.

Further, St. Jude portrays Enoch through the quotation as a preacher of repentance to the unrighteous. Enoch does no preaching in the text of Genesis, though Sirach possibly alludes to this (W. Sir. 44:16). The Enochic literature, however, repeatedly describes Enoch's "walking with God" as his preaching of righteousness to the wicked and corrupt generation that surrounded him. Finally, the first chapter of Enoch, where St. Jude draws this quotation, is a midrashic[11] commentary on Deuteronomy 33:2, which describes Yahweh coming forth in judgment from ten thousands of His holy ones. Saint Jude, therefore, is not quoting the general idea from the Deuteronomy text but rather the particular interpretation and application of this text from 1 Enoch. While this interpretation may have been widespread, St. Jude explicitly places this interpretive word in the mouth of Enoch himself.

Beyond these direct references to Enoch, the New Testament books also contain a number of allusions and references to various parts of the text. These are particularly concentrated in the Epistles of Ss. Peter and Jude, and, as one might expect, the Apocalypse of St. John. Perhaps less expectedly, St. Matthew's Gospel features several references to Enochic material. Many of these surround the way in which Christ speaks of the Son of Man as an apocalyptic figure. Others, however, are simpler, such as the meek inheriting the earth:

Blessed are the meek, because they will inherit the earth. (Matt. 5:5)

But for the elect there will be light and joy and peace, and they will inherit the earth. (1 Enoch 5:7)

---

11   "Midrash" was a particular popular mode of textual commentary at the time of the composition of the Book of Enoch (see the Glossary).

In some cases, these allusions, once understood, bring out an added dimension of meaning. As just one example, Jesus' Parable of the Wedding Banquet ends with the unworthy one being bound hand and foot and thrown into the outer darkness: "Then the king told his servants, 'Bind this one hand and foot, take him away, and cast him into outer darkness, where there will be weeping and gnashing of teeth'" (Matt. 22:13).

This precise phrasing—of being bound hand and foot and thrown into darkness—is used to describe the fate of Azazel, the prince of demons, in 1 Enoch: "Then in the second place, the Lord said to Raphael, 'Bind Azazel hand and foot and throw him into the darkness.' And he made a hole in the desert which was in Dudael and threw him there" (10:4).

This connection reveals that the fate of the wicked person is to share in the fate of the rebellious spiritual powers, as Christ states elsewhere in that Gospel (Matt. 25:41). In fact, this fate, the lake of fire, itself seems to have its origin as an image in the Enochic literature (e.g., 1 Enoch 54:6).

Significance to the Early Church

The Church's reception of 1 Enoch may surprise many modern people who assume anything outside of a rigid "Old Testament canon" was basically rejected. It is relatively well known that because of the authority the text has always exercised within Ethiopian Judaism, it was immediately received into the Old Testament of Ethiopian Christianity, centuries before the Council of Chalcedon. Beyond this, however, 1 Enoch found wide use in the ancient Church. The Epistle of Barnabas twice cites 1 Enoch as Scripture: Barnabas introduces one set of quotations with "for the scripture says" and the other with "for it is written" (4:3; 16:5).

Saint Justin the Philosopher, in the mid-second century, refers more than once to the Watchers story as reflected in 1 Enoch and related literature. He is likely our most important witness to the separation between Christianity and other Judaisms[12] that took place during his lifetime. In 1 Enoch, the Son of Man plays a central role as the second hypostasis of Yahweh, which likely doomed the book to immediate repudiation by non-Christian Jewish communities.[13] However, in his *Dialogue with Trypho*, St. Justin makes a tantalizing reference that another central emphasis of 1 Enoch was also a point of contention among Jews. Trypho accuses St. Justin, and thereby Christians, that their "expositions are mere contrivances, as is plain from what has been explained by you; nay, even blasphemies, for you assert that angels sinned and revolted from God" (79).

Tertullian, writing about AD 200, defends the authoritative status of 1 Enoch in part by saying that nascent Rabbinic Judaism had rejected it because of its many prophecies pertaining to Christ (*On the Apparel of Women*, 1.3). Also, in the late second century, St. Irenaeus of Lyons gives a fairly detailed account of the teaching of 1 Enoch regarding the origin and fate of the powers of darkness, ascribing this teaching to the prophets (*Adv.*

---

12 In the Second Temple period, the religious practice of Judean people in various places was highly varied. There was no single Judaism or a single religion of which all Jewish people were a part.

13 As we will see, in this and other extra-biblical texts from the Second Temple period, Yahweh, the one God of Israel, was believed to exist as multiple Persons. The second of these Persons, or hypostases, was identified by early Christians as Jesus of Nazareth, the Christ.

Haer. 10.1). Another second-century Father, St. Athenagoras of Athens, describes Enoch as a prophet and makes great use of the book's descriptions of the angelic realm (*Legatio*). Origen states that he had previously accepted 1 Enoch as Scripture but later found that others did not consider it so; thus he moderated his stand (see *De Principiis* 4.1.35; *Contra Celsus* 54).

Significance to the Post-Nicene Church

A number of scholars are familiar with this widespread ante-Nicene acceptance of 1 Enoch as Scripture, since many Fathers and other writers throughout the first three centuries recognized the teaching of the book as authoritative and also argued for the validity of attributing its authorship to Enoch. However, modern readers often presume that this acceptance shifted in the post-Nicene Church, with 1 Enoch marginalized and set aside along with the rest of the Enochic material. This is incorrect on at least two counts. First, the teachings of 1 Enoch represent the earliest textual witness to principles of Christology, angelology, demonology, hamartiology (the doctrine of sin), and eschatology that became doctrinally normative for the Christian Church. The ubiquitous understanding of demons as "fallen angels," for example, testifies to this influence. While 1 Enoch does not function as Scripture and is not read in the Church liturgically, many of its central teachings passed through the textual witness of the New Testament and of the early Fathers, eventually coming to rest on the authority of the Church rather than on the authority of the book itself as a document.

In the second place, despite this dynamic, in various places throughout the later history of the Orthodox Church, the authoritative use of 1 Enoch arises without controversy. For example, the great eighth-century Byzantine chronicler George Synkellos, a close adviser to St. Tarasios, the Patriarch of Constantinople, used 1 Enoch's text for the early portions of his *Chronography*, thereby indicating that he viewed it as accurate world history. A generation later, St. Nikephoros, Patriarch of Constantinople, identified 1 Enoch as one repository of the teachings of the apostles not written explicitly in the New Testament—an apostolic apocryphon. This means that as late as the ninth century, the Church remembered that the earliest written record of these apostolic traditions regarding angels, demons, sin, and the end of days is, in fact, the Book of Enoch. It is evident that 1 Enoch and other significant Second Temple literature preserved through the centuries by the Church occupy a place in relationship to the Old Testament similar to the place that the Apostolic Fathers hold in relation to the New Testament.

I. THE BOOK OF THE WATCHERS

Textual History

What is now the first section of the Book of Enoch or 1 Enoch, comprising the first thirty-six chapters, is known as the Book of the Watchers. Internal evidence indicates that this and the other portions of 1 Enoch were originally separate documents recording independent traditions, and clear manuscript evidence shows that the Book of the Watchers circulated independently in Greek. This portion of the Book of Enoch is known in Ethiopic, along with the rest of the book, as well as through

Greek fragments. Additionally, the Dead Sea Scrolls at Qumran included the Book of the Watchers in both Greek and Aramaic. This variety of textual evidence allows us to have a high level of confidence about the reading of the book itself and its history; it dates back to the third century BC or earlier.

The Book of the Watchers is likely the part of 1 Enoch best known in the contemporary world, at least in the broad strokes of its content. The central portion of the text concerns the rebellion of the Watchers, a group of angelic beings who consorted with human women and brought forth the giants, the Nephilim. Less well known are the details and the remainder of the text, which concerns the Day of the Lord and Enoch's tour of cosmic geography.

Who Are the Watchers?

Use of the term *Watchers* to describe a group of angelic beings occurs in several places outside the Book of the Watchers proper. "Watcher" is used to describe "one of the holy ones" three times in the Book of Daniel. King Nebuchadnezzar dreamed that he would be struck mad and live like an animal for a time until he accepted Yahweh as God Most High: "I continued looking in the vision of the night while on my bed, and suddenly a watcher, a holy one, descended from heaven.... This sentence is the decree of the watchers, and this decision is the word of the holy ones . . . because the king saw a watcher, a holy one descending from heaven" (Dan. 4:13, 17, 23). Nebuchadnezzar's affliction is the decree both of the Most High (v. 24) and of the Watchers (v. 17), referring to the divine council surrounding Yahweh's throne.

"Watchers" occurs throughout the Enochic literature, as well as in texts such as the Damascus Document (2:18). Philo of Byblos describes a class of celestial intelligences called *sope shenayim*, the Watchers of Heaven (cited by Eusebius, *Prep. Evang.* 1.10.1–2). The designation of "Watcher" likely indicates a role for these beings similar to our conception of guardian angels. They were assigned to guard and protect humanity and instead turned to its corruption.

Contents

The beginning of the Book of the Watchers, and 1 Enoch as a whole, introduces the speaker as Enoch and identifies the book as a record of the visions he received after his translation from earth to heaven. He writes these things not for "this generation," but for one that is far distant (1:2). This stands in contrast to the visions of St. John's Apocalypse, which are written to his contemporaries about "things that will soon happen" (Rev. 1:1). No one should assume, however, that the Book of the Watchers is an eschatological work from our perspective; the original readers of the written text of 1 Enoch were living millennia after Enoch himself. While the work concerns events already ancient by the time it was put into written form, it is not written to and for those who experienced those events but for later generations.

CHAPTERS 1–5

The body of the first five chapters constitutes a midrashic commentary on Deuteronomy 33 describing the Day of the Lord, the Day of Judgment. God appears with His angelic army to execute judgment, setting all things right (compare with Matt.

25:31–32). Mountains melt away like wax before the fire, and valleys are lifted up (1:6). The wicked are destroyed, and the righteous are vindicated (vv. 8–9). Saint Jude cites 1 Enoch 1:9 in his own description of the coming judgment and the Day of the Lord:

> And Enoch, seventh from Adam, also prophesied about these people, saying, "See, the Lord comes with ten thousands of His holy ones to do justice to all: to condemn every soul that is impious among them for all their impious works which they have committed in an impious way, and of all the rash things that impious sinners have spoken against Him." (Jude 14–15)

Chapters 2–5 are exceptionally short and argue for the just condemnation of the wicked of the whole earth—not based on the commandments of the Torah, which of course did not yet exist in Enoch's day and were given only to Israel, but based on the testimony of every aspect of nature. This includes the stars, the seasons, animals, and even plants. Several other places elaborate this understanding of all humanity's accountability following from the revelation of God in the creation, notably Romans 1:20–22 and 10:14–18. The condemnation in 1 Enoch concludes, "But as for you, you have not been patient, and you have not done the commandments of the Lord. You have transgressed and spoken blasphemous, grave, and rash words with your unclean mouths against His Greatness. Oh, you hard of heart, may you never find peace" (1 Enoch 5:4). Saint Paul's view of individuals from the nations who kept the commandments apart from knowledge of the Torah echoes this understanding (Rom. 2:12–16).

After this midrashic introduction, the text proper begins in chapter 6. The next six chapters represent an elaboration of Genesis 6:1–4, which states that the "sons of God" took wives from the "daughters of men" and that giants existed on the earth.[14] An unidentified speaker narrates the story of the Watchers' fall in the third person: Shemihazah calls together a group of two hundred Watchers at Mount Hermon in order to hatch a plan together. This group is divided into regiments of ten, each with a leader, and the leader of the two hundred is called Shemihazah in Aramaic. In the same sections, the leader is also named Asael/ Azazel, who seems not to be numbered among the two hundred but to be their organizer and the hatcher of their scheme.

Rather than protecting and aiding humanity in finding repentance and a return to God, the Watchers, under Shemihazah, seek to corrupt humanity. This corruption begins with sexual immorality in a ritual context, the drinking of blood, the sacrifice of animals to demonic beings, and ultimately human sacrifice with its accompanying cannibalism (1 Enoch 7:3–6). The offspring of this corruption are the giants, the Nephilim,

---

14 The background of chapters 6–11 of the Book of the Watchers preserves stories such as that of the Mesopotamian *apkallu* and other ancient Near Eastern traditions that describe similar events. The apkallu, or the Seven Sages, are a series of divine spirits in Babylonian myth who revealed mysteries of knowledge to human kings and were punished for it. The Greek story of Prometheus is in many ways similar.

who came to dominate and enslave humanity and force them to serve them (v. 3). Further, in parallel with the genealogy of Cain in Genesis 4:17–24, the fallen Watchers teach humans secret knowledge for which they are not prepared, such as the weapons of war, means of seduction and immorality, sorcery, and divination (1 Enoch 8:1–3).

The early Christian Church fully took on board this tradition of the fallen Watchers. As mentioned earlier, St. Irenaeus of Lyons identifies it as the apostolic teaching regarding the origin of sin and corruption in the world (*Apostolic Preaching* 18). While in modern times, many people generally believe that the devil led some sort of angelic fall in a primordial, pre-Creation era, this idea comes not from Scripture or the Fathers but from Puritan poet John Milton. While the text of 1 Enoch itself did not continue to carry canonical authority in much of the Orthodox Church beyond the third century AD, the Church accepted the tradition of sin and corruption spreading in the world through Cain's line, and even later authors referenced it in various ways, although they rejected the interpretation of Genesis 6:1–4 in particular (e.g., St. Augustine in *City of God*).[15]

In response to these horrors and demonic oppression, the people of the earth cry out, and four of the seven archangels who stand before the throne of God receive these cries (chapters 9–11), addressing them to the gates of heaven and to God

---

15 Saint Augustine not only rejected Enoch's interpretation of the origin of the Nephilim directly (*City of God* 15.22–23), but as the preeminent Latin theologian for the patristic era, he cemented that rejection in much of the West. Nonetheless, he maintained the traditional interpretation of the figure of Cain and his genealogy regarding pre-Flood sin and corruption (*City of God* 15.1, 5, 7–8).

Himself (9:1–2). Ultimately, of course, the people make their pleas to the God of Israel, but they do not view their supplications to heaven, to the throne, and to the holy ones of God's divine council as being at odds with this understanding. The text clearly communicates here the view that prayers and petitions to God Himself can pass through heavenly intermediaries. The Book of Job also references this practice when Eliphaz asks Job who will address his plea to Yahweh, the God of Israel: "Cry out, and who will answer you? Or to which of the holy ones will you appeal?" (Job 5:1). The Apocalypse of St. John likewise presents angels bringing the prayers of the saints before the throne of God (Rev. 5:8; 8:4).

This is precisely what the four archangels then do: they bring these petitions to the God of gods, Lord of lords, King of kings, and God of the ages (9:4). In response, the Most High gives assignments to each of them, showing that the intermediation goes both ways: Yahweh responds to prayers through the same heavenly beings through which He governs creation. God sends Sariel to Noah to give him instructions regarding the coming of the Flood. He commissions Raphael to deal with Azazel, binding him hand and foot and burying him in a ravine to dwell in darkness until the judgment, when he is thrown into the fire.

Azazel here is not the name of the demonic figure to whom sins are sent in the Day of Atonement ritual as practiced in Israel. Raphael's mission involves what is done with both goats used in that ritual. God commands him to write all the sins of the world over Azazel (10:8) and also instructs him to heal and purify the world from the corruption that Azazel has caused

(v. 7). First Enoch 10:8 reads, "The whole world was made desolate by the works of the teaching of Azazel. To him, ascribe all sins." In describing the eschatological atonement of Christ, St. John borrows this language: "The one who practices sin is of the devil, because from the beginning the devil has sinned. For this reason the Son of God was revealed: in order to destroy the works of the devil. . . . We know that we are from God, and the whole world lies under the evil one" (1 John 3:8; 5:19).

God then assigns the Archangel Gabriel to destroy the Nephilim, the giants. Gabriel does not do so directly but pits them against each other in wars until the Flood destroys them (10:9–10). Michael is sent to capture and bind Shemihazah and the other sinful Watchers, imprisoning them in the abyss until the Day of the Lord, when they will be judged. Both 2 Peter and Jude reference Michael's binding of the rebellious Watchers and their imprisonment:

> Because if God did not spare the angels who sinned, but cast them down to Tartarus into chains of darkness to be imprisoned for judgment; and if He did not spare the ancient world, but saved Noah, one of eight, the preacher of righteousness, bringing the flood on the world of the impious. (2 Peter 2:4–5)

> And the angels who did not keep their first position, but left their own household, He has reserved in everlasting chains under darkness for the great day of judgment. (Jude 6)

Yahweh, the God of Israel, then goes on to describe the age to come, which will occur when all sin and uncleanness has been cleansed from the earth in eschatological atonement, beginning with these angelic missions (1 Enoch 10:16—11:2).

Saint Irenaeus cites this description in an interesting way in his discussion of the messianic age. He writes that the Apostle John, according to those who knew him, taught that Christ said the age to come would be one of abundance, using an overflowing plenty of food as an example and mimicking the language of 1 Enoch 10:19: "Trees of joy shall be planted, and they shall plant vines. And he who plants a vine upon [Earth in those days] will produce wine in vast multitude." Most readers of St. Irenaeus have assumed that he recorded some previously unknown saying of Jesus, heard secondhand through St. Polycarp. Modern interpreters view these words as Irenaeus taking a chiliastic position, or describing belief in a literal earthly kingdom under the rule of Christ. The speaker, however, in 1 Enoch 10:19 is the Lord. It is far more likely, then, that given Irenaeus's authoritative use of 1 Enoch elsewhere, he is here saying that St. John cited 1 Enoch 10:19 Christologically—in other words, St. John saw the one speaking to the archangels in this verse as God the Son. This way of reading Old Testament texts is ubiquitous in the Fathers, but modern readers miss it here because of the presupposition that 1 Enoch is not Scripture.

CHAPTER 12 AND FOLLOWING: ENOCH AS PROTAGONIST
The beginning of chapter 12 shifts to presenting Enoch as the protagonist of the remainder of the Book of the Watchers. In chapters 12–16, the Watchers plead with him to request mercy for themselves and their children, the giants, from God. None of them are repentant, but they want a lesser punishment. Enoch

travels to the area around Dan and Mount Hermon, both associated with the evil and corruption of the Nephilim, and from there, he accesses their prison. He brings their plea before the God of Israel, who tells him in no uncertain terms that due to their continued rebellion and wickedness, they will receive no mercy, and their punishment will be eternal.

The somewhat cryptic reference in 1 Peter—Christ's proclamation to the imprisoned spirits—describes Christ's descent into Hades in a way similar to the second journey there by Enoch:

> Because Christ also suffered once for sins, the righteous one for the unrighteous, so that He might bring us to God, being put to death in the flesh but made alive by the Spirit, in whom also He went and preached to the spirits in prison, those who before were disobedient, in the days when God patiently waited, in the days of Noah, while the ark was being built, in which a few, that is, eight, souls were saved through water. (1 Pet. 3:18–20)

The gospel is the preaching of Christ's victory over the demonic powers, sin, and death. Christ proclaimed this victory to the imprisoned fallen angels to announce their doom as Enoch had, though now that doom was fulfilled.

In the midst of this condemnation, the spirits of the giants that have come forth at their deaths continue to roam the earth to afflict man (1 Enoch 15:8—16:1). This is the understanding of the origin of unclean spirits in the Old Testament and of demons in the synoptic Gospels. The condemnation also contains a statement from God that He did not create women among the spirits of heaven, in contrast to the creation of woman from Adam among humanity (15:6–7). Christ echoes this truth in His statement that angels "neither marry nor are given in marriage" (Matt. 22:30; Mark 12:25).

ENOCH'S JOURNEY: CHAPTERS 17–36

The remainder of the Book of the Watchers, chapters 17–36, is the description of Enoch's journey with the seven archangels through the heavens, the earth, and the underworld. It is a gazetteer of cosmic geography. Specifically, Enoch journeys to the north, south, east, and west, with the underworld and the heavens overlapping the geography of the earth. Chapters 17–19 give a brief summary of the entire journey, while the following chapters then break down the journey through the cosmos in greater detail.

First Enoch 20 begins with a listing of the seven archangels. Saint Raphael refers to the seven in Tobit 12:15; St. John's Apocalypse also references these seven spirits who stand before the throne of God (Rev. 1:4). They are:

Uriel: known in Second Temple literature as a very prominent archangel, mentioned in Scripture only in 4 Ezra/2 Esdras.

Raphael: in charge of the spirits of men; he figures prominently in the Book of Tobit (1 Enoch 20:3).

Reuel: takes vengeance on the stars, meaning that he is responsible for the discipline of other angelic beings (v. 4).

Michael: in charge of Israel, the elect (v. 5).

Gabriel: in charge of paradise as well as the "serpents and the cherubim" (v. 7).

Remiel: in charge of raising the dead; likely a reference to shepherding departed spirits to their destination (v. 8).

Sariel, elsewhere called Samael: in charge of the spirits who sin against the Spirit (v. 6).

These seven spirits serve as guides on Enoch's tour. Uriel, identified as the spirit in charge of Tartarus, shows it to Enoch, who describes Tartarus as the place where the fallen stars, the imprisoned Watchers, are chained until the end of days (1 Enoch 21:1–10). Nearby in the underworld, Enoch sees the mountain of the dead, which is Sheol or Hades. Angels escort the spirits of the dead to the mountain to dwell in caves hewn out from the rock. Saint Raphael describes the caves as being for the righteous dead, the unrepentantly wicked dead, the martyrs, and those who died apart from the truth of God, respectively (22:9–13). The righteous will someday be set free, and the martyrs will receive justice and salvation, but the unrepentant wicked will be condemned to perish for all generations, along with the fallen angelic beings. The final group, who died apart from truth, will remain in Hades forever.

Enoch sees two further details: The souls of the righteous, though in Hades with the rest, have a spring of refreshing water with them as they await the coming of the Lord (22:2, 9). Outside the cave of the martyrs, one spirit, whom Raphael identifies as Abel, leads the others in crying out for justice (22:6–7). The New Testament points to this tradition, an interpretation of Abel's blood—his life—crying out from the earth (Gen. 4:10), multiple times (Matt. 23:35; Heb. 12:24; Rev. 6:9).

In chapters 24 and 25, Enoch sees the mountain of God, and

at the summit sits God's judgment seat, where He will sit to render the final judgment at the end of days. Enoch and Raphael then travel to the center of the earth, the location of Zion and Jerusalem (26:1–6). This is early written documentation of the tradition that Jerusalem is the "navel of the world" and stands at its center.[16] Christ's Crucifixion there is taken to represent salvation wrought in the middle point of the earth (Ps. 73/74:12). Next to the holy city is the Valley of Hinnom, Gehenna, which will be the eternal abode of the unrepentant wicked after the final judgment, and Sariel describes what he will do with the wicked on that day. The righteous and the martyrs will dwell in that holy city, the New Jerusalem (1 Enoch 27:1–4). In its midst grows the Tree of Life, from which all will eat in the age to come (26:3; see also Rev. 22:1–2).

Finally, Enoch is taken to see Paradise, which St. Gabriel describes to him as the place from which his father and mother of old were exiled (32:6). The text describes the trees and the beauty of Paradise in great detail, but Enoch sees no residents (28:1—32:2). He describes it, however, as the Paradise of the righteous, indicating that the righteous, whom he saw earlier in the watered cave of Hades, will someday be brought here. This vision finds its fulfillment in the Harrowing of Hades, in Christ's descent, which St. Peter alludes to (1 Pet. 3:18–20). Within Paradise, Enoch sees that the "tree of wisdom" still stands (32:3–5). The tree's continued presence reaffirms here that the tree of the

---

16 This is a spiritual identification of the central place of Jerusalem in Scripture, not based on a limited knowledge of geography. Jerusalem—specifically, the Church of the Holy Sepulcher—as the center of the world remains a tradition in the Orthodox Church to this day, despite full knowledge of the geography of the globe.

knowledge of good and evil is not itself a wicked or evil thing, but, like the knowledge given by the Watchers, its knowledge was not meant to be seized by man but rather given by God at the proper time.

The Book of the Watchers concludes in chapter 33 with Enoch visiting the very ends of the earth and seeing all the visible and invisible creatures of God. The last three chapters offer another summary and the command for Enoch to record what he has seen. It ends in a way that reemphasizes the independent nature of this portion of the text.

Significance to Modern Readers

The Book of the Watchers not only records the traditions for which it is famous, such as the Watchers, the Nephilim, and the Flood; it also describes the spiritual geography of the entire creation. The New Testament writers and the Fathers presupposed this reality in their understanding of events within the invisible creation, the spiritual world. Further, the book describes how these spiritual locations overlay the visible creation. The Book of the Watchers sets the table for the coming of Christ, the Messiah. The next section of 1 Enoch, the Book of Parables, focuses on the Son of Man, who is to come and fulfill all things.

II. THE BOOK OF PARABLES

Textual History

The second major portion of 1 Enoch is the Book of Parables, which now constitutes 1 Enoch 37—71. This numbering is somewhat misleading, as the Book of Parables proper—three "parables" or visions received by Enoch—really only makes up chapters 37–59. Chapters 60–71 appear to be the incorporation of another, independent source into the Book of Parables. This material is primarily designated as the Book of Noah, or sometimes labeled as portions or fragments of a Book of Noah. However, it is not just another book that has been incorporated with all the others into 1 Enoch. The speaker shifts from Enoch to Noah, attesting to its independence. Yet within those chapters, at several points the identity of the speaker shifts back and forth between Noah and his forefather Enoch—sometimes abruptly. Further, material in the final chapters of the Book of Parables seems to be attempting, by way of a summary, to unite all the material as a unit.

The Book of Parables had achieved its present form by the first century BC. This likely indicates that both the three visions of Enoch and the Book of Noah represent older material that has been incorporated here and edited together. The Book of Noah material is likely the oldest, based on the sometimes awkward means of its incorporation: the later editor felt free to work with the Enochic material but not with the Noahic material, which is preserved intact, even where it creates difficulties.

The Son of Man and His Coming

Two major themes weave throughout the Book of Parables. The first is the description of a figure—the Son of Man, the Elect One, the Messiah, the Righteous One—who is divine, eternally preexistent with the Most High. This figure has been hidden from everlasting and revealed only to the elect, indicating Israel or, more likely, the faithful within Israel. This leads to the second major theme, the coming of this figure among men, which will culminate with his enthronement on the throne of the Most High, the resurrection of the dead, the judgment of the heavens and the earth, and the initiation of the age to come. Even in this broad-strokes summary, readers might get the impression that this all seems a little too "on the nose" in terms of finding later Christian Christology and eschatology in a pre-Christian document.

A misunderstanding of the New Testament, or portions thereof, causes this skepticism: the belief that the early Church was in some sense starting from scratch or simply starting over, revealing a whole new theology and new facts to produce a new religion. However, in reality the substance of the Christian religion had already existed and been believed and practiced for centuries by the time of the birth of Jesus Christ in Bethlehem. All the New Testament documents share the theme that Jesus of Nazareth is the messianic, divine Son of Man in whom faithful Judeans already believed. The Book of Parables gives us one particularly clear window into their understanding of the preexistent, divine Messiah during the Second Temple period.

First Enoch 37 begins by identifying the forthcoming Book of Parables as the "second vision" of Enoch, the seventh from Adam. This connective tissue frames the previous Book of the Watchers as Enoch's first vision. In the following verses, which introduce what is to come, however, this second vision is reframed as three "parables" that Enoch received. The language of parables, as well as frequent references to wisdom within these chapters, places the book within earlier Hebrew wisdom traditions. But this is not a wisdom genre distinct from the apocalyptic genre of the Book of the Watchers; while categorizations are sometimes helpful, genres blend throughout the Scriptures. One particularly apropos example is Proverbs 8 and its depiction of preexistent Wisdom begotten by God. "Apocalyptic" represents a divine perspective on earthly events, and Enoch communicates the wisdom he gains from his apocalyptic visions to those on earth through parables.

Chapter 38 begins with a preface describing what will occur at the end of days. The depiction of judgment here is twofold: First, the kings and the mighty on the earth will perish and come to an end. Second, the wicked who rejected the Lord of Spirits will be driven from the face of the earth and will have nowhere to go or to hide. While this event will be described later, already the text makes a clear distinction between these "rulers" who "possess the earth" at the present time and the unrepentantly sinful. This distinction not only is verbal but also concerns their fate: the unrepentantly sinful are driven not only from the presence of the Lord of Spirits, being unable to bear it, but also from the presence of the righteous, who themselves shine with the light of His glory, particularly from their faces (vv. 3–4). The wording regarding the permanence of their fate is also important: they are not now *unable* to repent; rather, none of them *will*. The rulers and possessors of the earth, in contrast, perish utterly and are destroyed. All of this happens when the Righteous One appears before the eyes of the righteous (v. 2). The Righteous One is here clearly delineated from the Lord of Spirits, and the righteous to whom He appears are those who have participated in the works of the Lord of Spirits (v. 2).

The First Parable

The parables are framed within a vision Enoch receives after he is taken up in a whirlwind and sees the heavens and the angels in their places. The Book of Parables here goes further than the Book of the Watchers in depicting Enoch beholding "the Elect One of righteousness and of faithfulness" (39:6; see also 1 Pet. 2:6; 1 Cor. 1:30). He dwells under the wings of the Lord of Spirits, and his characteristic attribute is righteousness. All the righteous, through their participation in his righteousness, become "flaming lights" (vv. 6–7). Before the throne of the Lord of Spirits, Enoch sees a thousand thousands and ten thousand ten thousands who never sleep (i.e., they are immortal), endlessly praising God (39:12—40:2; see Rev. 5:11).

On the four sides of the throne, Enoch sees four of the archangels performing particular tasks with their voices. Saint Michael unceasingly praises the Lord of Spirits, St. Raphael endlessly praises the Elect One and blesses the elect ones who are His brethren, and St. Gabriel endlessly intercedes for those who dwell on Earth and makes supplications for them. He is further identified as the leader of the powers of heaven, leading them in precisely this task of intercession. The fourth, the Archangel Phanuel, is said to fight back the satans[17] who wish to come and accuse those who dwell on the earth. He accomplishes this through the repentance and hope of the people on earth, which he conveys through prayer to the Lord of Spirits (1 Enoch 40:4–9).

---

17 The word *satan* in Hebrew means "enemy" or "adversary." Sometimes it is used with the definite article, "the Satan," to refer to a particular demonic being. It can be used more generally, including in the plural, to refer to demonic enemies of various kinds.

These angelic assignments reveal a pattern to the under-standing of worship in this period: it consists of praise offered to God Most High; praise offered to His Elect One, through whom the saints are made righteous and receive blessings; inter-cessory prayers and supplications; and prayers of repentance with the hope of reconciliation. It is not difficult to see how this understanding of worship passed directly into and formed early Christian worship, with the Elect One identified as the Lord Jesus Christ. Heaven intercedes for the earth, and the congrega-tion of the righteous on earth intercedes for the rest of creation.

Throughout the Book of Parables, themes regarding the Messiah and traditions regarding the second hypostasis of Yahweh, the God of Israel, are drawn together into one single figure. This figure is identified not only as Isaiah's Elect One, Servant, and Anointed One and Daniel's heavenly Son of Man, but also as Wisdom, despite the latter being grammatically fem-inine. Enoch takes a familiar theme from midrashic commen-tary—Wisdom seeking a dwelling on earth and finding none—and applies it to the Elect One. Wisdom comes to earth, and humans reject her, then she returns to be enthroned in the heav-ens. In the process, however, she ends up dwelling with a certain few who are not the ones she first sought, but who desperately need Wisdom (1 Enoch 42:1–3). Saint John uses these same themes in the prologue to his Gospel (John 1:9–13). Much of the remainder of the first parable focuses on the movements of celestial bodies, which will be a greater focus in the following Book of Luminaries. Here, however, the stars are identified not only with the angelic beings but with the destiny of the righ-teous (1 Enoch 43:4—44:1).

Second Parable

The second parable begins by describing the Day of the Lord, here referred to as "that day,"[18] when the Elect One will sit to judge on the throne of glory, which is the throne of the Lord of Spirits Himself (1 Enoch 45:3; see Matt. 25:31–32). The result of this judgment is a transformed and renewed heavens and earth (1 Enoch 45:4–5; Heb. 12:26–28; 2 Pet. 3:12–13; Rev. 21:1). The Elect One judges the rulers and possessors of the earth, the wicked spiritual powers and principalities in the heavenly places, and the wicked of the earth. The purification of the earth, in particular, becomes a blessing to man, reversing the cursed state brought about by sin (1 Enoch 45:5).

Chapter 46 then describes a scene parallel to Daniel 7. Enoch beholds the Ancient of Days and with him another being like a Son of Man (46:1). Enoch asks who the Son of Man is, and his angelic guide tells him that he is identical to the Elect One and the Righteous One whom he saw previously. The Son of Man is further identified as the one who has the right of the firstborn from the Lord of Spirits (v. 3). This single figure then is both the divine one that Enoch had seen earlier and this human figure now with the Ancient of Days. He also has the character of the one who reveals the hidden treasures (compare with Col. 2:2–3). In His judgment, the Son of Man is prophesied victorious over the rulers of the world, casting them down from their thrones and into Sheol, using the parallel language of Isaiah regarding the fall of the devil (1 Enoch 46:4–6; compare with

---

18   See 1 Enoch 45:3; compare with Matt. 7:22; 24:36; 26:29; Mark 13:32; 14:25; Luke 10:12; 17:31; 21:34; Rom. 2:16; 1 Thess. 5:4; 2 Thess. 1:10; 2:3.

Is. 14:9–11). The Son of Man casts them down for not extolling and praising the Son of Man and for not acknowledging from whom they had received their kingdoms (1 Enoch 46:5).

The text further describes the coming heavenly judgment, when the Son of Man will cast down and destroy the principalities and powers that have enslaved the nations. In her song of praise in the Gospel of St. Luke (1:52), the Theotokos uses the specific language here: "[he] shall raise up the kings and the mighty from their seats . . . and he shall put down the kings from their thrones and kingdoms" (vv. 4–5).

The Son of Man does not perform this judgment independently from the Ancient of Days; Enoch immediately describes the Ancient of Days sitting on the same throne and opening the books to render judgment, so the activity of judgment is one (1 Enoch 47:3–4). Though the title Son of Man or Son of Adam points to a human nature for this being, at the same time Enoch continues to describe him in divine terms:

And at that hour the Son of Man was named in the presence of the Lord of Spirits and his name before the Ancient of Days. Even before the sun and the signs were created, before the stars of heaven were made, his name was named before the Lord of Spirits. He will be a staff for the righteous with which for them to stand and not to fall. And he will be the light of the nations and the hope of those whose hearts are troubled. All who dwell on the earth will fall down and worship him, and they will praise and bless and celebrate with song the Lord of Spirits. For this reason, he has been chosen and hidden before him

from before the creation of the world and forevermore.
(1 Enoch 48:2–6)

The Son of Man is the recipient of worship, but that worship
is not given in addition to the worship of the Lord of Hosts; it
is one worship (Phil. 2:11). This section culminates with the
first identification of the Son of Man as the Messiah, Christ,
the Anointed One (1 Enoch 48:10). Saint Symeon, in his identification of Jesus as Messiah (Luke 2:32), echoes the language
Enoch uses regarding the Son of Man.

A recurring motif in the Book of Parables is the Elect One
producing a fountain of wisdom that flows like water (1 Enoch
48:1; 49:1). Saint John in his Gospel uses this language in relation to Christ on multiple occasions (4:14; 7:37–39; also Rev.
21:6). The Spirit of Wisdom indwells him (1 Enoch 49:3), des-
ignating him as the Elect One and allowing this life-giving flow
of Wisdom. As He has already been represented as Wisdom,
this Spirit of Wisdom is His Spirit, but also the Spirit of the
Lord of Spirits. Saint John's Gospel focuses much of its latter
half on the Holy Spirit whom Christ will send, but also refers
to the Spirit coming to rest and stay upon Christ at His Baptism as the marker of His identity as the messianic Son of Man
(1:32–33).

Before the judgment of that day, Enoch presents a period of
time during which humans are able to see the fate of the wicked
powers and of unrepentant sinners and find repentance themselves—even the worst of them (1 Enoch 50:1–4). After the
judgment, however, there is no more repentance or mercy (v. 5).
Enoch also explicitly ties the resurrection of the dead to this

day of judgment. Though the Book of the Watchers describes the realms of the dead and the abodes of their eventual fate, it does not discuss the bodily resurrection in that context. Here, however, Sheol and Hades will give back those whom they have received (51:1; compare with Rev. 20:13). Throughout these judgment descriptions, the text describes the figure on the throne alternately as the Lord of Spirits or Ancient of Days and as the Son of Man or Elect One, parallel to the way in which St. John's Apocalypse describes God and the Lamb seated on the throne (e.g., Rev. 4:1–6; 7:17).

The remainder of the second parable describes the fate of the wicked. Angels of punishment prepare a fiery pit or gorge with chains and scourges of punishment. Enoch asks about this lake of fire, and he is told that it is not being prepared for sinners who dwell on the earth, but for Azazel and the wicked spiritual powers, the rulers of the earth (1 Enoch 53:5; 54:4–5; 55:3–4; compare with Matt. 25:41). These rebellious powers have made themselves subject to Satan and have deceived and led astray into sinfulness those who dwell on the earth (1 Enoch 54:6).

This second parable depicts these hostile powers and the empires they govern as mountains made of various metals, combining several of Daniel's visions regarding world empires (52:1–9). The mountains melt like wax before the Elect One. The unrepentant wicked who dwell on earth end up sharing this same fate: they flee to the lake of fire because of their inability to withstand the glory of God, either directly or as reflected in the faces of the righteous. They go to that place of torment to hide from what they perceive as worse torment by the righteousness of the Lord of Spirits and His Anointed.

The Third Parable

In the final brief parable, Enoch describes the fate of the righteous following the judgment: they are now free of oppression by wicked spirits and the sinners who serve them (53:7). Their life is described as eternal, not merely in the sense of being unending, but of such a quality that time cannot be numbered (58:3–6). Peace and justice characterize this life without end (v. 4). It will also be a life of unending light. The light, righteousness, and peace proceed from the Elect One who stands before the Lord of Spirits, who will become as bright as the sun, dwelling on the earth with the righteous forevermore (compare with Rev. 21:23–24).

Significance to the Church

While the Book of Parables within the Book of Enoch is written in an apocalyptic style similar to that of the rest of the book, it makes important theological points. Likely the most important one is the bringing together of two major themes common in Second Temple literature. The first of these is the theme of the Son of Man, the divine but also human figure from the Book of Daniel who is enthroned and judges the world on the Day of the Lord. The second is the Messiah, the king from the line of David who was expected to come and restore the Kingdom of Israel on the earth. The Book of Parables in a direct and unmistakable way identifies these two as being the same person.

Though this identification of a single Son of Man/Christ figure was not universal in the first century AD, it had become prominent. The way in which the Gospels show Christ referring to Himself as the Son of Man, while also clearly invoking

the traditions concerning the Messiah, presupposes this identification. This is not to say that Christ, God Himself, needed
the Book of Enoch to understand His own identity. Rather, the
drawing together of these traditions allowed those who heard
and experienced Jesus to understand that He is the Son of Man,
the Christ.

III. THE BOOK OF NOAH

Textual History

The latter portion of the Book of Parables (chapters 60–69)
includes a "Book of Noah," an independent Enochic tradition
already in written form by the time it was incorporated into the
Book of Enoch's text. This is evident from a few distinct features: First and foremost, the speaker shifts from Enoch to his
descendant Noah. Occasionally the speaker shifts briefly back
to Enoch, but in each of these cases, the remark involving him
appears to be a later editorial insertion. If these passages were
merely oral traditions about Noah, the composer of the Book of
Parables would have felt free to adapt and streamline it, fitting
it into the overall narrative as he did with all the other Enochic
traditions incorporated into the text. As traditions are transmitted orally, they tend to shift and change in the details. But
once they are written down, they become more settled. That the
composer felt the need to preserve the Book of Noah so intact,
despite its awkward interface with the other material, implies
that the book was already in written form.

The Book of Jubilees mentions a Book of Noah (10:13; 21:10)
that seems to correspond in content to this material. While this
information may seem like scholarly ephemera regarding the

composition history of 1 Enoch, it is important for two reasons: First, it marks the Book of Noah as a work written a century or more earlier than the rest of the Book of Parables, pushing it back into at least the second century BC. Second, it means that the material within the Book of Noah has two contexts: As preserved in 1 Enoch, it has a function within the Book of Parables. It also, however, has its own context, having previously circulated independently. It carried enough prominence to merit its preservation here.

Noah as Protagonist

Chapter 60 begins with the shift to Noah as the speaker in his five-hundredth year. This transition is a bit awkward, as the first verse is clearly an attempt to integrate the Noah material into the Book of Parables. By verse 8, however, Noah clearly refers to Enoch as his grandfather, the seventh from Adam. Enoch's vision, which was the origin of the three parables, here incorporates a vision Noah received immediately before the onset of the Flood. Upon receiving the vision of the Ancient of Days enthroned and surrounded by the angelic hosts, he experiences the same kind of extreme distress the Old Testament prophets experienced when receiving their prophetic calls.

Here, however, Noah's distress is described in graphic terms, with Noah so afraid in the face of the holiness of God that he loses control of his bowels (v. 3). He describes this as a near-death experience in which he dropped dead and his soul left his body for a moment (v. 4). Saint Michael's intervention brings Noah back to himself, and he tells Noah that until the day of Noah's vision, God's patience and long-suffering had prevailed over the wickedness of man. But a change would occur on that coming day. Built into the life of this text is a comparison, then, between the coming of the Flood in Noah's day and the coming of the Day of the Lord at the end of the age, which undergirds much of the New Testament understanding of the delay in Christ's coming.[19]

Old and New Testament References

Saint Michael then tells Noah about the coming Day of Judgment in terms that clearly apply more to the Day of the Lord than to the coming Flood. Here the Flood that Noah will experience is seen as a sort of sign or preliminary fulfillment that ensures the truth of the greater prophecy of the end of days. In preparation for that day, Noah sees the Lord of Spirits separate two beasts, Behemoth and Leviathan. Behemoth is an earthly beast, and the Lord throws him into a desert waste named Duidain, east of Paradise. The sea beast is Leviathan, whom the Lord throws into the abysses of the sea. These two beasts are described in Job 40:15—41:26. Their separation is a polemical inversion of the Babylonian account of creation, in which the dragon that represents the heavens and the one that represents the earth come together and mate in order to create the cosmos. Here, the Lord of Spirits separates them and casts them down.

While the God of Israel dwells in a lush garden on His holy mountain, the beasts come to reside in opposite places—the depths of the sea and a desert wasteland. When Noah seeks to understand their identities, St. Michael shows him the angelic

---

19 Matt. 24:27–29; Luke 17:26–30; 1 Pet. 3:19–20; 2 Pet. 3:9; see also Rom. 1:18.

spirits associated with the winds, the thunders (see Rev. 10:1–7), the mists and rains, and the other elements of creation. These two beasts, then, are wicked spirits operating within these created elements, which have been subjugated to chaos, destruction, and death. Though they, as evil spirits, operate in the world until the end, at the end of days they come back together to feed (1 Enoch 60:23). Saint John portrays the coming together of the beast from the sea and the beast from the earth at the end in his Apocalypse (Rev. 13:1–18). Both these spiritual forces, of tyranny on one hand and chaos on the other, continue to operate in the world but will be fully revealed in the last days.

Pagan Gods and the Old Testament

In addition to the broad description of their character and activity, the two beasts draw directly on ancient Near Eastern divine depictions—pagan gods. "Behemoth" is the plural form of the Hebrew *behema*, a word that means "a beast, an ox, or cattle." The plural is used as a superlative, so Behemoth would be the "Great Beast," the "Great Ox," or the "Great Bull." Every culture in the ancient Near East made use of this "bull of heaven" imagery to express the power of their gods. Female gods are frequently described as heifers, and younger gods—divine sons such as Baal—are calves. The most common form of idolatry in ancient Israel employed this bull and calf imagery, as in the episode with the golden calf (Ex. 32:1–4). Leviathan, likewise, is an ancient demonic being, derived by way of *Lotan* from the Ugaritic *Litanu*. The name likely finds its origin in the verb "to writhe" (as the Arabic *lawiyu*), related to Leviathan's traditional depiction as a seven-headed sea serpent. Leviathan is a spiritual being, an embodiment of chaos and destruction, and is typically portrayed as female; 1 Enoch 60:7 explicitly says it to be so.

In Baal myth, Baal himself slays Leviathan to establish order in the world. She, therefore, typically appears in the Scriptures within anti-Baal polemic texts. Job 3:8 describes the wicked who tempt the patience of Yahweh, the God of Israel, as those who seek to "rouse Leviathan," thereby bringing about the final judgment. Psalm 73/74 takes the great feat supposedly accomplished by Baal and ascribes it instead to Yahweh: "It was You who broke the heads of Leviathan into pieces; You gave her as food to the peoples of Ethiopia" (v. 14). Unlike the parallel Baal and Marduk traditions, however, the God of Israel slays Leviathan for the benefit of humanity out of His love and compassion. Other texts belittle Baal's accomplishment by showing Yahweh treating Leviathan like a fish he catches (Job 41:1) or as a pet with which he plays (Ps. 103/104:26). Isaiah refers to the tradition of Leviathan rising in the last days and describes Yahweh slaying her with a sword, putting to an end her power over the nations (27:1).

Next in the Book of Noah, Noah sees a vision, parallel to Enoch's preceding visions, of the final judgment. The Lord of Spirits Himself seats the Elect One on the throne of the Lord's glory (1 Enoch 62:2). Before this judgment, all the dead are raised—every person who has ever lived, regardless of the means of their demise or the status of their remains. Not one human is lost (61:5; see Rev. 20:12–13). Nonetheless, the focus of judgment here is not the wicked among humanity but the rulers and possessors of the earth. God judges these principalities and powers, not the humans whom they misled, and their punishment is to share the fate ordained for the wicked of humanity (1 Enoch 62:9–13; 63:1–11). These principalities and powers are also distinguished from another group of spirits that Noah sees suffering the same punishment: namely, the Watchers (64:1–2). First Enoch, in all its parts, describes not one but multiple spiritual rebellions as well as a variety of evil spiritual forces, with different origins for their evil.

"Election" in the Book of Parables

Throughout the Book of Parables, the Son of Man is the Elect One and the Righteous One. He has existed from the beginning but was hidden in the presence of the might of the Most High (62:7). In past times, he was revealed only to the elect before his coming revelation as the Messiah (see Col. 1:25–26; John 1:1–2, 18), when he will gather the elect and the righteous to dwell with him forever (1 Enoch 61:3–4; 62:8). While it may be immediately tempting to understand "the elect" and "the righteous" here in terms of modern Protestant theological use of those categories, a number of features of the text of 1 Enoch make this impossible.

The Book of Parables describes the humans facing punishment and the powers and principalities who ruled over them as "their [the demons'] elect and beloved" (56:3–4). "Elect" in Second Temple Jewish literature is not a way of describing a group or an individual member of a group. Obviously, the Son of Man in 1 Enoch was not selected out of some group of sons; he is unique. This idea is in keeping with the election of Israel in Scripture. Israel was not simply one of the nations (as listed in Genesis 10) who was selected above all the others. Rather, Israel was unique among the nations.

One should not conclude then from 1 Enoch's language that the Lord of Spirits and the powers and principalities picked teams for their respective sides at some point in the past. Rather, the terms "righteous" and "beloved" are key here. The language of election is the language of imaging[20] and of sonship—in particular, of firstborn status. The Son of Man is the Elect One because He is the Image and Son par excellence of the Lord of Spirits. His elect are those who, by imaging Him, participate in His righteousness, are justified, and so become sons of God. The elect and beloved of the demonic powers, in contrast, are those who image them on the earth, participating in their rebellion and being corrupted by it, and thus becoming their children. It is by this reasoning that those spiritual powers who have not rebelled can be called "elect angels" (see 1 Tim. 5:21). This understanding that children of God and of light exist in the world, as well as children of Belial and darkness, is a commonplace of Enochic literature. This status is both actualized and revealed by imaging (1 John 3:1–15).

Enoch and the Divine Council

After this first vision, Noah beholds the state of the earth in his own days—corrupted and filled with wickedness. He knows that the destruction of the world he saw in his first vision is imminent, and so he cries out, seeking wisdom. He cries out

---

20 We often think of the image of God as a sort of status bestowed on human beings by God. Instead, serving as God's image in the world is an active pursuit to which humans are called. We are called to image God by representing Him to the rest of His creation and to other people, and by representing the rest of the creation to Him in prayer and intercession.

not directly to God, however, but to his grandfather Enoch (1 Enoch 65:2–4). Enoch not only was taken into the heavens and given the vision to share with humanity—an experience common to all the classical Hebrew prophets—but is also seen here to have an ongoing role as a member of the angelic council that surrounds the throne of the Lord of Spirits.

Enoch now serves for his descendant Noah the function that the archangels served for him in his own apocalyptic journey. Like the archangels, Enoch is not a figure with special powers in his own right but rather serves as a messenger for the Lord of Spirits (vv. 5–11). This understanding of the departed saints, already present centuries before the Christian era, would continue in the Church in the understanding of their appearances to those on earth in times of trouble and distress.

Waters as Punishment and Healing

The text here portrays the Flood itself as God removing His restraint from the waters. More specifically, the waters represent chaos and destruction, and spirits of chaos and destruction are associated with them. But the Lord of Spirits has assigned angels over these powers of the waters to prevent them from destroying the earth (66:1–3). When He removes the restraint, the waters come and destroy everything. God uses the waters, however, to do good. The release of their destructive force punishes the powers of the waters on the earth; at the same time God heals the body of the earth (67:8) by removing the agents of evil and their evil works, thus purifying and healing the world.

The Flood's purification of the earth from the rebellious spirits' evil in the days of Noah, then, is a testimony to a future, greater fulfillment. The day will come when the waters themselves will be purified and healed through the destruction of the powers over them (67:11–12). This cleansing of the waters from evil powers is fulfilled at the Baptism of Christ: the waters of chaos and death become the waters of purification, refreshment, and rebirth in baptism (see 1 Pet. 3:18–22). We see this understanding in the hymnography at the Great Blessing of the Waters: "Today the substance of water is made holy, / for the Master is washed in the Jordan. / When the River sees Him, it stops its flow and bursts forth" (Greek Orthodox translation).

At the time of the Flood, the unrepentant wickedness of the fallen Watchers is so abhorrent that even Ss. Michael and Raphael will not intercede for them, for to do so would be to take their side in rebellion against the Lord of Spirits (1 Enoch 68:1–5; see also 1 John 5:16–17). Next follows another list of the leaders of the rebellious Watchers, numbered at twenty—with Azazel separately as the twenty-first (1 Enoch 69:1–3). The text details the secrets of knowledge that these angelic beings taught to humans in order to further their self-destruction. Notable inclusions are weapons and armor for war, the preservation of secrets in writing, abortion, and magical oaths. The book describes the covenant with Noah following the Flood as an oath, a pact between the Lord of Spirits and the spirits superintending the various elements of the creation. He allows them to function as normal while restraining the forces of chaos and destruction until the end of days (vv. 16–25).

God's preservation of the world is, then, the restraint of supernatural and human evil within the cosmos, and the relaxing of that restraint is a form of judgment: God gives over humanity to its own evil devices and to those powers whom it has worshipped and obeyed. The covenant with Noah sealed by the rainbow, then, is not only a promise not to allow another flood of water but a promise to restrain the forces of wickedness until the last days, so that the situation in Noah's time will not recur until then (Gen. 8:20–22). The Book of Parables then concludes with Enoch ascending back to heaven to stand before the divine throne, as well as with a parting benediction retained from the earlier, independent text.

Significance to the Church

The Book of Noah as it has been incorporated into 1 Enoch is a very early artifact of tradition. Not only does it give us a glimpse of those early traditions, but the text of 1 Enoch gives us an example of how the incorporation of preexisting written traditions took place in the Second Temple period. By framing its narrative around Noah, the Book of Noah portrays Enoch in terms directly parallel to the later Christian understanding of the intercessory ministry of departed saints. The book's presentation of the reason for the delay of the coming of the Lord, in parallel to the days of the approaching Flood, is as timely today as it was two millennia ago.

THE FINAL THREE SECTIONS
OF THE BOOK OF ENOCH

Textual History

The last three portions of the Book of Enoch—the last three material elements that have been incorporated into the text—are considerably shorter than the first two, which most likely represent the most ancient traditions. These three sections are called the Book of Luminaries, the Book of Dreams, and the Epistle of Enoch. They also represent more diverse elements in regard to their teachings. The Book of the Watchers and the Book of Parables (including the Book of Noah) represent apocalyptic traditions both historical, in describing the origin of evil, and eschatological, in describing its final destiny. These apocalyptic traditions became formative for Jewish communities in Ethiopia, Egypt, and even in Palestine (such as at Qumran).

But the latter portions of the Book of Enoch represent those communities' reflections on the history of Israel and their place in it, as well as the ordering of their communities. Enochic literature historically produced such prophetic communities with features that would be incorporated into later Christian monastic traditions—not coincidentally beginning in some of the same regions of the world. As we have already seen, several New Testament texts, including St. Matthew's Gospel and the General Epistles, are grounded more deeply in Enochic Judaism than the Torah-based Judaism of the Pharisees, which evolved into Rabbinic Judaism centuries later.

IV. THE BOOK OF LUMINARIES

THE BOOK OF LUMINARIES currently constitutes chapters 72–82 of 1 Enoch. Its primary purpose is to lay out the basis of the Enochic calendar. Ultimately, this is a 364-day solar calendar, divided into four quarters of three thirty-day months each, with a single day inserted between the quarters. In the book, God grants Enoch a vision of the heavenly host, the sun, moon, and stars, and their paths through the heavens during

the various quarters, or seasons, of the year. The conception of
the heavenly host as angelic beings traveling in chariots harmo-
nizes with the general Second Temple view of the sun, moon,
and stars. These angels are tasked with two things: participation
in God's governance of creation (Gen. 1:16; Ps. 135/136:8) and
communicating on God's behalf, especially regarding times and
seasons (Gen. 1:14; Ps. 103/104:19).

After a detailed accounting of dates and seasons, laying out
the calendar in prose, the Archangel Uriel applies what might
otherwise be merely an obscure curiosity of ancient timekeep-
ing (1 Enoch 80—81): Uriel repeatedly describes the movements of the sun, moon, and stars as following divine "laws."
Their regularity and obedience are perfect, in contrast to the
way humanity conducts itself regarding the law of God. The
text speaks of certain stars that will transgress their laws and
be cast out of heaven to the earth, along with the disobedient
who dwell on the earth (81:3–4). To sin is, therefore, to separate oneself from the order of God's creation. These angelic
beings—the sun, moon, and stars who travel in chariots—
record all the deeds of men on heavenly tablets or books (81:1–
4; see Rev. 20:12).

The Book of Luminaries concludes with Enoch delivering
the books containing his visions to Methuselah to be preserved
for posterity (81:5—82:3). The story of the delivery of the texts
appears to be connective tissue that was inserted later, when the
Book of Luminaries was integrated into the Book of Enoch as a
whole.

Significance to the Church

The Book of Luminaries presents one position in a fierce disagreement within Second Temple Judaism over the proper calendar to follow in celebrating Jewish festivals. During that period, the Sadducees, who controlled the temple in Jerusalem, used the Julian calendar—the Roman civil calendar. Most other Jewish communities of the period considered the use of a pagan calendar to be a compromise with Rome. The Pharisees observed the festal calendar laid out in the Torah as precisely as possible. But because the Torah presents a lunar calendar of 360 days, whole months would need to be added every so often to keep the calendar on track.

Certain groups within Second Temple Judaism considered the 364-day Enochic calendar described by the Book of Luminaries to be mathematically perfect, though we now know it is lacking one and a quarter days in the year. This perceived mathematical perfection argued, in their minds, that this calendar was from God, as opposed to other imperfect calendars, which came from man. The community at Qumran, which produced the Dead Sea Scrolls, went into the desert as dissidents expressly to follow the Enochic calendar.

This level of dedication to a calendar may seem extreme to contemporary readers—at least to those not familiar with the heated battles in the twentieth century over the Orthodox Church's calendar. What the debate reveals, however, is a certain view of the importance of the cycle of feasts and fasts of the Church. The times and seasons of the year are not simply human measures of human devising but should accurately reflect the order that God has built into His creation. A person who follows the correct calendar should, by the discipline of its observances, be brought into the order of creation. Like all the disciplines given to God's people, the calendar represents a means of pursuing salvation.

V. THE BOOK OF DREAMS

THE NEXT SECTION after the Book of Luminaries is the Book of Dreams. Now chapters 83–90 of 1 Enoch, the Book of Dreams consists of Enoch relating a series of his visions to Methuselah, his descendant; thus the introduction of Methuselah at the end of the Book of Luminaries serves as a segue.

Enoch's first dream vision is related in chapters 83 and 84. In it, he sees the coming Flood and the destruction of all flesh for its wickedness. Enoch says he had this dream as a youth and told it immediately to his grandfather Malalel. In response to the dream, Enoch goes out and prays to the Lord of Glory (1 Cor. 2:8; James 2:1) that He would spare for Himself a righteous remnant on the earth (1 Enoch 83:8). This vision brings the Flood story into the narrative of the righteous preserved remnant that flows through St. Elias's doubts, the Old Testament prophets, and eventually into the ministry of St. John the Forerunner and St. Paul's understanding of Israel. Further, Enoch here directly connects the remnant with the faithful angelic host and the wicked with those angels who have fallen into sin, incorporating spiritual warfare into the wrath of the Flood (83:11; 84:4–6).

The Animal Apocalypse

The greater body of the Book of Dreams consists of the Animal Apocalypse. This is not some sort of massacre of wildlife, but rather an apocalyptic vision that depicts the history of the world from beginning to end in the form of interactions among a variety of animals, both wild and domestic. As with most apocalyptic literature, the intent here is not merely to tell the history of the world by means of an allegorical fable, but to bring together the events both of material history and of the spiritual realm into one narrative. Apocalyptic literature does not view history as a chain of earthly cause and effect, occasionally interrupted by divine intervention. Rather, cause and effect ripple through both the visible and the invisible realms, with each affecting the other and with spiritual beings crossing over from one to the other in regular interactions.

Enoch relates this vision, the Animal Apocalypse, to his son Methuselah as well. It begins with a bull who comes out of the ground and a heifer who also "comes out," clearly intended to represent Adam and Eve. The story then describes their sons and descendants as bulls, including Enoch himself (1 Enoch 85:3–10). At this time Enoch beholds a star falling from heaven (86:1), connecting the fall of the devil to events surrounding Adam and Eve and the expulsion from Paradise. This star lays hold of Cain, the black bull, and begins to operate through him (86:2; see also 1 John 3:12).

Shortly thereafter, Enoch sees many stars fall to earth and begin, in a rather graphic fashion, to impregnate various heifers (1 Enoch 86:3–4). The pregnant cows then give birth to all manner of wild, bloodthirsty beasts. This event clearly represents the fall of the Watchers and the beginning of the Nephilim. The text later describes the dividing of the nations at the Tower of Babel: God entrusts the wild animals, representing the seventy nations, to seventy shepherds and warns them that their deeds in shepherding these animals will be recorded for later judgment (89:59–60; see also Deut. 32:8).

All the humans before the Flood are described as bulls, likely connected to the symbolism of Behemoth, the bull of heaven, the great beast. Adam and Eve were created as both spiritual and earthly beings, and despite the fall into sin, their spiritual nature lingers in the greatly extended lifespans described in the genealogies of Genesis before the Flood. One exception to this rule is Noah, who is born as a bull but becomes a man (1 Enoch 89:1). We will say more about the special nature of Noah in Enochic literature in the discussion of the Epistle of Enoch, 1 Enoch's final portion.

The seven archangels punish the fallen angels, and the Flood destroys wicked humanity and the Nephilim (88:3—89:8). The bulls of Noah's sons then sire the nations: Shem begets another white bull, representing Abraham, and he is the last bull described in the descent of man in the Animal Apocalypse (89:10). Abraham, this last and unique white bull, represents the last of the type of man begun with Adam, carried through the line of Seth, and ending with Noah and Shem. His son Isaac is a white calf who sires a wild boar and a white sheep, representing Edom and Israel, respectively (v. 12). From this point forward in the narrative, Israel and all his descendants are depicted as sheep, in contrast to the wild beasts of the nations, many of them predators or scavengers. From this point forward in the narrative, God is the Lord of the sheep, that is, the God of Israel (see also Heb. 13:20). The identity of the remnant of Israel as "sheep" is also a recurring theme throughout the Gospels.[21]

Within the narrative of the Animal Apocalypse, the Egyptians are wolves, and the Lord sends the sheep to pasture among them. Despite the responsibility of the shepherd of Egypt—and thereby the Egyptians—to protect the sheep, they turned and preyed on them (1 Enoch 89:13–15; see also Matt. 7:15; 10:16). Moses is here presented as one of the sheep (1 Enoch 89:16 and following). While subtle, this emphasis reflects a theme within Enochic literature: demoting Moses and thereby the Torah as definitive for faith and life. Previous figures up to Abraham and even, by extension, Isaac are bulls. David and his descendants will be rams. Moses, as well as Aaron, are simply sheep like the others. It is the Lord Himself who delivers the sheep out of Egypt.

Beginning with the sin involving the golden calf and continuing through the rest of the narrative, many of the sheep are blinded (1 Enoch 89:33). The language is important: These are not sheep that had been born blind, but sheep that have been blinded by their wickedness and rebellion. Their blindness is not a fault of their creation but a punishment brought about by hard-heartedness (see Matt. 12:22; 15:14; 23:16–26; John 9:39–41; 12:40).

As already mentioned, as the history of Israel continues to unfold, first Saul and then David appear as rams (1 Enoch 89:42–48). Solomon, another ram, builds the temple, which is

---

21 See Matt. 9:36; 10:6; 15:24; 25:32–33; 26:31; John 10:1–16, 26–27; 21:16–17.

described as a low house and a high tower. The purpose of the house is sacrifice, described here as a wide table spread before the Lord of the sheep. Sacrifice, then, is understood as the Lord feeding His sheep (v. 50). Saint Elias—the Prophet Elijah—is a sheep whom the other sheep attempt to kill before he is brought up to Enoch in heaven to dwell with him there, connecting these two figures (v. 52). As the northern and southern kingdoms are judged, Enoch in heaven intercedes through prayer for the sheep below, that the Lord would have mercy on them (v. 57).

God sends the sheep into exile, giving them over to the shepherds of the nations, who then give the sheep over, each in turn as the empires succeed one another, to be devoured (v. 68). The temple is destroyed (vv. 66–67). The narrative describes the rebuilding of the temple under Ezra and Nehemiah, but here it clearly rejects the second temple as unclean—another emphasis of the Enochic literature (vv. 72–73). The blinding and deafening of the sheep is continuous and ongoing until it produces a latter-day generation that is utterly unable to see and hear the Lord of the sheep (90:7).

The Animal Apocalypse ends on a note of eschatological promise, despite the wickedness of the deaf and blind sheep and the swarming beasts of the nations feeding on the few innocent lambs. Finally, the man charged with recording the deeds of the shepherds reveals them on the last day to the Lord of the sheep, and in response, He rends heaven and earth (90:17–18). All the books are opened, and judgment ensues, facilitated by the seven archangels. First, judgment begins with the devil (v. 21), then the other stars who fell, the Watchers (v. 24). Next the Lord of the sheep judges the seventy shepherds of the nations

(vv. 22–23, 25; see also Ps. 81/82). All those judged are thrown into an abyss of fire. Once the wicked spiritual powers have been judged, the blind sheep who through wickedness refused to see and hear receive the same fate (1 Enoch 90:26–27; see also Rev. 20:9–15).

Anticipating the Messiah and the Transformation of Humanity

Two images follow of the Messiah, who will come later. The first is of a new temple, the second temple having been discarded as unclean. This temple builds from the symbolism of the promised temple of Ezekiel but associates it clearly with the messianic age (90:29–36). Significantly, this house is filled not only with the righteous sheep but also with all manner of wild animals and birds from the other nations (v. 33); entering the house restores their sight (v. 35). These are not the animals that were perfect, but the ones that did not persist in hardening themselves and so were healed. Those within this new house are then transformed because the Messiah is born among them, the greatest and most powerful white bull who is worshipped by all (v. 37). His birth among them transforms the sheep into white bulls, like Adam and Eve and the other humans of old (v. 38). Enoch awakens from his dream and glorifies the Lord of righteousness for this second vision, then weeps at the memory of his first and the destruction of the Flood (vv. 39–42).

Significance to the Church

Five hundred years before St. Athanasius, before the Birth of Christ, Enoch's vision here anticipates that the Incarnation of the Son of Man will restore and transform the human race in His image. Like the rest of 1 Enoch, the Animal Apocalypse identifies the origin of evil with fallen spiritual beings who deceive, manipulate, and ultimately come to control the actions of humans. The "fall" of humanity is not a single event or transition but an ongoing corruption, weakening, and decline of the human race. When Christ perfectly united His divine nature to our human one in His Person, He cleansed, purified, strengthened, and reinvigorated humanity. Through Christ, all humanity is reinvigorated in our shared battle against our spiritual enemies.

VI. THE EPISTLE OF ENOCH

Textual History

The final portion of the Book of Enoch, comprising what is generally numbered as chapters 91–108, is commonly referred to as the Epistle of Enoch. Though *epistle* gives the idea of a letter, these chapters are not a letter written by Enoch. Rather, they purport to be a record of Enoch's parting words to his son Methuselah and his extended family. Depending on the translation, 1 Enoch may end with a brief, two-verse chapter 105, continue through to chapter 108, or jump from the former ending to chapter 108. Some translations incorporate all the material, numbering chapters 105–108 as verses of chapter 105. These variations are based on our somewhat scattered manuscript evidence.

The complete Book of Enoch is found in the Ge'ez language in the Old Testament of Ethiopian Bibles, and partial Greek and Aramaic manuscripts of earlier provenance also exist. It appears that in at least some languages, fragments of the Enoch tradition were appended to the end of 1 Enoch after its five major parts were edited together. But it is unclear whether these were written fragments added to texts in the scribal process or if they were fragments of oral tradition incorporated into the text in written form for the first time.

Contents

The main body of the Epistle of Enoch, before the various endings, consists of Enoch relating to his family a vision that lays out the future history of the world as a series of weeks, because he has been told he is about to ascend to the heavens. The vision begins with Enoch's own era and continues until the end of days and the Final Judgment. After describing this future, Enoch then gives counsel and direction to his family on how to live in the coming ages. These homiletical applications are, of course, aimed primarily at the readers of the text in those latter times. This means that the Epistle of Enoch, written in the Hasmonean period (circa 150 BC), gives us an early and prime example of apocalyptic preaching during the Second Temple period. As we will see, the Epistle of Enoch contains clear connections in both form and content to Christ's own preaching as recorded in the synoptic Gospels, justifying and facilitating their apocalyptic interpretation.

The basic themes of this preaching are set out in what is now chapter 91 of 1 Enoch. Enoch calls on his children to walk in and practice righteousness (v. 3). This is particularly important because of the great wickedness on the earth during their lifetimes (v. 5). The text, as should be clear from its date of final composition, is not aimed primarily at antediluvian peoples. The judgment of wickedness in the Flood will be succeeded by a second period in which wickedness will rise to a climax, eventually to be answered by a Final Judgment (v. 6). The initial readers of the text in this form were living in these latter days. This Last Judgment includes the resurrection of the dead, when the righteous will receive eternal life and the wicked will go to eternal darkness (92:3–5). Enoch then approaches this theme homiletically along two different lines.

The Prophecy of Weeks

The first of these is the prophecy of weeks. Enoch speaks of the entire history of the cosmos from its beginning as a series of "weeks," though not necessarily to indicate any particular period of time nor to associate that period with a multiple of seven. One unfortunate diversion in interpreting the apocalyptic literature within Scripture is the overliteralization of numbers and time periods. Any reasonable reading of 1 Enoch and other Second Temple apocalyptic literature makes it clear that such a literal interpretation is not defensible. Enoch claims to have this knowledge of history from reading the heavenly tablets, which represent a tradition found throughout the ancient Near East, most commonly expressed in the English Bible as the Book of Life.[22] The focus of the weeks is not on the quality of the era that the epoch represents; rather, it is on a transitional figure or event that arises at the end of one week, which then begins the next.

---

22   See Luke 10:20; Phil. 4:3; Rev. 3:5; 13:8; 17:8; 20:12–15.

WEEKS 1–6

And so, the first week ends with the birth of Enoch, the seventh from Adam, who obviously within the Enochic tradition is a figure of primary transitional importance (1 Enoch 93:3). The second week ends with "the First End," the Flood of Noah, in which a man is saved (v. 4). The third week ends with the call of Abraham, who will become a "plant of righteousness" that grows and blossoms forever (v. 5; compare with Rom. 11:16–24). The fourth week ends with the giving of the Torah as a result of "visions" (v. 6). Here the appearance of Yahweh, the God of Israel, to Moses is considered at least as significant as the written text itself. The end of the fifth week features the building of the temple (v. 7). In the sixth week, Israel falls into apostasy, a man (Elijah) ascends to heaven, and at the end, the temple burns to the ground and "the whole race of the chosen root" scatters in exile (v. 8).

WEEK 7: THE RISE OF THE APOSTATE GENERATION

The seventh week, then, is the period of time when the Book of Enoch was compiled. This period is marked by the rise of "an apostate generation," all of whose deeds are apostasy (v. 9).[23] At the end of this week, the Messiah appears (1 Enoch 93:10). The great increase in evil results in the end of God's long-suffering and the revelation of His wrath (91:7; see Rom. 1:18). This coming of the Messiah has two primary effects on the following week: First, the nations give up their idols, and God casts down the gods of the nations and hurls them into the fire of eternal

---

23   See also Matt. 11:16; 12:41–45; 16:4; 23:36; 24:34; Mark 8:12, 38; 13:30; Luke 7:31; 11:29–32, 50–51; 16:8; 17:25; 21:32; Acts 2:40.

punishment (1 Enoch 91:9). Second, His coming also represents the beginning of the resurrection of the dead, who, upon their resurrection, receive Wisdom (v. 10).

WEEK 8 AND ON INTO ETERNITY

The next period, the eighth week, is the age of righteousness (v. 12; see Romans 1—5). It is a period of spiritual warfare, a battle against sin. At the end of the week, those who practice righteousness receive houses within the house of the Great King in Glory (1 Enoch 91:13; see also John 14:2–3). In the ninth week, the entire earth will be judged, and sin will be put away forever—the earth passes away and is reborn (1 Enoch 91:14). In the tenth, God judges the heavens—the Watchers and the other rebellious powers (v. 15); the heavens pass away and are replaced with a new and eternal heaven of purity (v. 16; see also Matt. 24:35; Luke 21:33; 2 Pet. 3:13; Rev. 21:1). Weeks without end then follow (1 Enoch 91:17). The separation by the age of the coming of the Messiah from the Final Judgment is an important feature of Second Temple apocalyptic literature, even outside of explicitly Christian contexts. In light of these ages to come, Enoch exhorts his children to walk in righteousness through their time on earth (vv. 18–19).

A Series of Woes

Enoch's second homiletical approach is laying out a series of woes that will come upon sinners as the Day of Judgment approaches (94:6—100:13). These woes are not merely condemnations of the world outside the Enochic community; rather, Enoch proclaims them to his people as a series of warnings not to be misled by the evil practices of the surrounding world. In form and function, these woes parallel those of St. Luke's Gospel (6:24–26; see also Matt. 11:21; 18:7; 23:13–36; 26:24) and St. John's Apocalypse (8:13; 9—11; 12:12). As in the case of St. Luke's Gospel, many of Enoch's woes relate to wealth and influence, Mammon, as a false god (94:7–8; 96:4–6, 8; 97:8–10; 98:2, 11). Beyond this recurring theme, the text describes a wide range of sins: blasphemy, bearing false witness, persecution, and even taking vengeance. Judgment here involves the scales of justice being balanced and the wicked suffering loss as they receive their own wicked deeds upon themselves.

Enoch goes on to describe violence filling the whole earth and then the judgment itself, when the blood will run up to the chests of horses (100:3; compare with Rev. 14:20). In the midst of this judgment, however, the righteous have two reasons to take comfort: First, God will assign a guardian angel to protect each one of them from the wickedness of the world (1 Enoch 100:5). These angels bear witness in heaven to the deeds of the wicked against those whom they protect (100:10; see Matt. 18:10). Second, the righteous will participate in the resurrection, no matter how long they have lain asleep in the grave (1 Enoch 100:5).

In chapters 101 and 102, Enoch invokes the awe of the created order and from it argues for greater awe, fear, and reverence for its Creator, expressed through obedience. He then describes the fate of the righteous and the wicked while they sleep in the grave, before the resurrection. The souls of those who have died in righteousness will live before God until the time comes for them to awaken (103:4). The souls of those who die in their sin, though the world may think them to have been blessed in life, will go down into Sheol and then into chains, burning flames, and the Great Judgment, which will last for all generations forever (vv. 5–8). Though the righteous suffer many things in this life, they are not forgotten. The angels of heaven ever intercede for them, and their names are written in the tablets of heaven (104:1). The text of 1 Enoch proper then ends with a command not to alter or change or add to Enoch's writings nor to believe those who do (104:10–11; compare with Rev. 22:18–19).

Significance to the Church

The Prophecy of Weeks, sometimes called the Apocalypse of Weeks, makes explicit the understanding of history resident in much of Second Temple Judaism. Ancient cultures typically viewed the history of the world as an endlessly repeating cycle: nations, empires, and civilizations rose and fell. The structure of the world changed through cycles. Even the gods rose to prominence, then were defeated by a succeeding generation of divine beings. The Prophecy of Weeks, however, sees history as having both a beginning point and an ending point. Certainly, history repeats itself, and certain patterns recur. But history is progressing toward a destiny and a goal. History has an aim. God is guiding His creation toward a blessed end.

ADDITIONAL MATERIAL

As previously mentioned, in some versions of the text of 1 Enoch, additional material has been appended to the end. In some cases, this material is broken off as an appendix; in other cases, it is incorporated as chapters 105:3—108; elsewhere it is incorporated as additional verses of chapter 105. This material is clearly of a different origin from the Epistle of Enoch and does not continue its flow; instead, it represents a particular Noah tradition found in other Second Temple texts regarding his unique birth and nature.

This unique birth then raises the question of whether Noah himself is, in fact, one of the Nephilim, albeit one whose ways were righteous. There are variations on all these details within the surviving written expressions of these traditions, and they seem to serve two functions vis-à-vis the text of Genesis: First, they serve to answer the question of the reemergence of the Nephilim and giant clans after the Flood, which within the narrative of the Old Testament was sent to destroy them all. Second, it interprets Noah's corrupt generation not as a temporal generation but as a race (Gen. 6:9). This allows the idea of the Nephilim's corruption of the whole earth, save the righteous Noah, to be read quite literally.

In the particular version of the story appended to 1 Enoch, Noah, at his birth, has white woolen hair and bright skin, and a light shines from his eyes (105:2). Though he is a newborn, he speaks. His father, Lamech, panics, thinking that Noah is not human but a being of a different nature and the offspring of one of the angels of heaven (vv. 3–4). He brings that concern to Methuselah, his father, to find out the truth. Methuselah goes on a pilgrimage to a place where he can pray to Enoch, his own father, in the heavens to inquire of God through him (vv. 6–7).

Through Enoch, God reveals to Methuselah that Noah and his three sons will be the means through which humanity will survive the coming judgment of the Flood and that Noah is, in fact, Lamech's son (vv. 12–15; 17–19). He adds, however, that Noah's progeny will also eventually beget giants on the earth like those who troubled the earth in his day (v. 16). Finally, he gives Methuselah a book, once again reiterating the fate of the righteous and the wicked as previously described in 1 Enoch, and a final benediction.

CONCLUSION: SIGNIFICANCE OF THE BOOK OF ENOCH TO THE CHURCH

First Enoch, then, is not a single work of a single genre. Rather, it is a collection of ancient apocalyptic traditions transmitted for some centuries orally, then as independently written documents, and finally as one collected text. Outside of Ethiopia and Eritrea, 1 Enoch is not canonical; it is not read publicly in the worship of the Church. On the other hand, as this chapter demonstrates, these traditions and their written form have shaped major portions of the New Testament, such as St. Matthew's Gospel, the Johannine corpus, the Petrine Epistles, and Jude.

The work is best seen, then, as St. Nikephoros I, Patriarch of Constantinople, stated in the ninth century: as an apostolic apocryphon.[24] It can be described as "hidden" because it is not read publicly. It is, however, apostolic because it represents in written form traditions that formed a part of the apostolic teaching, as attested by St. Irenaeus of Lyons and others directly

---

24 Literally, "a hidden thing." In St. Nikephoros's usage, *apocryphon* more commonly means "private" rather than "public." He saw the Book of Enoch as a text that influenced the apostles without being openly cited, with the exception of St. Jude.

connected to the apostles by chronology and spiritual father-hood. It is a vital part of the tradition in which the Scriptures, particularly the New Testament, were formed. It is also a vital part of the tradition in which the Scriptures were passed on to the Fathers. First Enoch can, therefore, be a vital part of our own understanding of the Scriptures in their original context and world.

CHAPTER THREE

Slavonic Enoch (2 Enoch) and the Apocalypse of Abraham

Preserved Enochic Literature outside St. Nikephoros's List

ENOCHIC MATERIAL" is not merely a conventional way of naming a particular group of texts. As previously noted, the Book of Enoch, or 1 Enoch, is itself made up of a series of earlier texts and oral traditions. Beyond the scope of that book in its fullest form, a number of other texts contain related traditions. The Book of Enoch has a certain pride of place within this literature, not only thanks to its popularity; it is the lone book in this category that St. Nikephoros of Constantinople identified as an apostolic apocryphon. This means it has a greater reliability than some other texts, theologically and also for St. Nikephoros historically.

Two Enochic works that do not share this status but have nonetheless been preserved are the book now known as Slavonic or 2 Enoch and the Apocalypse of Abraham. Both texts have been preserved in the Slavonic language in broadly Christian, rather than Jewish, circles. They were used authoritatively by certain schismatic groups who were condemned as heretics, which has left their memory somewhat sullied. Regardless of who precisely preserved them, however, this literature bears witness to ideas, currents, and traditions from the pre-Christian world of Second Temple Judaism. Many of these traditions also expand on themes contained in 1 Enoch and elsewhere. Though less valuable theologically than 1 Enoch and not included in St. Nikephoros's list, these two books are still worthy of consideration as a repository of Enochic traditions.

2 (SLAVONIC) ENOCH

Background

The full text of 2 Enoch, also sometimes referred to as the Slavonic Apocalypse of Enoch, is available only in Slavonic, and its use was widespread throughout the Slavic world. Twenty manuscripts copied between the fourteenth and eighteenth centuries have been preserved for us in libraries of Russia, Serbia, and Bulgaria. Further, these twenty manuscripts show distinctive features—meaning that they are not copies of each other but represent independent lines of copying. The text includes certain Greek etymologies that demonstrate its translation from Greek. Additionally, several untranslated Hebrew terms and emphases regarding Jerusalem, the temple, and sacrifices imply a Hebrew or Aramaic original from the pre-Christian era.

For some time, a scholarly debate raged about the antiquity of the text, with many scholars assigning its composition to the tenth century, based on the Greek factors. Recently, however, a few Coptic fragments of 2 Enoch have been discovered, demonstrating an earlier date of the text. This means that this

text was translated into Greek and preserved in Orthodox circles, ultimately translated into Slavonic; the Slavonic-speaking
Orthodox churches then continued to copy this text across a
vast geographical area for more than seventeen hundred years.
The manuscript evidence ends in the eighteenth century, not
because 2 Enoch was abandoned, but rather because of the
advent of the printing press.

Textual History

Second Enoch is an ancient Jewish text, but we know of it in the
present time only in Slavonic—specifically, an old Bulgarian
translation. The oldest of these Slavonic manuscripts dates to
the fourteenth century AD, and because the text seems to have
been preserved in part by the Bogomils,[25] its public reputation
has been damaged. Second Enoch is now commonly dated to
the first century AD for several reasons, many of them revolv-
ing around the way in which the temple is discussed. The book
shows no clear signs of Christian editing or direct references to
Christian doctrine, nor are there any indicators that the temple
had been destroyed.

Contents and Significance

Though similar in genre and in some of its contents, 2 Enoch
is not a sequel or continuation of the narrative of the Book of
Enoch, or 1 Enoch. It is a separate apocalyptic text describing Enoch's heavenly ascent in Genesis and the ten heavens
through which he passes, guided by angels. At the conclusion

25　The Bogomils were a heretical Christian group in the medieval Bal-
　　kans. See the Glossary.

of his ascent, God speaks to Enoch face to face and reveals to him the mysteries of his age, from the expulsion from Paradise to the Flood of Noah. Enoch is then sent back to earth to teach what he has learned to his descendants. The text concludes with Enoch essentially receiving a successor in Melchizedek.

The overall pattern of the book sets Enoch as an alternate Moses. Moses is not mentioned, nor is the Torah, even in the section that consists primarily of ethical teaching. Second Enoch, then, shows all the earmarks of a sectarian document. It likely emerged from a Judean sect who attributed their cosmology and way of life to God's direct revelation through Enoch. Tying their own way of life to Enoch and the antediluvian age is a sort of theological trump card over other Torah-based Jewish sects. The book gives us a witness into another form of Second Temple Judaism whose traditions resonated with at least some Christians and Christian communities. Not only was 2 Enoch preserved over the centuries; the book also shows clear parallels between its cosmology of the ten heavens and various medieval cosmologies of the heavens.

Cosmology and Astrology

The cosmology of the early portion of 2 Enoch is an important window into Second Temple Jewish understandings of the relationship between angels and visible, material phenomena, as well as the stars of the heavens and pagan gods. Various angelic beings, some righteous and some fallen, preside over the heavens. The angels of the first heaven control the four winds, rain, snow, and hail. The fourth heaven contains the angels of the sun and moon as well as the heavenly host, which sings as a choir.

The sixth heaven contains the angels who oversee the elements of creation, like mountains, rivers, the sea, and crops, as well as the angels who write the deeds of humanity in books, awaiting the judgment. The eighth heaven contains the constellations, in particular the twelve signs of the zodiac, and the ninth heaven contains the houses of the zodiac. It is worth noting that the highest levels of heaven here, immediately below the throne of God, are not occupied by archangels but by the zodiac. Many Second Temple Jewish groups saw astrology as a means by which God communicates to humanity.

Relatively unique is 2 Enoch's placing of the location of punishment for the fallen angels within the heavens, though the text also refers to these particular heavens as being under the earth. In the second heaven, Enoch encounters a group of rebel angels who are bound in darkness, awaiting punishment. In a scene similar to the one that unfolds with the imprisoned Watchers in 1 Enoch, they ask Enoch to pray and intercede for them, but here he refuses. The third heaven contains both Paradise, the destination of righteous humans after their death, and Hades, the destination of the wicked. Second Enoch's depiction of the third heaven is consonant with St. Paul's vision (2 Cor. 12:2–4). In the fifth heaven, Enoch encounters another group of Watchers explicitly identified with those who descended to Mount Hermon and took for themselves the daughters of men. Enoch does not intercede for this group either; rather, he persuades them to repent and offer worship to God Most High. This distinction highlights the difference between regret and avoiding consequences on one hand and true repentance on the other.

As he and Gabriel pass through the seventh heaven, Enoch

gets his first glimpse of God Himself enthroned, albeit at a distance. At the conclusion of his ascent, in the tenth heaven, Enoch speaks to God directly, face to face, and God gives him all knowledge of the age that will end with the Flood. This revelation covers some of the same material as the heavenly ascents, but here it is structured around the seven days of Creation and a prophesied future eighth day. Each of these days is also associated with an age of a thousand years in the history of the world (compare 2 Pet. 3:8). In 2 Enoch, Satan and his followers (not including the Watchers, called *Grigori* in Slavonic, who will fall later) fall from their angelic estate on the second day of Creation, when he first conceives of the idea of rebellion. He then follows through on that idea by tempting Eve in Paradise.

Chapter 30 discusses another group of fallen angelic beings in a subtle way. The narration of the fourth day of Creation— the sun, moon, and stars and their appointment to govern— makes explicit not only the sun and moon but also five other heavenly beings named Kronos, Aphrodite, Ares, Zeus, and Hermes, in descending order. These are references both to angels and to planets, and those planets are explicitly related to the zodiac. While some may find it shocking to find an account of the God of Israel creating the Greek gods, this is essentially an interpretation of texts such as Deuteronomy 32:8 and 4:19, which describe how, at the Tower of Babel, God assigned heavenly beings to watch over and shepherd the nations. These beings included the sun, moon, stars, and other angelic beings associated with various constellations. The nations of the world, however, began to worship these spirits as gods in and of themselves, including the Greeks' worship of beings named Kronos,

Aphrodite, Ares, Zeus, and Hermes. The Scriptures repeatedly affirm that the gods of the nations are demons (Ps. 96:5; 1 Cor. 10:20). The text of chapter 30 does not endorse the worship of Greek gods; rather, it presents them as created angelic beings who have fallen and become hostile principalities and powers in the world.

When Enoch returns to teach his descendants the wisdom he has received at the end of his ascent, he takes a positive, virtue-centered approach to ethical life, promoting particular virtues rather than issuing a series of bare commandments that focus on incorrect, sinful behavior. Enoch rhetorically moves back and forth from issues of the calendar and the movements of the heavens to ethics on earth. His approach demonstrates that correct human conduct is built into the cosmos, as are the laws of nature. The consequences of virtuous or depraved living, then, are internal rather than the subject of external judgment. Enoch gives particular attention to refuting the idea—implying its popularity at the time of composition—that one could behave as one wished while depending on the intercessions of holy figures for salvation.

The final portion of 2 Enoch continues the parallel with Moses in the Torah by describing an independent priesthood. The book employs the concept of the Melchizedek priesthood, well developed in Second Temple literature. Enoch gives the priesthood to his son Methuselah, who passes it on to his son. The critical figure, however, is Melchizedek, here a great-grandson of Enoch: he is virginally conceived by the wife of Nir, Methuselah's son and the priest, and is born from her after her death. Saint Michael the Archangel takes Melchizedek and shelters him in Paradise from the Flood, returning him afterward to continue his true priesthood in the age to come. Some manuscripts of 2 Enoch then conclude with a brief description of Noah's Flood.

Influence on the New Testament and the Church

Though not as influential or authoritative a text as 1 Enoch, 2 Enoch is a repository for a number of Second Temple Jewish traditions. It therefore forms an important link in the development of various ideas that find a particular form in the New Testament and in the writings of the Fathers. Within Second Temple Jewish circles, seeking the intercessions of angelic holy ones and human saints was a common practice. Second Enoch is an early testimony to the tradition that Melchizedek represents a messianic priesthood that supersedes the Levitical. The text also testifies to the differentiated understanding of the falls of angelic beings and their nature. It reflects a fully developed understanding, similar to Philo's, of the connection between angelic spirits and the cosmos, including a Jewish form of astrology.

THE APOCALYPSE OF ABRAHAM

Textual History

Like 2 Enoch, the Apocalypse of Abraham is a Second Temple Jewish text now preserved only in medieval Slavonic manuscripts. Also like 2 Enoch, the text passed through the hands of the Bogomils along its historical road of transmission. Despite the Bogomil association, scholars generally agree that the Gnostic text called "the Apocalypse of Abraham," which

St. Epiphanius mentions in his *Panarion*, is not the same text we now possess under the same name. The work Epiphanius describes does not match the contents of the extant Apocalypse of Abraham, though detailed comparison is impossible. However, some relationship between the two may exist.

The exact origins of the current work are likewise difficult to nail down. The Apocalypse of Abraham contains words and names that are clearly transliterated Hebrew or Aramaic, unlikely to be found and accurately preserved from a Greek original; thus the text is almost certainly of Semitic origins. The treatment of atonement ritual the book suggests is generally taken to imply that the temple has been destroyed, arguing for a date after AD 70. At the same time, there is not a great deal of clear interaction with Christianity, which suggests a date before the split between Christianity and Rabbinic Judaism around AD 150. Based on its lack of reference to Christianity as a separate tradition, the Apocalypse of Abraham seems most reasonably to be a Jewish text from around the period of AD 80.

Additional arguments on the dating of the Apocalypse often center on the state of development of various Jewish traditions in the text as compared to other Second Temple literature and to Talmudic Judaism. While this seems a sensible approach, several complicating factors render it ineffective. This view presumes that all these disparate traditions existed within an undifferentiated Judaism in the Second Temple period. In reality, countless Judaisms flourished at that time, carrying different elements and sometimes conflicting traditions regarding cosmology, the end of the age, and the relative importance of various biblical figures. Likewise, such a developmental approach assumes that the beliefs of the Judaisms all evolved along similar trajectories so that a throughline can be constructed to assist in dating various texts. Not only is there no such throughline, but most of these Judaisms proved to be developmental dead ends and did not survive the end of the Second Temple era.

Understanding of Atonement

The Apocalypse of Abraham opens with an expanded version of the call of Abraham that focuses on an anti-idolatry polemic. Abraham's father, Terah, is portrayed as being an idol carver, and Abraham has misgivings. He throws an idol into the fire and tells it to save itself. Of course, it does not. His father objects that the idols are a means of embodying the powers and elements of nature, which are greater than the idol itself. Abraham points out that these forces are all in a balance, each one countered or overcome by another, and therefore none of them can function as a first principle. Ultimately, Abraham is warned to leave, and fire from heaven destroys Terah, his idols, and his workshop.

The action of the Apocalypse centers around an act of sacrifice that Abraham must undertake. This sacrifice is patterned around the Day of Atonement as described in Leviticus, with the opposition of the demonic Azazel to Abraham reflecting the two goats. An angelic being named Yahoel guides Abraham to Mount Horeb for the sacrifice. Yahoel says, and his name implies, that he is a being who bears the name of the God of Israel (compare with Ex. 23:20–22). Yahoel is another example of a second power in heaven, like 1 Enoch's Son of Man—a second hypostasis of Yahweh, the God of Israel, who bears that name but is distinguished from Him.

Azazel, the figure mentioned in the Levitical atonement ritual, is here presented as the devil in quite literal fashion. Though initially in the form of a raven, he enlarges into dragon form; Azazel is depicted as the one who deceived Eve in Paradise. As in 1 Enoch's understanding of the atonement, sin is placed upon Azazel, and he receives its consequences by means of the sacrificial ritual that Yahoel performs with Abraham. The ritual thereby removes sin from the world so that the world can be purified and healed. The Apocalypse of Abraham, then, foresees a cosmic atonement that both precedes the Mosaic covenant, here represented by Horeb, and concludes and fulfills it.

Understanding the Apocalypse

The Apocalypse of Abraham is precisely what the title immediately implies. Following the atonement portion, the apocalypse proper begins. Abraham takes a visionary journey through the cosmos that is revelatory. He journeys to the heavens and beholds the throne, the *Merkavah*, of God, surrounded by the four living creatures as depicted in Ezekiel (Ezek. 1:1–28). Yahoel stands between these creatures, and they direct their worship and attention to him, suggestive of later use of the creatures in iconography of Christ and the four Gospels. When seen from above, the angels are the unseen movers behind the sun, moon, stars, and other elements of the natural world. Abraham then takes what seems like a tour of the cosmos, but it is a sort of manufactured prototype of the cosmos from which God created the actual one.

Abraham then sees the expulsion from Paradise, with Azazel in the role of the devil in his dragon form. The fruit of the Tree of Knowledge of Good and Evil is described here as a cluster of grapes. The expulsion of humanity from Paradise is the first and paradigmatic exile, and here it and the Babylonian exile of Judah are portrayed as people being handed over to Azazel, the unclean spirit of the wilderness. In the ritual of the Day of Atonement, as described in Leviticus 16, the goat for Azazel, with the people's sin placed upon it, was sent out into this wilderness to return sin back to the evil spirits that are its source. This correlates with St. Paul's description of excommunication from the Christian community as being handed over to Satan (1 Cor. 5:5; 1 Tim. 1:20). Humanity has desired evil, and so our punishment is that we are given precisely what we want (see Rom. 1:24). In the Apocalypse of Abraham, the first and prime example of someone fully possessed by Azazel is Cain. Because he belongs to Azazel, he persecutes God's people, who are represented by Abel (compare 1 John 3:12–13).

After a description of the destruction of the temple clearly depicting the events of AD 70, the book prophesies a twelve-part age that will follow before the coming of the end. The interpretation of these final five chapters is extremely difficult, owing both to their somewhat cryptic language and to the fact that many of the identifications that seem symbolic do not fully work out if pressed. The closing of this section is relatively straightforward and includes the expected elements: The final trumpet will sound. The Messiah will come and destroy his enemies, Azazel and his followers. The Last Judgment will take place, and God's people will be delivered into the life of the age to come.

The Coming of "a Man"

Before this final judgment, however, the Apocalypse of Abraham prophesies the coming of "a man." The description of this man and his activities renders the whole section confusing. When this man comes, Azazel, the pagan Gentiles, and some of the descendants of Abraham worship him, while Abraham's other descendants persecute and beat him. After the beating, the man is once again worshipped. On one hand, it is tempting to immediately identify this as an anti-Messiah, the man of perdition or man of Belial[26] who is found in several Second Temple works. Because this text was written after the beginning of Christianity within Judaism, it may even be tempting to understand this figure as a negative depiction of Jesus of Nazareth as understood by a non-Christian Jewish author.

But this easy identification is problematic because of the explanation given to Abraham regarding the man's identity. God Himself tells Abraham that this man is the relief He granted to Abraham's people from the Gentiles and that God will set up this man, one of Abraham's descendants, in the final stage of the last age. This explanation opens the possibility that this man and the Elect One, the Messiah, are the same person. In the context of the book, the relief here mentioned implies relief for Judeans from the persecution of the outside world, beginning with Cain.

One possible approach that makes sense of the text is that it is written by a non-Christian Jewish author who is not averse to Jesus of Nazareth. In the Christian period, a distinction was

---

26　Many Second Temple Jewish texts describe an anti-Messiah. The New Testament applies several of the traditional Jewish titles for this person to the coming Antichrist (e.g., 2 Thess. 2:1–12).

made between the Christians who followed Jesus as the Messiah and many other Jewish sects that did not, but enmity was not universal. The characterization of Jesus as a man who was beaten, rather than killed, may well indicate a lack of belief in the Resurrection. Nonetheless, the author of the Apocalypse, in the face of external persecution symbolized by the destruction of the temple, thought the conversion of Gentiles to Christianity could make them potentially more sympathetic to the Judean people. The portion of the text surrounding "the man," then, could be a brief digression to describe the phenomenon of Christianity, which, at the time of the writing of the text, was still an intra-Jewish phenomenon. Yet it was important enough to require explanation from a non-Christian Judean in terms of the unfolding plan of God.

Significance for the New Testament

Though not included on St. Nikephoros's list, the Apocalypse of Abraham testifies to certain modes of interpretation and thought within Second Temple Jewish communities. A number of these modes are reflected within the pages of the New Testament, albeit transformed in light of the coming of Jesus Christ. First among them is the idea of a final, eschatological Day of Atonement that will involve the final defeat of demonic powers and purification from sin. This understanding of atonement becomes a major theme in St. Matthew's Gospel, Hebrews, and 1 John. Additionally, the Apocalypse of Abraham gives an all-too-rare window into non-Christian Jewish thought after the onset of the Christian era, but before the historical process that produced the Talmud and Rabbinic Judaism.

CHAPTER FOUR

The Book of Jubilees and Other Enochic Literature

Overview

IN ADDITION TO THE WORKS discussed in the previous chapters, other materials from the Second Temple period are categorized as Enochic literature because they share themes with the texts compiled under Enoch's name. This classification is the only commonality between the texts treated in this chapter, as they were written in different languages by diverse groups across the course of several centuries. Further, no single community considered all these texts to be authoritative.

Each work represents a written record of preceding oral traditions. Third Enoch is a last-ditch attempt by later Rabbinic Judaism to reappropriate the Enochic traditions that were being abandoned to Christianity. This attempt ultimately proved unsuccessful from the perspective of later Judaism. Nonetheless, this background makes 3 Enoch an essential witness to the changes in the formulation of Talmudic Judaism as well as to particular areas of contention between Jewish and Christian communities.

The other texts in this chapter are ancient codifications of these traditions. Jubilees is a repository of traditions regarding the pre-Flood world, apocalyptic information, and the broad sweep of patriarchal history up to and including the Exodus. The Book of Giants integrates particular elements of the Enochic tradition into one specific community's ritual and religious life. The traditions of the assembled people of God were a constant, consistent unit through ancient Israel and into the Second Temple period, and these texts represent the written record of a portion of it.

THE BOOK OF JUBILEES

Background

The Book of Jubilees is an ancient Jewish work from the Second Temple period. As a text, it played a significant role in the religion of the first century AD. Josephus made heavy use of it in his *Antiquities*. Jubilees is also a repository for a vast collection of Jewish religious and historical traditions, providing a window into Jewish people's understanding and practices during this period. Many of the book's ideas appear in the New Testament, casually mixed with the text of the Hebrew Scriptures themselves. In a handful of places, the New Testament authors seem to cite Jubilees directly, and many of the earliest Fathers reference it as well. Though it is less well known than 1 Enoch, it is no less influential or essential.

Textual History

The Book of Jubilees was written in the middle part of the second century BC, very likely in Palestine. The earliest known manuscript portions are in Hebrew and Aramaic and were found among the Dead Sea Scrolls. A significant portion of the text also exists in Latin, and a great deal of the Greek can be reconstructed from patristic citations. The entirety of the text of Jubilees is also available from Ethiopian sources in a Ge'ez recension titled "Book of Divisions." It is generally considered canonical by both Ethiopian Jews and Christians, resulting in its preservation in various codices. Comparing the text in these multiple languages allows for a high degree of certitude regarding its state in the Second Temple period as the New Testament authors would have known it. Jubilees and the Enochic literature share many links in themes and content. The book was so foundational to Qumran's community, which produced the Dead Sea Scrolls, that it is the third most commonly found text there, following Genesis and 1 Enoch.

Content

At its core, Jubilees is an expansionistic retelling of Genesis and Exodus. It operates under the same principle in many sections as the Aramaic Targums, a series of translations into Aramaic of the original Hebrew texts of Old Testament books. These Targums not only translated the words but also expanded the narratives with additional traditions that interpreted the content of the Hebrew original. In a similar manner, Jubilees incorporates other elements, even whole stories, into the biblical text. Elsewhere it greatly condenses and summarizes the material of Genesis and Exodus, seemingly in places of less interest to the author. In the places that maintain the original text of Genesis and Exodus, even in the Hebrew fragments of Jubilees, the work does not match either the traditional Hebrew text or the Hebrew text that underlies the Greek Old Testament.

This implies that the author of Jubilees reworked other, undiscovered, independent texts or traditions. This variation points once again to the fact that in the Second Temple period and at the time of Christ, no set text of the Hebrew Scriptures existed. Instead, the Hebrew Scriptures represented a broader tradition that included several forms of the books that would later make up the Hebrew Bible and the Christian Old Testament.

A Window into Second Temple Religion and the Torah

Beyond this early witness to the text and understanding of Genesis and the early portion of Exodus, Jubilees makes several significant contributions to understanding Jewish religion in the Second Temple period. It does this in two primary ways: through the traditional material in the text and through its arrangement. Jubilees purports to record Moses' vision at Mount Sinai when he received the Torah from the Angel of the Presence. Therefore, the book presupposes that Moses' knowledge of the primordial history in Genesis came to him through a visionary experience. Apocalyptic themes abound, though *apocalyptic* is a feature throughout the Scriptures. The reason for the title of the Book of Jubilees is its organization and structure.

As for the writers of the other Enochic literature, the calendar was of crucial importance to the author of Jubilees. Jubilees retroactively describes the history of the world to Moses' era in light of the structure that the Torah itself gives to time. Therefore, it divides primeval history according to weekly sabbaths, festal cycles, sabbath years, and jubilee years, although, strictly speaking, these cycles and feasts had not yet been instituted. This results in anachronisms such as the patriarchs celebrating the Feast of Tabernacles in Canaan centuries before the wilderness wanderings that inspired it.

Jubilees, however, taking its cue from the Creation of the world in Genesis 1 as a week ending in a sabbath, sees these structures of measurement as built into time itself. Therefore, these measurements have existed since time was created—since the beginning of this age, whether or not humanity recognized their existence. This understanding, in turn, suggests something about the nature of the Torah. If the moral, religious, and even temporal structures in the Torah are embedded in creation itself, the Torah then is not legislation but revelation. Saint Paul parallels this conception of the Torah in his argument in Romans 1 and 2. There he states that the God of Israel is knowable from creation itself, so that Gentiles who have been attentive to that creation can become a Torah for themselves (Rom. 2:14).

Thematic Content: Bridging the Visible and Invisible Worlds

Thematically, much of Jubilees focuses on the spiritual beings of the invisible creation: the ranks of angels, the origins of demons, and especially the origins of disembodied demonic spirits. God assigns angels to every aspect of creation, from the skies to the seas to the winds, and also as guardians of people and nations to administer His rule. The book narrates the story of the origin of the demon Mastema, as well as the story of the Watchers, in a way that parallels other Enochic literature: as angels who left their former estate, entered into sexual congress with human women, and produced the race of giants destroyed by the Flood in the days of Noah and later by the descendants of Abraham. However, the story goes further in describing how some of those spirits were allowed to remain upon the earth, explaining the unclean spirits of the Hebrew Scriptures and demons described by Tobit and the synoptic Gospels.

Mastema, a leader among the giants, bargains with God before their impending destruction, asking God to allow him and one tenth of the demonic spirits to remain in the world to test humanity and afflict those in whom wickedness is found (Jub. 10:8). God consents to this arrangement because He intends to use the evil spirits, who had played a part in corrupting humanity, to bring humans to repentance. This is how Second Temple Judaism understood the evil spirit who came "from God" to afflict Saul (1 Sam. 16:14–16, 23; 18:10; 19:9). Mastema's bargain with God, however, has an expiration date: at the Last Judgment, these spirits will be punished for eternity in the abyss.

The story of Mastema in Jubilees shaped the understanding of demonic powers for the original audience of the Gospels. In Mark 1:23–26, the unclean spirit recognizes Jesus Christ's identity and immediately asks if He has come to destroy them all; that is, the demons associate the arrival of Christ with the time of the end. In his confrontation with the Gerasene demoniac, St. Matthew records the demons asking if Christ has come to torment them "before the time" (Matt. 8:29). Saint Mark records the demons pleading with Christ not to send them out of the land (Mark 5:10). Saint Luke makes clear that the alternative to the demons' continued dwelling on the earth is confinement in the abyss (Luke 8:31), which lies in the depths of the sea.

Though Jesus casts the demons into the swine, they meet their end in the water (Matt 8:32; Mark 5:13; Luke 8:33). Because God Himself strictly limited the activity of these demonic spirits, the fact that Christ is able to command and punish them is prominent in the Gospels precisely as evidence of His identity as Yahweh, the God of Israel.

The calendar structure of the Book of Jubilees as a whole integrates this understanding of the angelic and demonic powers by linking the happenings in this world and in the spiritual world. In this age, events are the product of human participation either in the work of Yahweh, the God of Israel, or in the rebellion of the evil spiritual powers. Because humans are constituted of both body and soul, they bridge the invisible and visible creations by overlapping these two worlds' events. In the Book of Jubilees, the casting down of the Watchers into the abyss accompanies the defeat of the Rephaim and the Amorites by the armies of Israel. While this overlapping of seen and unseen is true as a general principle of history for the Jubilees author, it is nowhere truer than in the context of worship in its various cycles: the heavens and earth unite as one when humans worship with the angels. This is also the understanding of the Orthodox Church: the worship of the Holy Trinity is continuous in heaven always and at all times. When people gather to worship, they enter into this heavenly worship already in progress.

New Testament Influence: Allusions from St. Stephen and St. Peter

In several instances, New Testament authors reference traditions contained within Jubilees. However, it would be difficult to demonstrate that Jubilees is a source. Both texts may merely be drawing on a common tradition. But in these cases, the Book of Jubilees represents the earliest known textual form of the tradition in question.

Saint Stephen's speech in Acts 7, for example, repeatedly refers to traditions that are not found in the biblical texts of Genesis and Exodus but are included in the Book of Jubilees. He speaks of Jacob's remains and those of all the patriarchs being brought back to the tomb at Shechem: "And Jacob went down into Egypt; and he died, he and our fathers. And they were carried into Shechem and buried in the tomb that Abraham bought for a sum of money from the sons of Hamor in Shechem" (Acts 7:15–16; see Jub. 46:9). He describes Moses' age of forty at the time he killed the Egyptian, as recorded in Jubilees (Acts 7:23; Jub. 47:10–12), as well as the forty years Moses spent in Midian (Acts 7:30; Jub. 48:1). Saint Stephen states that the law was given "by angels," a tradition recorded in Jubilees in an earlier form (Acts 7:53; Jub. 1:27). Suffice it to say that St. Stephen narrates Israel's early history in a way that parallels the Book of Jubilees.

Second Peter likewise appears to reference the Book of Jubilees, in addition to the clear allusions to elements of the Enochic literature regarding Sodom and Gomorrah and the fate of the fallen angels (2:4–10). Saint Peter refers to Noah as a "preacher of righteousness" here, despite there being no account in Genesis 6—7 of Noah preaching to anyone (2 Pet. 2:5). Jubilees not only describes Noah as a preacher to his corrupt generation but records one of his sermons (Jub. 7:20–39). The language of Jubilees 1:29 parallels the description of "a new heavens and a new earth" in 2 Peter 3:13. This particular expression of the restoration of creation is not spelled out in any known sources before Jubilees. Saint Peter, as mentioned earlier, also cites the maxim that to the Lord, "one day is as a thousand years" (2 Pet. 3:8). Jubilees likewise records this expression (Jub. 4:30).

New Testament Influence: Possible Direct Citations

Several verses in the New Testament appear to be something closer to direct citations. Possibly the most important of these is from Christ Himself in St. Luke's Gospel. Jesus quotes the Wisdom of God as saying, "I will send prophets and apostles to them, and some of them they will kill and will persecute" (Luke 11:49). Based on essential vocabulary, this appears to be an abbreviated quotation of Jubilees 1:12: "And I will send to them witnesses in order to witness to them, but they will not listen. And they will kill the witnesses. And they will persecute those who search out the Torah. They will leave everything, and they will change to do evil in my sight." In the context of Jubilees, God spoke these words to Moses, revealing that the Israelites would later go astray and murder His prophets.

Israel's murder of God's prophets is precisely the context for Christ's words in Luke (11:47–51). A second possible reference is included in St. John's Gospel: Jesus promises His disciples and apostles that when the Holy Spirit comes, He will cause them to remember all the things they had seen Jesus say and do (John 14:26). In Jubilees, God, following Jacob's vision at Bethel, tells Jacob in the same words that He will cause him to remember all the things in his vision to understand them later (Jub. 32:25).

Saint Paul, likewise, appears to reference the Book of Jubilees on a few occasions. In 2 Corinthians 6:15, at the end of a series of Old Testament quotations about the people of God being separate and holy to the God of Israel, the apostle appends the words, "I will be a Father to you, and you will be sons and daughters to Me" (2 Cor. 6:18). Many English Bibles footnote this text as a reference to 2 Samuel 7:14, in which Yahweh tells David that He will be a father to Solomon and Solomon a son to Him. But in the context of St. Paul's quotation, this makes little sense. The verse in 2 Samuel refers to the tradition of the king of Israel as the son of God, anticipating the Messiah. Saint Paul's citation is instead directed toward the entire people of Israel, explicitly toward men and women equally. He nowhere implies that they are made to be kings (and queens?) based on their holiness. The Book of Jubilees, however, provides a direct parallel quotation: God tells Moses that when the people of Israel keep His commandments, He will be a Father to them, and they will be His children (Jub. 1:24).

Saint Paul makes other passing references in his epistles to details found in the Book of Jubilees. In 2 Thessalonians 2:3, he refers to the coming Antichrist as the "son of perdition"—one of the titles given to the giants destroyed by the Flood (Jub. 10:3). In his Epistle to the Galatians, Paul uses the phrase "Gentile sinners" to refer to those outside the Christian community (2:15). This same phrase is found in Jubilees in a similar context (Jub. 23:23–24).

A further detail St. Paul cites in Galatians has caused considerable trouble to scholars who are devoted to a literal interpretation of biblical numbers. Paul states that the Torah was given 430 years after the confirmation of the covenant with Abraham

(Gal. 3:17). This does not match the typically constructed time-line of the Books of Genesis and Exodus that scholars use. It is also challenging to get that number to jibe with the dating in Exodus 12:40, which states that Israel was in Egypt for 430 years. The Book of Jubilees, however, in line with its structure according to cycles and years, records the period of time from the birth of Isaac to the giving of the Torah as precisely 430 years (Jub. 15:4). Because the timeline of Jubilees is composed with such precision, these verses likely are citing its information rather than a shared tradition.

The Apocalypse of St. John contains at least two allusions to the Book of Jubilees. The phrase regarding the identity of the Church as "a kingdom and priests" is used twice, rather than the more common "a kingdom of priests" or even "a royal priest-hood" (Rev. 1:6; 5:10). However, this wording is found in the Book of Jubilees as a promise to God's people Israel (Jub. 16:18). Additionally, Jubilees 2:2 speaks of angels giving voice when the Torah is given. These angels are assigned to specific aspects of creation—they are the "angels of the voices and of the thunder and of the lightnings." Repeatedly in the Apocalypse, as St. John stands in the heavens, at critical moments he hears "lightnings and voices and thunderings" (Rev. 4:5; 11:19; 16:18).

Influence on the Church

These are key and clear examples of the influence of Jubilees on the authors of the New Testament. Many more examples could be given, as well as countless points of connection to Orthodox worship and liturgy. As one example, one of the prayers of the Trisagion for the Departed begins with the words, "O God of spirits and of all flesh . . ." This is the phrase that begins Noah's prayer in Jubilees 10:3 as he asks for his children's and grand-children's deliverance from the power of demons. The Book of Jubilees also provides early testimony to the tradition of crown-ing at wedding festivals (Jub. 16:30).

Suffice it to say that the Book of Jubilees, regardless of canon-ical status, is a critically important witness to the interpretation and religious significance of Genesis and Exodus in the first cen-tury AD. It is invaluable as background to the apostles and New Testament writers in understanding their religious worldview and experience, because the texts that make up the Christian Scriptures are not timeless in their origins. Real men produced them in real times and places—men, times, and places chosen by God for this purpose. They cannot be understood outside of this divinely chosen context.

THE BOOK OF GIANTS

Textual History

Before the discovery of the Dead Sea Scrolls, the Book of Giants was best known as a text used by the Manicheans, a Gnostic sect with its origins in Persia. Mani, the founder, had been a mem-ber of the Elkasaites, a Christian group following the Jewish Prophet Elkesai in Mesopotamia, and then developed his own sect. Manicheanism spread far beyond its point of origin to both the East and the West. In the West, it is perhaps best known through the works of St. Augustine, a former Manichee him-self, who debated and wrote against Mani's followers in western North Africa. In the East, the discovery of the Book of Giants in a western province of China attests to the extent of its spread.

However, beginning in 1946, fragments of the Aramaic text of the Book of Giants were found among the Dead Sea Scrolls in four different caves, implying that a number of copies of this text had been preserved at Qumran. Thus the book not only predates its Manichean and Elkasaite usage but predates the existence of Manicheanism entirely. From these fragments, the arc of the text can be reconstructed, though admittedly many details have been lost. The Book of Giants is clearly a piece of Enochic literature, retelling another version of the traditions within the Book of the Watchers in 1 Enoch. The Aramaic fragments also reveal that the Manichees had altered the book's narrative repeatedly to fit within Manichean cosmology.

Content

As with the Book of the Watchers within 1 Enoch, the Book of Giants is an expanded retelling of the events in the background of Genesis 6:1–4. A group of angels assigned to shepherd humanity instead engage in sexual relations with animals and with humans, bringing forth monstrous giants. The giants and their angelic parents spread evil, violence, and corruption throughout the world, eventually resulting in the judgment of the Flood of Noah on the entire cosmos. The narrative as it plays out here is set not in the days of Noah but of Enoch, who makes an appearance in the story.

The unique element of the Book of Giants in the context of other Enochic literature is its focus on the possibility of repentance. Not only is Enoch assigned to preach repentance to humanity before the judgment comes; even the Watchers and the giants are given an opportunity to repent. God sends dreams to a number of the Nephilim, particularly two named Ohya and Hahya. The giants, however, are so corrupted that when God gives them revelatory dreams for the purpose of bringing about their repentance, they are completely unable to understand them, even when they pool their wisdom with their formerly angelic parents.

The confused fallen angels and Nephilim then delegate one giant, Mahway, to go and ask the Prophet Enoch to explain to him the mysterious dreams. Enoch, like God, wants to see the giants and their parents repent, so he gives them their dream interpretation on two tablets. There is here a clear parallel to the later Israelites who receive the presence of Yahweh, the God of Israel, on Mount Sinai with fear and confusion: they send Moses in their place to the top of the mountain, and he returns with the two tablets of the Torah, which detail the means of their repentance. Yet despite this mercy extended to the giants and the Watchers, the vast majority of these beings, faced with upcoming destruction in the Flood, choose to continue in their rebellion rather than repent. Named among the monstrous giants are Gilgamesh and Humbaba, who are also found in the Gilgamesh epic.

Significance for the Church:
The Opportunity for Repentance

The Book of the Giants is yet another document attesting to the universal understanding of the background of Genesis 6:1–4 in the Second Temple period and the early centuries of the Christian Church. In addition, however, this text reflects the idea that no one—not even a demon—is ever too far gone to be able to repent. The possibility of demonic repentance has never been the mainstream teaching of any major sect of Judaism or of Christianity; however, as an extreme representation, it makes the point that certainly no human is past turning from evil and returning to God. This message would have been of great relevance in a period of Jewish history marked by compromise, dissolution, and integration into the surrounding nations' pagan way of life. It remained important with the coming of the Christian gospel and the opportunity for every person to repent in response to its call.

3 ENOCH

Textual History

What is now called 3 Enoch is not a third book of Enoch in the sense of a continuation of 1 Enoch and/or 2 Enoch. As with those two texts, 3 Enoch represents its own separate narrative. That said, it is a work highly dependent on the preexisting Enochic traditions, especially 1 Enoch. As discussed earlier, the New Testament and the early Church Fathers carried forward many themes of this literature into early Christianity, and these elements of Second Temple Jewish tradition held on within non-Christian Jewish communities for centuries, in some cases even to this very day.

Third Enoch, composed in the fifth century AD, is nothing more or less than the last major textual attempt within Rabbinic Judaism to reinterpret and assimilate the Enochic traditions into the newly forming Talmudic orthodoxy. By that point, Christianity and Judaism had become separate ways of life and of being in the world. At this point also the tide of opinion within

Christianity was beginning to further marginalize the Enochic literature, despite its earlier Christian popularity. This created a window in time when the author of 3 Enoch likely thought it plausible to redeem the literature and its traditions.

Third Enoch is a short text, and it focuses directly on the idea of two powers in heaven, that is, that there are two persons, or hypostases, of the God of Israel. Obviously, this element of Jewish tradition, prominent in the Enochic and other Second Temple Jewish literature, was elaborated into the Christian doctrine of the Holy Trinity. This development led to non-Christian Judaism's rejection of its entire line of thought, inquiry, and interpretation of the Hebrew Bible by the end of the second century AD. The Talmud itself, the foundational written record of the oral traditions of the early rabbis, handled the "two powers" in at least two different ways. In one case, the Old Testament texts that had been interpreted as representing two hypostases of Yahweh were instead interpreted as two manifestations of the one God of Israel. The other talmudic interpretation is that the second person in the Hebrew Bible is actually a high-ranking created, angelic being, and those who seek to elevate this angelic person to the same level as God are idolatrous heretics.

Content

Third Enoch represents a variation on the second approach. The text presents itself, like the tractates that make up the Talmud, as the record of a tradition handed down from centuries earlier. Third Enoch is narrated by Rabbi Ishmael, a major second-century figure in the development of Merkavah mysticism. The text describes his ascent to the seventh heaven and what he sees there; the content of the vision is the primary focus and purpose of the text.[27] Pausing before entering the final and seventh realm of heaven, Ishmael is greeted by the Metatron, the greatest angelic being most closely related to the God of Israel.

The rest of the text primarily concerns Ishmael asking Metatron his identity, which he apparently finds more interesting than beholding God Himself enthroned. Metatron first says that he has seventy names according to the seventy nations of the world, placing him above the princes of those nations and giving him a universal jurisdiction and ministry. When Ishmael inquires more deeply, however, Metatron identifies himself as Enoch. He narrates how in response to the wickedness of the world before the Flood, Enoch was taken away not only into heaven but also into the Glory of God Himself (*Shekinah*). Upon being taken into the presence of God, Enoch was transformed into the angelic Metatron.

Influence on Judaism

Though brief, 3 Enoch attempts a profound purpose: it seeks to take the figures described in so much of Second Temple Jewish literature—the Angel of the Lord, the Son of Man, the Metatron, the Angel of the Presence—and to integrate them with the apocalyptic figure of Enoch. By doing this, the book hopes to make all these diverse traditions fit into the new synthesis of Rabbinic Judaism. While this grouping together and identification of figures functions at the level of ideas, it cannot actually make these concrete Second Temple traditions conform to the

---

27 The heavens are described and enumerated differently here than in 2 Enoch.

Talmudic vision. Third Enoch's attempt, then, to reappropriate previously important and popular Jewish literature into a post-Christian system ultimately fails. Nevertheless, the document itself bears witness to the ongoing influence of the relevant ideas within Judaism—even the Judaism that had rejected Jesus of Nazareth as the fulfillment of these ideas.

CHAPTER FIVE

The Testaments of the Twelve Patriarchs

The Meaning of "Testament"

THE WORD *testament*, for most English Bible readers, likely first brings to mind the Old and New Testaments of the Christian Bible. In that usage, "testament" translates the Greek *diatheke*, more often conveyed in English as "covenant." The Old Testament, following on the Torah and the covenant given at Sinai, is the record of a covenant destined, in Christ, to become "old." The prophets of the Babylonian exile, particularly Jeremiah and Ezekiel, promise a new covenant, greater than the old, and the New Testament has one central theme—the issuing of that covenant.

Testament, however, is also used to describe a genre of extra-biblical literature; here the word is meant more as it is used in the phrase "last will and testament." As a prime example, in Genesis 49, Jacob summons first Joseph's sons, then all his own sons to give parting prophetic words as he prepares for his own death. These words are not only good advice from his years of life or remembrances of their shared past; he characterizes each son and grandson and lays out the path not of their individual lives, but of the shared life of the tribes that will come to bear their names.

Textual History

Using Genesis 49 as a format, in the Second Temple period extra-biblical testaments proliferated for various people in the Scriptures, beginning with Adam himself. Among these, a group of testaments ascribed to the sons of Jacob—the founding fathers of the twelve tribes of Israel—arose to special prominence. Various textual and historical factors indicate that these Testaments of the Twelve Patriarchs did not always exist as a unit; certain individual testaments within the whole seem to have circulated independently. The New Testament authors at least allude to, and in some cases even quote, several of these testaments. They were written originally in Hebrew, and many Hebrew fragments have been discovered in various locations. They were also preserved, copied, and recopied at monasteries and other ancient libraries, and they find a place in St. Nikephoros of Constantinople's list of books worthy to be read in the home.

Signs scattered throughout the testaments serve to identify the date of original composition as somewhere in the first half of the second century BC. Certain apocalyptic portions of the texts describe a succession of world empires that ends with the Seleucid Greeks. There are no clear references to the Maccabean revolt or the Hasmonean dynasty, but some scholars have found allusions within the messianic material that are reminiscent of the portrayal of John Hyrcanus[28] (circa 130 BC)

28　John Hyrcanus was the most prominent Hasmonean ruler over Judea. See the Glossary.

in other sources. This similarity, however, can work in either direction: the text may describe John Hyrcanus as a paradigm for the Messiah, or other literature may present John Hyrcanus in messianic terms drawn from works such as the Testaments of the Twelve Patriarchs. In either case, the first half of the second century BC within Syria seems secure as a time and place of composition for the earliest form of the testaments.

Some debate remains as to their original language, though there is good reason to believe that it was Aramaic, likely with Syrian origins. Certain late Hebrew copies of the text exist, including fragments among the Dead Sea Scrolls, but they show signs of having been brought over into Hebrew rather than being copies of the original. The more common Greek text of the testaments shows certain elements of alteration—sometimes particularly Christian editorial activity. In most cases, these edits are easy to isolate because they have the nature of parenthetical comments. For example, an inserted phrase will indicate some element of the text finding prophetic fulfillment in Christ. In the ending of the Testament of Dan, an addendum simply says that all the things prophesied therein had later come to pass. It would be difficult to mistake additions of this kind for original wording.

The earliest full representation in Greek is a tenth-century manuscript from Mount Athos, while one from the seventeenth century comes from the library at St. Catherine's Monastery at Sinai. The Mount Athos manuscript, from the Koutloumousiou Monastery, has a particularly useful copy of the Testament of Levi. The tenth-century copyist had access to both an Aramaic and a Greek form of the text, which differed somewhat.

He copied the Greek wording then used notations to indicate the differences in the Aramaic, making this testament our best witness to both forms of the text. Parallels in content and emphasis are particularly common between the Testaments of the Twelve Patriarchs and the Johannine literature in the New Testament. While there is no evidence of direct literary dependence between these testaments and St. John's writings, conceptually they are drawing from similar wells of Second Temple Jewish thought. They were translated into Aramaic and Greek and thence into Armenian, Slavonic, and other languages from the Hebrew.

Content

As a whole, the Testaments of the Twelve Patriarchs serve as a series of treatises on virtues and vices. They expand on stories from Genesis, as well as later historical developments among particular tribes, to present an individual son of Israel as an exemplar of either a passion or an antithetical virtue. In content, therefore, the testaments are a sort of precursor to certain forms of monastic literature as exemplified in St. John Cassian's *Institutes* and *Conferences*. Not only do these works describe various virtues and vices, but they also prescribe ascetic practice as the means of progress from one to the other. It is not a coincidence that monastic settlements preserved these texts. The reading of the testaments and similar works set a trajectory for monastic literature and naturally led to their preservation.

Significant portions of the Testaments of the Twelve Patriarchs are also made up of apocalyptic, visionary material. This material is narrower in focus than in texts such as the Book of

Enoch, with their tours of the cosmos and relatively elaborate eschatologies. The apocalyptic elements of the Testaments instead focus intently on the coming of the Messiah and what He will accomplish. Within this focus, individual testaments emphasize various elements, such as Levi's concern with the priesthood and Dan's with the Gentile nations. The Testaments of the Twelve Patriarchs, then, represent a merger of apocalyptic and wisdom traditions from the Judaisms of the Second Temple period. Refracted through the revelation of Christ in the New Testament, these traditions would blossom into the wealth of early monastic literature.

The testament of the patriarchs' father, Jacob, is oriented primarily toward the future—toward the tribes that would bear the names of his sons—rather than to his sons themselves. In contrast, as the Testaments of the Twelve Patriarchs move through the sons of Israel, the contents are grounded in a meditation on the life of the particular patriarch, at least where the information is available within Scripture or elsewhere in received tradition. The testaments are not exegetical works; these meditations serve as the jumping-off point for a brief discussion of elements of these men's lives and what they represent to the wise reader going forward.

I. TESTAMENT OF REUBEN

THE OVERRIDING EVENT of Reuben's life in the Book of Genesis is his attempt to usurp authority in his family through a sexual union with one of his father's concubines (Gen. 35:22). This attempt led to his disinheritance, despite his being the firstborn. It also places Reuben, in the dramatization of his testament at the time of his death, in a unique position to speak to his descendants about the perils of lust. The episode is here dramatized in some detail: how he caught sight of his father's concubine Bilhah while she bathed, how lust took root in his heart, and how he began to plot a way to be with her.

The Testament of Reuben also gives a detailed description of Reuben's repentance after his misdeed. This repentance took the form of an extended period of mourning over his sin accompanied by fasting, here described as refraining from eating meat and drinking wine. Reuben spent seven years in this state of repentance before emerging on the other side with an experience of forgiveness and reconciliation. As a pre-Christian Jewish text, it is worth noting that this period of penitence obviated the death penalty to which Reuben would have otherwise been liable. The death penalties of the Torah were applied only to the unrepentant. Also worth noting is the fact that Reuben's firstborn status is not restored, nor does he seek its restoration, despite his repentance and reconciliation. He accepts the loss as the consequence of his grievous sin.

The Testament of Reuben also shows an awareness of what would later, in Christian monastic circles, become known as the "blameless passions": human capacities that, if pursued to excess or as ends in themselves, have the potential to become sinful and thereby twist the person into something less than human. For Reuben, these capacities are the seven parts of the spirit of man received at birth: Every human receives a spirit that animates the body. The first part of this spirit is life itself, the soul, which makes the body alive. The next five parts are the five senses—sight, hearing, smell, and taste, but with speech in the place of touch. Humans are able to receive knowledge and wisdom through speech. Touch appears to be part of the seventh and final part as these senses unfold: procreation and sexual intercourse. Reuben sees this sensuality as being as integral as the others to human life.

Misogyny in the Text

Any discussion of the Testament of Reuben must address what seems, on its face, to be a reasonably clear case of misogyny. What is now its fifth chapter begins with the words, "Women are evil." It must be noted, however, that this statement is misogynistic only if it is accompanied by a corresponding belief, stated or unstated, that men are not evil. In the context of the ancient world, where women were not seen as having agency and were therefore innocent, Reuben's statement and the following explanation can be seen as a correction that actually confers a sense of agency to women rather than treating them as merely the object of men's lusts.

Legislation governing human sexuality in the Scriptures is notably aimed entirely at men (e.g., see Leviticus 18). In the social setting of the Scriptures, men held power and authority in society, and women were subject to them, meaning that the onus for sexual morality fell on men. Women had no ability to give or deny consent that the surrounding culture acknowledged. What Reuben adds to this picture is that the situation, by the second century BC if not at other times, had become more complex.

If male lust were met by female dedication to purity and chastity, there would be an additional check on masculine wantonness. The reality, as Reuben points out, is that women are just as subject to the temptation to sexual immorality as men are. He gives the fall of the Watchers as just one example of women's sinful capacity. Male lust meets female lust more often than it meets female chastity, enabling a man who has given in to the desires of the flesh to find a willing partner. This situation was particularly true in an ancient world that commonly accepted prostitution. Even in a mutually desired affair, Reuben presents the responsibility as falling more heavily on the male participant.

Lessons from Reuben

Reuben uses this argument to double down on the commandment that men must govern themselves and their own chastity rather than expecting women to do it for them. He does not argue that women are evil and therefore marriage is to be avoided. His argument is not for male virginity but for extramarital chastity and devotion to the wife of one's youth. Although the wife was most often chosen for a young man without his involvement, this reality is irrelevant to the moral call of the Testament of Reuben.

II. TESTAMENT OF SIMEON

IN CONSIDERING SIMEON, one might expect that the paradigmatic event in his life is the massacre of the men of Shechem, when, in response to the rape of their sister Dinah, Simeon and Levi killed the men of the city, only to be rebuked by their father (Genesis 34). Though not stated explicitly, the text of Genesis strongly implies that the Davidic kingship ultimately arises from the tribe of Judah because of the sins of his three older brothers. However, neither the Testament of Simeon nor the Testament of Levi discusses the change in Reuben's firstborn status.

Rather, the Testament of Simeon attributes to Simeon the intent to murder his brother Joseph, with Judah interceding to instead sell him into the slavery that led Joseph to Egypt. Simeon therefore becomes the brother who represents the passion of envy. He holds jealousy toward Joseph not only because he feels his father favors him, but because of Joseph's handsomeness, winsomeness, and, ultimately, his goodness as a person. Joseph's goodness inspires an evil within Simeon that parallels Cain's jealous gaze falling on Abel.

Unlike his older brother, Reuben, Simeon finds forgiveness and redemption from the passion of envy not through repentance and fasting but through Joseph. The testament retells, from Simeon's perspective, the series of encounters in Egypt between the brothers and Joseph after Joseph's ascent to power. Simeon treats Joseph's ruse—of suspecting them as spies and imprisoning them—not as a game, a prank, or vengeance on Joseph's part. Rather, Simeon deserves that treatment because of his murderous intent. The taste of those consequences allows Simeon to experience Joseph's forgiveness, and the love he receives in response to his hate is liberating.

There is no small debate around a certain prophetic reference in chapter 6 of the Testament of Simeon, which states,

Then Shem will be glorified, because God the Lord, who is great in Israel, will appear upon earth as a man. By himself will he save Adam. Then all the spirits of error will be handed over to be trampled upon, and men will have command over evil spirits. Then will I arise in gladness, and I will bless the Most High for His wonders, because God has taken a body to eat with human beings and to save human beings. (6:5–7)

Scholars immediately tend to label this bit of text as an interpolation by Christians. This is not necessarily the case, however. Parallel statements about God appearing on earth, even in human form, for the salvation of humanity are common in Second Temple literature. The theophanies surrounding the Mount Sinai event, which occurred after Simeon's time, involved appearing, redeeming, even eating with human beings. This is not to deny that for early Christians, these words would have been taken as a direct prophecy of the coming of Jesus Christ. Rather, it is to say that this statement follows the contours of countless other examples of pre-Christian literature that the early Church later interpreted in the same way.

Lessons from Simeon

For the Testament of Simeon, envy and jealousy are passions that consume and seize control of the mind of the person who allows them to take root. Given enough time and preoccupation, envy will drive someone to commit acts of vengeance over minor slights that a right-minded person would never commit. This passion, however, has a direct cure: brotherly love drives out jealousy and envy. This healing can begin, as with Simeon, not by finding love within oneself, but through receiving love, even—or maybe especially—from the unloved.

III. TESTAMENT OF LEVI

THE TESTAMENT OF LEVI presents strong evidence of originally being an independent composition. Notes on one of the manuscripts at Mount Athos, as well as fragments recovered among the Dead Sea Scrolls at Qumran, indicate that another Aramaic Testament of Levi stands apart from this one, that one representing earlier material later integrated into this larger Testament of the Twelve Patriarchs. The Testament of Levi also represents a subtle shift in genre: a portion of the incorporated material is an apocalyptic description of Levi's heavenly ascent and consecration as a priest.

The author of the Testament of Levi faces a certain problem of anachronism. Within the Book of Genesis, Levi himself has no particular priestly role over his brothers. The Levites receive the priesthood when God takes it away from the elders of the people after the episode with the golden calf in Exodus. Specifically, the Levites take up arms alongside Moses, their fellow Levite, to render judgment upon the guilty (Ex. 32:27–28). Later in the Torah, Phinehas receives the high priesthood after slaying the Israelite man who fornicated flagrantly and publicly with a foreign, pagan priestess (Num. 25:1–9). The author resolves the problem of drawing these developments back in time to Levi himself by recasting the story of the rape of Dinah at Shechem (Genesis 34) in the pattern of these later events. Here, unlike in Genesis, Jacob has arranged a marriage between his daughter Dinah and a foreigner. Levi leads the killing of men of Shechem not as an act of vengeance, but rather out of his zeal for ritual purity. As a result, he becomes the high priest.

Levi receives the high priesthood at the end of a heavenly

ascent, when angels vest him with the garments of the high priest as later described in the Torah. The story here presents this priestly investiture as eternal and permanent. Levi's heavenly vision is of his descendants and of the emergence of the exercise of their priesthood, and here the characteristic vice belongs to the later priesthood, not to Levi himself. Levi sees the whole history, up to the time of the writing of the Testament of Levi, from the perspective of the later priests' pride and arrogance, which results in corruption.

Unlike other traditions from the Second Temple period, the answer to Levitical corruption offered here is not to institute another priesthood such as that of Melchizedek. Rather, the testament prophesies a future priest who will take up the tarnished priesthood of Levi and restore it to its pure state. This priest will reign forever and have no need of a successor for all generations. This amounts to a tradition, repeated in various other Second Temple literature, of an expressly priestly Messiah or priestly Savior, since *Messiah* as a title indicates specifically only kingship.

Relation to 1 Enoch

Levi is one of several testaments that directly refer to the Book of Enoch. In the Testament of Levi, the patriarch's vision allows him to understand the Apocalypse of Weeks found in 1 Enoch to gain further detailed information concerning the future of his priestly descendants. Certainly, Levi and the other testaments refer to, retell, and reframe stories from the Hebrew Bible in general and from the Torah in particular. Within the time of the patriarchs, however, none of this literature had yet been written.

Of all the texts that held authority in various Jewish communities of the Second Temple period, only 1 Enoch would have existed in any kind of written form for the sons of Jacob to cite.

Lessons from Levi

The testaments of both Levi and Judah are concerned with the relationship between king and priest in Judea, and they express this emphasis in terms of the relationship between the brothers and their offspring. In many places the Testaments of the Twelve Patriarchs reiterate the command that every tribe must remain in covenant with the tribe of Levi, placing Judah and its king under the authority of Levi and the priesthood. These two testaments mention future kings setting up another priesthood—possibly a reference to the various pagan cults that were allowed to flourish under Solomon and the divided monarchy. Based on the time of writing, this inclusion likely represents a justification for the Hasmonean dynasty, who, though Levites, took the kingship for themselves.

IV. TESTAMENT OF JUDAH

WITHIN THE TESTAMENT OF JACOB in the final chapters of Genesis, Jacob singles out Judah for special attention as the tribe from which David, his dynasty, and ultimately the Messiah will come. The books of 1 and 2 Samuel (1 and 2 Kingdoms in the Septuagint) obviously concern David himself, but the books of Judges and Ruth also lay the groundwork for the Davidic monarchy and its lineage. As noted previously, however, within the Testaments of the Twelve Patriarchs, Judah takes second place to Levi and the priesthood. The testaments of Levi and Judah directly state Judah's secondary status several times, but it is also described more subtly, through narrative, in Judah's final words to his progeny.

Judah presents himself in his narration as a warrior who leads men into battle. His bravery in doing so illustrates his chief virtue and also sketches the outline of ancient kingship in an ideal form. Judah relates a series of exploits, battling wild beasts, pagan kings, and warriors of all kinds. Most of these escapades are not recorded in Scripture, and a handful of them actually seem to be borrowed from other biblical figures. For example, Judah kills a giant with a hurled stone and kills a lion with his bare hands. Though Judah himself will not reign as a king over his brothers, he is presented as a kingly figure awaiting a kingdom.

Nevertheless, unlike Levi, Judah is ultimately a flawed figure. Both his foreign wife and his affair with his daughter-in-law, Tamar, whom he believed at the time to be a prostitute, represent his moral failure. In both cases, drunkenness was involved in his poor decisions regarding sexual morality. It is not a coincidence that Judah's virtues and flaws directly parallel those of his descendant David. Solomon also faced his downfall through the accumulation of foreign wives. Judah therefore advises his sons that two spirits seek to guide them in opposite directions—one toward truth and the other toward error. One of these is the Spirit of God, who produces virtue; the other is sinful passion.

The Testament of Judah goes on to establish an ordering of the tribes in glory. Levi, as in the other testaments, is in the first place. Judah comes second as the lineage of the kings of Judah;

then Joseph, forefather of the kings of the Northern Kingdom of Israel by Ephraim; then Benjamin, the last tribe of the Southern Kingdom; and so on through the sons. This ordering and this glory will come at the time of the resurrection of all flesh. The resurrection, in its turn, will follow the coming of the final messianic king, who will pour out His Spirit on all flesh.

Lessons from Judah

More clearly than the rest of the testaments, the Testament of Judah exhibits the theme that the sons of the patriarchs are the images of their fathers. This is true in both their virtue and their vice in a broad sense, with the patriarchs issuing warnings from their own difficult experience. Taking the testaments of Levi and Judah together, one sees the tradition of two messianic figures, one priestly and one kingly. This conception was so widespread in the Second Temple period that the New Testament reflects it in diverse ways, from St. John the Forerunner's question of whether Christ was the Messiah or if he should expect another (Matt. 11:3; Luke 7:19) to the entire framing of St. Luke's Gospel with St. John, son of a priest, and Jesus the Messiah.

V. TESTAMENT OF ISSACHAR

THE TESTAMENT OF ISSACHAR is one of the shorter testaments within the compendium. The Book of Genesis tells us relatively little about Issachar, so the focus is on its two bits of information: the author constructs a commentary on chastity within marriage and the virtues of agrarian life. While the circumstances of Issachar's birth were less than ideal, he himself is portrayed as one who lived a quiet and peaceful life in godliness and sanctity. He lacks Judah's great deeds of courage but is a figure more worthy of emulation.

The first story in Genesis concerning Issachar relates to his conception and birth (Gen. 30:14–18), when Leah gives Rachel mandrakes, thought to bring fertility, in exchange for the opportunity to sleep with Jacob that night. The other significant mention of Issachar in Genesis is within the Testament of Jacob (Gen. 49:14–15). This brief prophecy is interpreted as Issachar embracing life as a farmer, tithing from his first fruits to Levi and using his excess not for profit but to provide for the poor and needy. His diligent work is portrayed as heroic in and of itself, paralleling Judah's martial prowess; but unlike Judah, Issachar kept himself from falling into sin. The first two sins that he avoided are precisely the two into which Judah fell—sexual immorality and drunkenness. While the Testaments of the Twelve Patriarchs elevate the Levitical priesthood as the highest institution within the life of Israel and later Judea, they also present the humble, agrarian way of life as the best way of being in the world for most of humanity.

Lessons from Issachar

The brief story of Rachel and Leah and its context are here reinterpreted in relation to female sexuality. Rachel, in the preceding verses of the chapter, desperately desires to bear children. Leah already has several children, yet essentially bribes Rachel to let Leah sleep with their husband, Jacob, instead of her. Rachel makes the agreement despite being childless. The Testament of Issachar interprets this event as Rachel understanding sexuality to be intimately related to childbearing, while Leah seeks sex purely for the purpose of physical pleasure. Issachar is certainly not arguing for celibacy within marriage—Rachel's two children are a blessing to her from God and were conceived in the usual way after these events. Rather, the testament calls for chastity in marriage, which maintains the inherent connection between sexuality and childbearing, rather than marriage as permission to indulge the passion of lust.

VI. TESTAMENT OF ZEBULON

THE TESTAMENT OF ZEBULON is another testament that meditates upon the brothers' intended murder of Joseph and his ultimately being sold into slavery. Zebulon begins his testament to his children and grandchildren by saying that he has not, as far as he remembers, sinned other than in thought or in ignorance. These distinctions, between sins done in knowledge and those done in ignorance and between sins of thought and sins of action, form the frame of Zebulon's testimony. The rest of the Testament of Zebulon largely concerns the remedy for such sins.

The text dramatizes Zebulon's collusion with his brothers in the matter of Joseph in order to distinguish types of sins. Though Zebulon is not the direct agent of any actions taken against his brother, he is party to them, sympathizes with them, and does nothing to interfere or to prevent them from taking place. Additionally, Zebulon knew that what his brothers were doing was wrong, and he was moved with compassion. This explanation is not intended as a form of self-exoneration but the exact opposite: Zebulon considers himself to have greater guilt because he went along with what he knew was sin, even swearing with his brothers not to reveal the truth to their father.

Zebulon contrasts these sins of omission with the way he has lived the rest of his life. He claims to be the inventor of the boat, sail, and rudder. This seems somewhat unlikely, especially given the distance in time between his life and the Flood of Noah. More specifically, he presents himself as the first great fisherman, in a sort of parallel way of life to Issachar's: as Issachar works the land, Zebulon works the seas to bring forth food. Like Issachar, however, he engages in fishing not only to feed his own household or to generate profits; rather, he shares the fruit of the seas freely with those in need and provides all forms of aid and help.

Lessons from Zebulon

The sins of omission that Zebulon emphasizes are more subtle and perhaps less easy to resist than those of commission. It is, at the very least, difficult to imagine someone living a long life on earth without at some point entertaining sinful thoughts or failing adequately to confront the sin of others in some social situation. Faced with the seeming inevitability of such sins, Zebulon does not merely urge greater vigilance. Instead, he counters sinful passivity with virtuous activity. The means of resisting and atoning for the passive sins that are all too endemic to our lives is to engage in active love toward our neighbor (1 Pet. 4:8).

VII. TESTAMENT OF DAN

THE TESTAMENT OF DAN is immediately complicated by his tribe's apostasy. Beginning with the prophecies concerning Dan in the Testament of Jacob (Gen. 49:16–18), through its brutal siege of a city rather than the territory God allots to it (Josh. 19:47–48), to its descent into idolatry (Judg. 18:27–30), the Scriptures say nothing positive about the tribe of Dan. The Testament of Dan, unlike some of the others, does not fully attempt to read this condemnation back into the person of Dan the Patriarch. It does, however, see the seeds that will grow into that destruction and issues a warning based on his prophetic awareness of the fate of his progeny.

Dan reflects once again on the episode in which the brothers betrayed Joseph. Dan is the prime motivator of violence toward his brother because of his seething anger and wrath. Though his brothers were able to restrain him, the other tribes would not restrain his descendants—at least not as effectively. Dan's meditation reveals how anger is truly a passion, a spirit of hatred and violence that takes control of people, blinding them and driving them to destructive actions. Dan states that the spirit of anger that controls those consumed by wrath comes from the right hand of Satan.

Despite these words directed to his immediate descendants, Dan is fully aware that in the long term, the tribe that bears his name will renounce their God. He cites the Book of Enoch in prophesying that their prince will be Satan and that they will give themselves over to every kind of evil. This assessment of Dan as a tribe was near universal in the Second Temple period, especially since the Assyrians had destroyed it. When the Revelation of St. John lists the tribes of Israel, the apostle omits Dan and replaces it with Joseph's younger son Manasseh (Rev. 7:5–8).

Lessons from Dan

The Testament of Dan, however, despite the sureness of the prophecy of its destruction and the blunt statement in its final verse that the prophecy came to pass (7:3), is not hopeless concerning the tribe members' future. In fact, alongside the prediction of Dan's apostasy and destruction, the tribe's founder calls his people to find and follow their Savior. This Savior, however, is expressly the Savior of the Gentiles, of the nations. Through their apostasy and the resulting destruction by the Assyrians, the Danites will become Gentiles and lose their inheritance. Yet repentance and faithfulness to the Savior of the world will one day allow them to be redeemed.

VIII. TESTAMENT OF NAPHTALI

THE TESTAMENT OF NAPHTALI is another testament that circulated independently. A manuscript of the testament, without any other related testaments, was discovered at Qumran among the Dead Sea Scrolls. As with the Testament of Levi, Naphtali contains apocalyptic material that has been incorporated into the body of the testaments.

The Book of Genesis offers very little information about Naphtali, and the rest of the Hebrew Bible also contains relatively little. The Testament of Jacob in Genesis 49 includes only a couplet comparing Naphtali to a deer, which is used briefly as a motif within the Testament of Naphtali (2:1). But the couplet provides the occasion for a meditation on the way in which God equips all his creatures for their contributions to the created order. Naphtali also references the Book of Enoch's prophesied falling away of the tribe, but this is part of more general statements in 1 Enoch regarding the Northern Kingdom of Israel as a whole and the tribes that constituted it.

The central element of the Testament of Naphtali is a vision he receives at the Mount of Olives near Jerusalem. He sees Levi and Judah mount their way up into the heavens. In keeping with the ranking of the testaments as a whole, Levi becomes the sun and Judah the moon. The twelve rays beneath Judah's feet represent the twelve tribes over whom he reigns as king. Behemoth, the bull of heaven, appears as a great bull with eagle's wings that frightens all the brothers, but Joseph mounts it and ascends to heaven.

Joseph's son Ephraim was the center, ruler, and representative of the ten northern tribes. The vision depicts the destruction of the Northern Kingdom not as a fall or a waste but as a means of ascent, and not primarily for Joseph's descendants and the rest of the ten tribes. Rather, after this ascent, a great scroll appears to Naphtali that states the "Assyrians, Medes, Persians, Elamites, Gelachians, Chaldeans, and Syrians will gain a share in the twelve tribes of Israel through captivity" (5:8). Through the dispersion of the northern tribes, the Gentiles—all nations hostile to Israel, Judah, and Judea—come not only to find salvation but to become a part of the twelve tribes. This idea represents an important undergirding to St. Paul's discussion in Romans 11.

Lessons from Naphtali

The Testament of Naphtali at its closing reiterates in detail the recurring theme within the testaments that the tribes of Israel will find salvation through unity with Levi and Judah. Only through the authority of the Davidic king and the Levitical priesthood can humanity find deliverance from the powers of sin and death. The dispersion of the northern tribes, then, into the nations allows them to receive a share of Israel's inheritance by entering the Kingdom of the Messiah.

IX. TESTAMENT OF GAD

THE TESTAMENT OF GAD is another of the shorter testaments within the collection, and it is also another testament that meditates primarily on the episode of the plotted murder of Joseph and his sale into slavery. Unlike Dan, Gad considers this event through the lens of hatred rather than anger. Also, unlike Dan, the purpose of describing this hatred is not primarily to warn against it but to replace it with love for one's brother.

Lessons from Gad

Love and hate here are direct opposites, meaning that the text delineates hatred so that the outline of love can become clearer. Hate seeks to kill; love seeks to restore to life and to pardon those sentenced to death. Hate seeks to destroy; love seeks to create. Hate engenders jealousy and bitterness; love longs to see the other person prosper. Importantly, even when someone prospers through injustice or causes harm, love must continue, leaving judgment and repayment to the Lord. The chief mode of loving someone is to lift them continually before God in prayer.

X. TESTAMENT OF ASHER

THE TESTAMENT OF ASHER is the shortest of the testaments. As in the cases of Gad and Naphtali, the Torah contains relatively little information about Asher. This testament, there-fore, is not only brief but relatively general. It speaks of two ways in the world, one of good and one of evil. Many people are two-faced and pursue evil while speaking and presenting themselves as good. In the end, this avails nothing before the God who knows the hearts and deeds of all people.

Lessons from Asher

One important factor that differentiates the ways of good and evil, according to the Testament of Asher, is evil's duplicity. Not only are humans duplicitous in pursuing evil, but along the way the steps of evil themselves appear good yet hide evil within them: The enjoyment of possessions hides greed. Celebration and merriment hide drunkenness. Laughter and mockery hide grief and lamentation. Good, on the other hand, never hides its opposite: Truth never hides falsehood. Obedience does not hide rebellion. Sobriety does not hide dissolution. Within and beyond the pursuit of the good, one finds God Himself.

XI. TESTAMENT OF JOSEPH

JOSEPH IS A FIGURE of major importance within the Book of Genesis; his story takes up between a quarter and a third of the text of the first Book of the Torah. He is the central protagonist of the narrative of Jacob's sons, taking over the focus from his father Jacob even well before Jacob's death. His descendants, primarily the tribe of Ephraim, are the most numerous tribe. They form the center of the Northern Kingdom of Israel, and their territory contains its capital. Joseph and Ephraim, used interchangeably, appear in the Psalms and the Prophets to indicate the entire Northern Kingdom, both during its existence and following its destruction by Assyria. Joseph's prominence in the Torah reflects the relatively early date of its material, especially Genesis. Texts from later in history, such as the Testament of the Twelve Patriarchs, greatly reduce Joseph's prominence in favor of Levi, Judah, and Benjamin—the three surviving tribes that made up most of Judah and later Judea.

Because of its late date, the Testament of Joseph primarily approaches the patriarch, as the other testaments do, by finding a throughline in his story that exhibits a particular virtue or vice. As noted in the previous sections, many of these testaments are framed around the selling of Joseph into slavery and the sins related to his brothers' varied participation in it. But both within that event and in the rest of his narrative, Joseph is presented as virtuous. Later Christian interpreters will focus primarily on Joseph's movement from apparent death to life, or from humiliation to exaltation, as a story arc that reflects the life of Christ. But there is little of this mode of interpretation in the Testament of Joseph. The absence of this narrative connection to Jesus becomes important when assessing whether or not the messianic prophecies at the end of the book are later Christian interpolations.

The Testament of Joseph zeroes in on Joseph's time as a slave to Potiphar and the attempts by Potiphar's wife to seduce him; the vast majority of the text is just an elaborate retelling of that story with a great deal of added detail. Potiphar's wife attempts everything to get Joseph to sleep with her. She threatens him. She tortures him. She seeks to seduce him with words. She plots the murder of her husband so that she would be available to marry Joseph. She purchases love potions and attempts to use magic. Finally, she threatens to kill herself and frame Joseph for murder if he refuses to participate. When even that doesn't work, as in the text of Genesis, she frames him for rape instead and has him thrown into prison.

Joseph therefore represents the virtue of chastity, and he patiently endures the suffering caused by his determination to remain chaste. In return, God rewards him with a long and healthy life and with his wife, Aseneth. Interestingly, his children are not mentioned in any detail here, again reflecting the dissolution of the tribes of Ephraim and Manasseh. Joseph encourages his children, the hearers of his testament, not only to protect their chastity as he had, but also not to give in to anger or revenge when they suffer unjustly; rather, they are to pray for those who persecute them.

Messianic Prophecies in Two Versions

Joseph's story in the Book of Genesis surrounds divinely inspired dreams and their interpretation. The Testament of Joseph ends with his final dream and his interpretation of it. Two versions exist: one found in the Aramaic and the other in the Greek. The Greek version of the dream and its interpretation is much shorter, but in some ways more on the nose regarding its messianic prophecies and the Person of Jesus Christ. Thus many scholars think the Greek reflects a post-Christian version of the Jewish text. This supposition raises as many questions as it answers, however. There is no clear reason why Christians would omit most of the missing material, which surrounds the history of Judea from the exile to the time of its writing in the Hasmonean period. The Greek texts of the other testaments do not omit similar material. The small details in the messianic portion of the dream in Greek are precisely that: small details. The substance of the messianic prophecy is the same in both.

The Aramaic section omitted in the Greek describes this historical era of Judea, from exile to the Hasmonean period, in a manner similar to the animal apocalypse or Daniel's vision of the beasts. Animals represent Israelite tribes and nations; horns represent their kings. Following this narration, which constitutes the entire dream in the Greek, is a clear prophecy of the coming Messiah, who is a lamb born of a virgin from the tribe of Judah. While modern scholars may find this to be too accurate to be pre-Christian, the wording here in Aramaic or Greek is close enough to that of Isaiah 7 that the prophecy is clearly derivative of that found in the Hebrew Bible.

A variety of creatures attack this lamb—not the animals that represented the nations, but reptiles and creeping things—and he defeats them. The lamb represents the salvation of Israel and all the nations, if the people remain true to Levi and Judah. The phrasing of the Greek of Testament of Joseph 19:11, which refers to the Messiah as "the Lamb of God who will take away the sin of the world," seems an obvious interpolation to many scholars. But when St. John the Forerunner identifies Christ as this figure in John 1:29, the words are a symbolic means used to identify the Messiah. It seems, if anything, more likely that St. John was appealing to preexisting symbolism to identify Jesus as the Messiah than that St. John here was inventing an unknown image to communicate cryptically with his own followers. Nothing in either version of the Testament of Joseph would require it to be a post-Christian text. Non-Christian Judeans of the early Christian centuries did not disagree with Christians about the coming of a Messiah or the prophecies concerning Him; they disagreed with the Christian claim that Jesus of Nazareth was that figure.

Lessons from Joseph

The Testament of Joseph ends with Joseph predicting that the sojourn of the sons of Jacob in Egypt will inevitably become bondage and slavery. Joseph applies the example of his own trials as a slave in Egypt to them: if they endure patiently and remain faithful to God, He will deliver them and reward them at the end of their time of suffering. For Judeans standing at the end of exile, under Greek and later Roman domination, this theme had particular resonance. The Testament of Joseph was a promise that patient endurance, obedience, and faithfulness to God during their time of servitude would bring rewards at the time of the coming of the Messiah.

XII. TESTAMENT OF BENJAMIN

THE FINAL PIECE of the Testament of the Twelve Patriarchs is the Testament of Benjamin. The text is convoluted because of the ambivalent way the Hebrew Bible treats Benjamin and his decisions. Benjamin is Joseph's younger brother, the only other son of Rachel, their mother. Joseph loves him and is concerned that he may have faced ill treatment at the hands of his brothers, like that Joseph himself had faced. On the other hand, in Genesis 49 Jacob describes Benjamin as a rapacious wolf. His descendants in the period of the Judges proved treacherous and sparked a civil war within Israel. The rivalry between Saul and David and their respective houses was the culmination of a rivalry between the tribes of Benjamin and Judah.

The Testament of Benjamin deals with this ambiguity by clearly discriminating between Benjamin himself and his descendants. Benjamin relates the story of his separation from and reunion with Joseph, and this story is marked with all the tenderness and brotherly love of the Joseph narrative in Genesis.

Benjamin directly applies his own characterization as a wolf to his descendants, again citing the Book of Enoch as a source for the contours of his tribe's future sinfulness. Nevertheless, unlike most of the brother tribes, Benjamin remained with Judah and therefore went into exile rather than face Assyrian destruction. Benjamin compares his progeny's future loss of the kingdom and its restoration to his own separation from Joseph and their reunion. In the meantime, Benjamin needed to stay faithful to his brother's memory, just as Benjamin's tribe needed to remain faithful to Levi and Judah—even though the priesthood and monarchy were not functioning during the time of the exile.

Prophecy of the Messiah

The Testament of Benjamin includes one final prophecy of the coming Messiah, though it differs somewhat between the Aramaic and the Greek. In this prophecy also, the Greek includes additional details, but the broad strokes in both are the same. The shorter Aramaic form describes the coming of the Messiah as the point at which the spotless one will be seized by lawless men, and the sinless one will die for impious men. The Greek version fleshes this out by referring to the Messiah as the Lamb of God, the Savior of the world, and adding that the Messiah will use the blood of the covenant to save the Gentiles and Israel, and to defeat Belial and his servants.

Typically, scholars see the Greek expansion as a later Christian interpolation. This is certainly possible, though the Testaments of the Twelve Patriarchs elsewhere mirror the language used here. The expansion could, therefore, simply be a means of summarizing the messianic material of the whole work here at its end. In theory, either a Christian or a Jewish author could have constructed such a summary. Here the suffering and death of the Messiah—the major interpretive understanding of the latter portions of Isaiah in the Second Temple period—is not specifically joined, for example, to the Cross or the Resurrection. These would have been tantalizing additions if a Christian intended to make these prophecies appear more specific.

Lessons from Benjamin

Benjamin encourages not some virtue of his own but that his descendants emulate the virtue of his older brother Joseph. From the perspective of the time of writing of the text, Joseph is a patriarch of old whose life would be emulated by reading, meditation, and practice. Clearly, the pattern of reading the lives of the saints as guiding principles of human conduct had already developed within the Second Temple period.

Significance: A Key to Early Christian Understanding of Moral Teaching and History

In terms of understanding the teaching of the New Testament and early Christianity, especially the moral teaching, the view of history, and the makeup of the people of Israel, no work discussed in this book is more important than the Testaments of the Twelve Patriarchs. The understanding of sin and virtue presented in this composite text would have a profound influence on the monastic literature of the Christian Church, which not coincidentally preserved this text in her monastic foundations. When the New Testament describes Jesus of Nazareth as fulfilling the role of Israel's Messiah and Savior, it does so in terms laid out clearly in the Testaments of the Twelve Patriarchs.

CHAPTER SIX

The Ascension of Isaiah and the Assumption of Moses

In the Apocalyptic Tradition

THE PENCHANT FOR THE APOCALYPTIC displayed in Jewish writings of the Second Temple period, as seen in the proliferation of Enochic literature, continued into the Christian era. Many of the earliest Christian texts adopted the form, in large part resulting in its abandonment by nascent Rabbinic Judaism. This chapter will discuss two such texts— one of them really a set of texts—from the late first and early second centuries: the Ascension of Isaiah and the Assumption of Moses. Each of them, in certain ways, spans the developing divide between what became Rabbinic Jewish synagogues and Christian communities. The Church Fathers cite and reference both, and these books contain traditions that would continue in Christian teaching and also in forms of Talmudic tradition.

Background

The first of these books is now known as the Ascension of Isaiah. Its title, both as found within existing manuscript copies and as used by early Fathers who cited it, refers to the text as a whole. It is a composite work made up of three texts that appear to have been composed separately: the first appears to be of Jewish origin, while the latter two are distinctly Christian.

The first text, chapters 1 through 5, is the Martyrdom of Isaiah, which describes that event in some detail. The second text, now making up chapters 6 through 11, is the Vision of Isaiah, which recounts Isaiah's visionary experiences following his martyrdom as he traveled through the seven heavens. The third text, the Testament of Hezekiah, is not appended to the other two but rather inserted into the middle of the Martyrdom of Isaiah. This text is third because it clearly reflects Christian composition. Each of these works seems to have been written in the late first century AD, with the three of them compiled into something like their present form in the first half of the second century.

The second work discussed in this chapter is most often known as the Assumption of Moses, though sometimes as the Testament of Moses. In the list of St. Nikephoros and elsewhere, two different works are known by these two titles. The extant text that has come down to our day has been variously identified over the centuries by one title or the other. But Church Fathers such as St. Athanasius and later Byzantine writers cite this text as the Assumption of Moses; hence the preference for that title here. The book is a composition of the early first century AD and is therefore pre-Christian. It purports to be apocalyptic insight that Moses gives to Joshua at the time of Moses' death, describing history very nearly up to the date of its composition. Moses is here used as a rhetorical device to explain Israelite and Judean history from the perspective of the Torah.

THE ASCENSION OF ISAIAH

Chapters 1–5: The Martyrdom of Isaiah

Despite being a composite text, the Ascension of Isaiah is not terribly long. The original narrative of the first five chapters, the Martyrdom of Isaiah, seems clearly to be a recording of oral traditions regarding the prophet's manner of death that are not included in the Hebrew Scriptures. However, the Talmud and other later accounts from Rabbinic Jewish sources echo the broad strokes of the story. The specific method of his death, that he was placed inside a log and then sawn in two, is also referenced in the Epistle to the Hebrews 11:37.

Isaiah's martyrdom takes place explicitly in the context of spiritual warfare. After the death of Hezekiah, Manasseh becomes king and will prove a particularly evil one. Isaiah, as a prophet, is aware in advance of his character, so he gathers the community of the prophets and leads them out to the desert around the Jordan—not coincidentally the area in which St. John the Forerunner would later minister. Manasseh's rejuvenation of pagan worship in Judah gives an opportunity for Belial (or Beliar) to possess a pagan prophet named Belkira, a name that seems to be a corruption of a name meaning "lord of evil." It is also another name for the fallen archangel Samael, generally identified with Satan. This demon-possessed false prophet leads Manasseh's forces to track down and capture Isaiah, and he oversees the execution as Isaiah is sawn in half.

Christian Insertion: The Testament of Hezekiah

Another, separate document is inserted into the middle of the martyrdom story in the first five chapters. This later insertion, generally referred to as the Testament of Hezekiah, begins in Ascension of Isaiah 3:13 and includes chapter 4. This addition is overtly Christian, not only referring to the life of Christ and the disciples in detail but also using the phrase "the Christian Church" at one point (3:15). The Testament of Hezekiah records a vision that Isaiah received of the Incarnation, life, death, and Resurrection of Christ; the coming of the Holy Spirit; and the evangelization of the world by the apostles. It is presented as the reality underlying the prophecies of the canonical Book of Isaiah. Isaiah's revelation of these things to humanity fostered Belial's hatred toward him and thereby brought about his death. The latter portion of the vision describes the coming of the Antichrist, followed by the return of Christ, the resurrection of the dead, the Last Judgment, and the final establishment of the Kingdom. As in the Revelation of St. John, the Antichrist is reminiscent of Nero as Roman emperor.

Chapters 6–11: The Vision of Isaiah

The second portion of the main text is often called the Vision of Isaiah. Like the inserted testament, it is very clearly a Christian addition and likely was originally a separate tradition. Though always found as the second half of the text, the vision takes place before Isaiah's martyrdom rather than describing what happened to him afterward. It is an apocalyptic text that narrates Isaiah's heavenly ascent and journey in angelic form through the seven heavens and describes their contents.[29] His

---

29 The description here of the seven heavens is a different breakdown from those previously discussed in other texts. In the Second Temple period, no standardized cosmology of the heavenly realm existed.

journey includes enmity and a contest with Samael.

Before the throne of God, Isaiah sees both angels and Old Testament saints, beginning with Enoch, who no longer wear garments of flesh but instead wear new garments. They are now like the angels, and Isaiah sees many crowns, thrones, and garments awaiting the saints in the future. But they have not yet received their crowns or thrones because Christ has not yet completed His work. These saints, and the angels with them, will replace the angels of the "lower world," who had rebelled by rejecting God their Creator and presenting themselves as the only gods, demanding worship from humanity.

The Vision of Isaiah makes plain the state of Trinitarian understanding at the end of the first century AD. God the Father is the Great Glory upon whom no one can look. Christ is the Beloved, who descends in the Incarnation and then ascends in glory to where He was before. Isaiah also beholds the "angel of the Holy Spirit," a term that has caused some consternation among commentators. Influenced by an evolutionary view of doctrinal development, they want to interpret this as an identification of the Holy Spirit as an angel. A simpler answer is that the Holy Spirit does not have a physically visible form in the way that Christ does. The wording seems to be a circumlocution to indicate that Isaiah saw a representation, or image, of the Holy Spirit. All the angels and humans in the heavenly places give worship to Christ and to the Spirit, who then pass that worship on to God the Father. Unless someone obsesses over a literal, detailed reading of still-forming terminology, this portrayal is entirely consonant with Nicene Trinitarianism as described three hundred years later by Ss. Basil the Great, Gregory the Theologian, and others.

Significance to the Early Church

The Ascension of Isaiah concludes, in what is now chapter 11, with a summary of the life of Christ and of Isaiah's vision as previously recorded. Like the Testament of Hezekiah inserted into the first part of the text, this information is presented as the reality that underlies the canonical Book of Isaiah. In the pages of the New Testament and in much of early Christian writing, the Book of Isaiah holds a special place in its now seemingly clear foreshadowing of the Person and work of Jesus Christ. Isaiah therefore made an appropriate vehicle for early Christian writers to express the fulfillment of Old Testament prophecy and the future of the Christian hope.

THE ASSUMPTION OF MOSES

Textual History

The text now known in translation as the Assumption of Moses is difficult to assess. While the early manuscript from which it is translated bears the title "The Assumption of Moses," in terms of genre it is more of a testament, relaying Moses' parting words to Joshua, his successor. A mismatch between genre and title is not uncommon in this sort of literature, but in this case, ancient writers also refer to another document as the Testament of Moses. While it is possible that these are the same text, St. Nikephoros lists two separate works by those two names. Further, his list provides the length of each text, and the two differ significantly. There are no other known instances of St. Nikephoros listing two versions of the same text separately.

Further confounding the issue is the fact that the original ending of the extant copy of the Assumption of Moses is missing roughly its last third. The argument, then, that this is a testament that does not describe Moses being assumed into heaven and therefore must be the other ancient document runs afoul of this objection. When Moses refers to his coming death within the surviving two-thirds of the text, he refers to it as his assumption. It is therefore entirely plausible, even likely, that the missing ending included an account of Moses' ascent into heaven; thus this text is, in fact, correctly labeled. Another possibility is that at some point historically the two texts merged into one. While this could, of course, be the case, the present text is translated from a single sixth-century manuscript in Latin. This means that the surviving text predates the list of St. Nikephoros by roughly four hundred years.

Contents

Scholars may never determine the actual title of the extant text, or which ancient work on St. Nikephoros's list it represents. Nevertheless, this surviving text was considered, at least in the early ninth century, to be worthy of the attention of Christians. The content of the Assumption of Moses is essentially similar to that of any other apocryphal testament. Moses, in his final discourse to Joshua, predicts the entire course of the history of Israel, Judah, and Judea, down to the beginning of the first century AD.

Modern commentators have a tendency to read a kind of fatalism or predestinarianism into the Assumption. This represents an incredible overreading. The book presents Moses as knowing the entire history of Israel roughly fifteen hundred years in advance, but this is not necessarily an assertion of fact.

The work does not claim that the historical Moses actually knew and understood this history; the thrust of the text, rather, is that the first-century AD commentator understands that the history of Israel from Moses to his time has unfolded according to the providence of God. The writing of pseudepigraphic literature was not, especially in the Second Temple period, an attempt to deceive. Rather, it provided a frame for theological literature to make certain points regarding Israel and her history.

An overarching theme of the extant text of the Assumption of Moses is the culpability of Moses' descendants in the tribe of Levi, as well as the priesthood's culpability in the ongoing corruption within Israel, Judah, and Judea. The blame placed on the priesthood continues into the Hasmonean period, thereby ultimately implicating the Sadducees. This and other elements of the narrative may indicate that this text emerged within Pharisaic circles.

Moses' commentary to Joshua concludes with a prophecy of the coming of the Messiah. In chapter 10 the Most High arises from His throne to execute judgment and vengeance upon those who are first described as His sons (v. 3) and then later as the idols of the Gentiles (v. 7). Judgment comes upon the sons of God who have enslaved the nations through false worship. He casts them down and replaces them with the faithful of Israel, who become like the stars of heaven (v. 9). These righteous will stand before the throne of God, and their demonic tormentors will be punished in Gehenna (v. 10).

Significance to the New Testament

Ordinarily the discussion of these apocryphal texts would be purely the project of certain scholars in a niche field. But in this case the Assumption of Moses has direct relevance to the New Testament. The Epistle of St. Jude, in addition to quoting directly from 1 Enoch, also refers to an episode in which the Archangel Michael contested with Satan over the body of Moses (v. 9). Jude refers to this episode in an offhand way to demonstrate a point, implying that the story is generally known to his audience. The earliest authors who comment on this verse, Gelasius of Cyzicus and Origen, write that this tradition is found in the Assumption of Moses. The discovery of a manuscript with that title in the nineteenth century was therefore greeted with eagerness, though the relevant portion was missing.

SIGNIFICANCE OF BOTH TEXTS
TO THE CHURCH

THE CANONICAL NEW TESTAMENT refers to traditions contained within both the Ascension of Isaiah and the Assumption of Moses. Their composition in the first century, beyond those specific cited details, gives us a window into the understanding of Jewish communities at the time of Christ as well as that of the earliest Judean Christians. Possibly the most important element of these texts is the way in which they read the history of Israel and Judea.

Much of the debate between Christ and His opponents in the Gospels, as well as the framing of St. Paul's arguments in his epistles, is grounded in competing readings of the history of the people of God. The opponents of Christ and of the apostles believed that the sons of Abraham, and therefore the heirs to the promises made to him, are Judean people who strictly keep the commandments of the Torah that identify them as Israelites. But following Christ, St. Paul presents the true sons and heirs of Abraham as those who are like Abraham in their faithfulness. Texts such as the Ascension of Isaiah and the Assumption of Moses show that the Christian understanding of this history was not new in the first century AD, nor was it a disjunction from previous tradition. Rather, the early Church's understanding represents the ultimate flowering and fulfillment of the religion of the faithful of Israel.

CHAPTER SEVEN

The Books of Baruch

Who Was Baruch?

BARUCH, SON OF NERIAH AND THE SCRIBE of Jeremiah the prophet, appears to be a minor figure to most readers of the Hebrew Bible or the shorter form of the Christian Old Testament used by most Protestant communities. However, the more expansive Old Testaments used by Latin, Greek, and Slavonic traditions include a Book of Baruch. In addition, three more texts exist that bear his name, numbered Second, Third, and Fourth Baruch. These numbers are purely for reference, because no Christian tradition reads from all four publicly.

We know little about Baruch from the Book of Jeremiah, although his role as a scribe implies a level of education that would require him to have come from a well-placed family in Jerusalem. Jeremiah identifies a Seraiah, son of Neriah, as the chamberlain of Zedekiah, king of Judah (Jer. 51:59). Josephus makes explicit that this is Baruch's brother. Wealth and privilege in this case are relative, as Zedekiah was the final king of

Judah before the Babylonian exile, which took place during Baruch's lifetime in the sixth century BC. At this point, Judah barely existed as a vassal state of the Neo-Babylonian Empire and was kept on a short leash. Two separate archaeological finds uncovered bullae bearing the seal of a scribe named "Baruch son of Neriah." While, as with all finds, their origins cannot be definitively proven, these artifacts date to the right era and were found in the right place for them to have come from the Prophet Baruch himself. Tantalizingly, one bulla holds a fingerprint in the clay that could also belong to him.

In addition to the books that bear his name, a number of other traditions about Baruch have been passed down through the life of the Church. An early Jewish tradition identifies Baruch with the Ethiopian "servant of the king" who appears in Jeremiah 38:7. Though no direct connection is clear, it is interesting that this ancient tradition of Baruch's Ethiopian ethnicity is joined with what has become known as 4 Baruch in the canon of the Ethiopian Church. A later, widespread tradition in Syria and the Middle East among Jews, Christians, and early Muslims identified Baruch with Zoroaster. The idea is that Baruch, at the time of the destruction of Jerusalem and its temple, went even farther east than Babylon and there founded what became the dominant Persian religion. It is unclear if this tradition arose to explain certain similarities in Second Temple Jewish and Persian practices, the coming of the Magi to worship the infant Christ, the beneficence of Cyrus toward Judea, or all—or none—of the above.

Textual Histories

1 AND 2 BARUCH

The book titled simply Baruch, found in the Latin, Greek, and Slavonic canons among others, is often reckoned to be the original version of the Book of Jeremiah that the king destroyed in Jeremiah 36:27/43:27. Another closely related text, the Epistle of Jeremiah, is sometimes appended as the final chapter of Baruch and in other cases is listed separately. This text has a long history of use and reflection, either as canonical or as deuterocanonical, and so will not be addressed here. Instead, this chapter will focus on the other three major texts bearing Baruch's name, which are today far less well known.

The early Fathers and even many later ones tend to refer to the Book of Baruch, or 1 Baruch, as simply "Jeremiah" in quotations. It is also introduced this way when it is read liturgically in the Orthodox Church. The Book of Lamentations also is traditionally identified merely as "Jeremiah," even though it appears as a separate book in nearly all Old Testaments. The canonical books of Jeremiah, Lamentations, and Baruch are all frequently cited as "the prophecy of Jeremiah," as he is the prophet behind all three books.

When these Fathers refer to the Book of Baruch, they nearly always mean what is now known as 2 Baruch or the Apocalypse of Baruch. While 1 Baruch—the book in most Roman Catholic and Orthodox Old Testaments—is named for the scribe and also contains material from the Prophet Jeremiah, 2 Baruch purports to be Baruch's own prophetic visions. This series of apocalyptic visions, found in Syriac Bibles, uses Baruch's witness to the destruction of the first temple by the Babylonians as a narrative device to speak about the destruction of the second temple by the Romans in AD 70. Second Baruch was written in the late first or early second century AD and contains a number of thematic crossovers with 4 Ezra.

3 BARUCH

Third Baruch is likewise an apocalyptic text, dating to sometime in the second century, and was originally written in Greek. Scholars disagree on whether it is a Jewish or early Christian text, though we must remember that in the second century, particularly early on, there was not a strong distinction between these two communities. Like 2 Baruch, it uses the first temple's destruction as a veil through which to speak about the Roman destruction of the second temple without directly criticizing the empire. Though 3 Baruch is not found in Christian canons, the text was copied down through the centuries and survives in both Greek and Slavonic translations.

In 3 Baruch, Baruch, the Prophet Jeremiah's scribe, takes a journey through the heavens and describes his experiences of each.[30] This text was initially written in Greek, as attested by two Greek manuscripts from the fifteenth century from libraries on Mount Athos, which show clear signs of being two copies of the same original. More than twelve manuscripts of 3 Baruch exist in Slavonic, representing at least three strands of copying tradition.

---

30 As with other Second Temple texts, the description of the seven heavens in 3 Baruch is used as a literary device to teach certain spiritual and theological truths. In the ancient period there was no consistent breakdown of the structure of the heavens or the underworld that was accepted by all Jewish people or Christians.

Interestingly, one of the best Slavonic manuscripts, dating to the thirteenth century, comes from the library of St. Catherine's Monastery in Egypt. Its presence there shows the wide circulation of this text throughout the Orthodox world over a vast span of time. Origen references the text in *On First Principles* as the place to find a description of the seven heavens, attesting to the work's antiquity. Third Baruch, in distinction from other apocalyptic literature, contains a critical account of the early second-century AD view of Paradise and Hades as the locations of souls before the resurrection of the dead; the New Testament also references these places.

4 BARUCH

Fourth Baruch, sometimes called the "Remaining Words of Baruch" or literally, "Baruch's Leftovers," is found in the Old Testament of the Ethiopian Church. Internal evidence allows it to be dated with great confidence to around AD 136. Though only the Ge'ez manuscripts are part of liturgical or canonical texts, the text of 4 Baruch is also preserved in Greek, Armenian, Slavonic, and Romanian. Like the other literature attributed to Baruch, 4 Baruch appears to be using the Babylonian exile as an analogy for the state of affairs following Rome's destruction of the second temple in Jerusalem.

St. Nikephoros and the Books of Baruch

Saint Nikephoros, in enumerating the apocryphal books of the Old Testament, makes reference to "the pseudepigrapha of Baruch" as well as a list of other prophets, but it is not possible to discern a particular number of books of Baruch here. There are several reasons to conclude, however, that he was likely referring to what we now know as 2, 3, and 4 Baruch. These works are all prominently featured in subsequent manuscript copying and preservation activities, and 2 and 4 Baruch's canonical status in non-Chalcedonian churches likewise would have made them an obvious subject of St. Nikephoros's attention.

2 BARUCH

Content

Though 2 Baruch is patterned after the Book of Baruch and therefore included here, it was written near the end of the first century or at the beginning of the second century AD. Portions of the text are read as part of the Old Testament lectionary of the Syriac Orthodox Church. The genre is apocalyptic, centering around a series of visions Baruch experienced during his mourning of the destruction of the temple in Jerusalem by the Babylonians circa 586 BC. This destruction, as in the other texts named after Baruch, is a quite thinly veiled means of commenting on the destruction of the second temple in Jerusalem in AD 70.

The text is structured around three threes. Three times Baruch fasts, generally for seven days, then receives a vision, then communicates that vision to the rest of the people. These visions serve to relativize the importance of the temple in Jerusalem, as the prophecies regarding it here are more particular than, for example, in Ezekiel. From his vantage point in the sixth century BC, in Babylonian exile, Ezekiel had prophesied the building of a new temple. For many groups within Second Temple Judaism, the physical temple in Jerusalem, built after the return from Babylon, was a crucial center of piety and the foundation of religious practice. But 2 Baruch considers the material temple to be of secondary importance. From his point of view in the past, Baruch prophesies not only the rebuilding of the second temple but also its second destruction. Both temples are copies of the true temple that existed in Paradise and was revealed to Moses atop Mount Sinai. That true temple will finally arrive on earth with the Messiah.

Time as a Series of Ages

The major theme of the visions of 2 Baruch is the periodization of time, seeing history as divided into a series of ages, or eras. The destruction of the temple was not the end of everything— not even the end of God's covenant. Rather, it represented the end of a particular era; several of these eras occurred in the past, and another would come in the future. Second Baruch points to eras in which evil held dominion, as from Adam to Noah's Flood, the bondage of Israel in Egypt, the period of the Judges, and the reigns of wicked kings like Jeroboam and Manasseh. On the other side, the text reminds the reader of the ages of Abraham, Moses, David, Hezekiah after his repentance, Josiah, and the independence of Judea under the Hasmoneans. While contemporary readers might have a different evaluation of that last season, the author makes the point clear: suffering in an era of evil does not mean that God has abandoned His people or that they should abandon hope.

The visions reveal to Baruch that he, in the sixth century BC, stands at the beginning of a long period of tribulations. Within the Second Temple period when 2 Baruch was written, the faithful consistently understood the Prophet Daniel's great tribulation period (9:25–27) to represent the time between the destruction of the first temple and the coming of the Messiah. Second Baruch breaks this period down into a number of stages of subsequent history from the author's perspective. This begins with the Babylonian exile and moves on to describe the return under Cyrus, the reconstruction of the temple, the coming of the Seleucids, the desecration of the temple, and so forth. Despite the sufferings of this era, the messianic age is coming, culminating in the resurrection of the dead.

At the close of 2 Baruch proper, the Prophet Baruch sends two letters intended to communicate the substance of his visions and related exhortations to the now scattered people of Israel. The text of the letters is not included, leading to the assumption that their contents would be the preceding text of the Book of 2 Baruch. One of these letters goes to the two and a half tribes that had made up the Kingdom of Judah in their exile in Babylon: Judah, Levi, and Benjamin. The other is sent by way of a mystical eagle to the nine and a half tribes who had been long since dissolved by the Assyrians.

At some point in the transmission history of 2 Baruch, a letter purporting to be the letter of Baruch to the nine and a half tribes was added to the end of the book. In the current common numbering, this letter is designated as chapters 78–87. Though it shows clear signs of being a separate, later work, the letter is also clearly a dependent one, crafted to read like Baruch's actual letter. Because of this intentional crafting, the letter serves as a good summary of the way in which readers applied and understood the preceding text.

Influence on the Early Church

Second Baruch was written in a Jewish context to reckon with the destruction of the Jerusalem temple in AD 70. Nevertheless, it became an influential text in Christian circles rather than in nascent Orthodox Judaism. In reaction to Christianity, Orthodox Judaism gradually reduced the fervor and centrality of messianic expectation from the near fever pitch of the first century AD. Early Christian communities, however, continued to look forward to the return of Christ and to suffer persecution and struggle in awaiting that return. The view of the ages of history from the Second Temple era, as expressed in 2 Baruch, became the basis for the Christian understanding of the history of the world and its future.

3 BARUCH

Overview

Because of its place in Syriac-speaking churches, 2 Baruch is often referred to as the Syriac Apocalypse of Baruch. Similarly, 3 Baruch is commonly known as the Greek Apocalypse of Baruch, based on its language of original composition. It is also similar in genre, setting, and major theme to 2 Baruch. Though likely written later in the second century, 3 Baruch is still essentially a response to the destruction of the temple in Jerusalem. Its slightly more pessimistic view of earthly temples likely reflects a greater distance in time from that destruction. Because the true temple is heavenly, the perspective of 3 Baruch is that there is no reason for the second temple ever to be rebuilt, and it likely should not be.

Contents

In response to his sorrow at the temple's destruction, the Prophet Baruch is taken on a journey through the numbered heavens. Third Baruch as a whole is a very short text, so the descriptions of sacred geography are much shorter and less detailed than in, for example, 1 Enoch. Baruch travels through the first four heavens but is unable to enter the fifth. Only the Archangel Michael is given access to the great doors that lead into the fifth heaven. He passes through them to present the good works of humanity to God and later bring forth their eventual reward. Despite the destruction of the temple and subsequent suffering of God's people, differing rewards await the faithful and the wicked when the Day of Judgment comes.

Along the course of his journey, Baruch encounters Hades in the form of a dragon who consumes the dead, with imagery that recalls the curse placed on the devil in Genesis 3. Third Baruch takes a particular interest in the fall of the nations surrounding the construction of the Tower of Babel. Baruch encounters the demons—a composite of animal forms—who inspired the tower's construction, and he witnesses their punishment and suffering. The depiction is similar, though briefer, to that of the Watchers in Enochic literature, but associated with Babel rather than the Flood of Noah. Baruch also beholds a great phoenix—here a single, cosmic angelic being rather than an odd species of earthly bird—that covers the earth with its wings and is associated with the rising and setting of the sun.

Significance to the Church

Though 3 Baruch is a brief text, its central theme is clear: the heavenly temple, not the earthly one, is of primary importance. Though the temple on earth was twice destroyed, the heavenly temple, served by angelic beings in the presence of God, never ceased its function. The way for humans, at all times and in all places, to participate in that heavenly worship is to keep the commandments of God and to do good works in the world, which are borne as offerings into the presence of God. He will reward the faithful on the Last Day.

4 BARUCH

Background

Like the other works attributed to Baruch discussed in this chapter, 4 Baruch is set after the destruction of the Jerusalem temple by the Babylonians but written after the Romans' destruction of the second temple. Fourth Baruch is also a very short text, though it exists in two forms, one slightly longer than the other. The text is a part of the Old Testament of the Ethiopian Orthodox Church, where it forms a part of a larger work called the Lamentations of Jeremiah, a composite work that includes the Book of Lamentations from the Hebrew Bible, the sixth chapter of the Book of Baruch, a very brief bit of Jeremiah tradition related to his contest against the priest Pashhur, and finally 4 Baruch, which circulated separately. This form of the book is also used among Ethiopian Jewish communities and was inherited by Ethiopian Christianity.

Contents

Fourth Baruch is prophetic but not apocalyptic per se. That said, a few tropes echo other traditions in the material ascribed to Baruch. The story begins with Jeremiah receiving the word that the temple will be destroyed. God tasks him with preserving holy items and vestments from the raiding Babylonians so that they might someday be used again. This is a repurposing of a theme found throughout the prophets of the Hebrew Bible concerning the destruction of the first temple and the Babylonian exile: specifically, foreigners or their gods did not defeat Yahweh, the God of Israel. Rather, God carried out a judgment on His people through the Babylonians. This perspective applies equally to the Roman destruction of the second temple and later the entire city of Jerusalem.

Contrary to the canonical Jeremiah, which sees Jeremiah taken to Egypt at the time of the exile, in 4 Baruch he goes into Babylonian exile with the rest of the people while his servant Baruch, who will continue to record the events of the text, remains in the ruins of Jerusalem and its environs. The center point of 4 Baruch is the story of Abimelech, an Ethiopian character who appears in Jeremiah 38:7 (45:7 in the Greek) and who is identified with the servant of the king, Ebedmelech, in Hebrew. Abimelech falls asleep after the destruction of the temple and, like an ancient Rip Van Winkle, sleeps for sixty-six years. The Hebrew Scriptures and history present the exile as having lasted seventy years rather than sixty-six; scholars understand the latter number to reflect the composition of 4 Baruch around AD 136.

When Abimelech awakens, he has no idea how long he has slept, but he finds fresh figs. It was not the season for figs when he fell asleep, so he knows some time must have passed—probably only months, not necessarily years. Canonical Jeremiah called Israel a barren fig tree at the time of the exile (Jer. 8:13), and Abimelech therefore understands this new life to represent a sign of the resurrection of Israel and the imminent end of the exile. When Abimelech finds Baruch, Baruch tells him how long he has been asleep, and Abimelech then tells Baruch of the sign of the figs. Baruch writes a letter to Jeremiah, and an eagle carries it to him, along with the figs. The eagle arrives while Jeremiah is serving a funeral for one of the Judahite exiles, emphasizing the resurrection symbolism.

Receiving this news and this sign, Jeremiah is overjoyed, and the return from exile begins. The book ends, however, with entry into the land of Judea prohibited for those who have entered into mixed marriages. Historically, this prohibition is tied to the Judean people's antipathy toward Samaritans. In the former regions of the Northern Kingdom, the Samaritans were descended from Israelites who had intermarried with the non-Israelite people who had settled in the area. Rejection of the perceived impurity of intermarriage became a major issue in the time of Ezra among the returnees from Babylonian exile (Ezra 10).

Significance to the Church
Within the later context of the writing of 4 Baruch, whether in Christian or non-Christian Jewish communities, the book may have maintained the force of dissuading intermarriage with those outside the community. Such intermarriage represented a threat not primarily to a modern perception of ethnic purity

but of seduction to false religious and spiritual practice (as in 1 Kin./3 Kgd. 11:2). It would be difficult to confine this principle, however, merely to marriage. Likely, the intermarriage dissuaded here includes "marriage" to the things of this world in the present age, which might pull a believer away from the life of the world to come.

Compared to the apocalyptic visions of 2 and 3 Baruch, 4 Baruch is perhaps less blunt in its message. The visions and their explanations in the earlier two books convey in a very straightforward way a particular view of history and the promises of the world to come to those who endure faithfully to the end. Fourth Baruch, on the other hand, communicates more in the style of the classical prophets of the Hebrew Scriptures, in which prophetic utterances and signs serve to convey the message. This symbolic approach, interacting with the imagery of the Old Testament, is another example of the mode of interpretation used in the Gospels and the Acts of the Apostles.

Through the Second Temple period, a rich literature developed around the Prophet Jeremiah and his scribe Baruch. Out of all this literature, only a particular form of the Book of Jeremiah and the Lamentations achieved an authoritative status within Rabbinic Judaism. Various Christian communities received more of this literature, including the Epistle of Jeremiah and the texts named for Baruch. Baruch is, through reception, a sort of Christian prophet. Second Baruch in particular is a repository of understandings within Second Temple Judaism that were embraced by Christianity and ultimately left behind by Rabbinic Judaism.

CHAPTER EIGHT

Joseph and Aseneth

O NE OF THE MOST POPULAR Jewish texts of the ancient
world is Joseph and Aseneth. The book was written by a
Jewish author in the first century AD but was popular in both
Jewish and Christian communities; throughout history, it was
well known to literate Christians throughout the Orthodox
world.

Textual History

The text now commonly known as Joseph and Aseneth com-
bines the story of the romance implied in Genesis with the story
of Aseneth's conversion to the worship of Israel's God. The vast
majority of manuscripts of the text are in Greek and were preserved at Orthodox Christian monasteries, then later translated
into Slavonic and other languages. The oldest manuscript, however, is in Syriac, though it shows clear signs of translation from
the Greek original. This manuscript is part of a compilation—
created in the sixth century AD by a Syrian monk—called *A Vol-
ume of Records of Events Which Have Happened in the World*. The
text notes that the Syriac translation of Joseph and Aseneth was

made by an earlier monk who had found a "very old" Greek copy of the text in the library of the bishop of Aleppo. This particular manuscript survived the centuries in Egypt at the monastery of St. Mary El-Sourian, where it was taken after being purchased from a Syrian monastery by the abbot, Moses the Nisibene, in the tenth century. The Nitrian Desert provided near perfect conditions for the preservation of ancient manuscripts.

As evidence of its widespread popularity, the Greek text is found in several manuscripts at St. Catherine's Monastery from the tenth to the seventeenth centuries, at multiple monasteries on Mount Athos from the fifteenth century, at Mar Saba Monastery from the seventeenth to the nineteenth centuries, and in Romania from the sixteenth and seventeenth centuries. Additionally, two modern Greek illuminated manuscripts have been preserved at Mount Athos from the sixteenth century.

Background

Among the texts discussed in this book, Joseph and Aseneth is of a unique genre: it is essentially a romance between the Patriarch Joseph and his wife, Aseneth, the daughter of an Egyptian priest (see Gen. 41:45, 50–52). Genesis 41:45 says that in Egypt, Joseph married Aseneth, the daughter of Potiphera, the priest of On. On is not an Egyptian god but rather the ancient name of Heliopolis. The city served as a major religious center throughout Egyptian history, and, as the later name implies,[31] it was primarily devoted to the worship of Re, the sun god. In fact, Potiphera's name means "given by Re." The text of Scripture never clarifies whether this is the same man as the Potiphar whom

---

31 Helios is the Greek name for, and god of, the sun.

Joseph had previously served as a slave. This identification is possible, but the Egyptian name is the equivalent of the Hebrew Nathan or Nathanael and therefore may have been common at various points in Egyptian history. Aseneth's name is derived from the Egyptian for "belongs to Neith." Neith was a prominent Egyptian goddess in the period involved in primordial creation and was known as the goddess of wisdom and fate.

Aseneth became Joseph's wife and the mother of his two sons, Manasseh and Ephraim, the latter of whom was given firstborn status through the blessing of Jacob (Gen. 48:15–20). Ephraim became the primary, most populous, and ruling tribe of the Northern Kingdom of Israel throughout its life, and Ephraim is used particularly in the Psalms and Prophets as a way to refer to all the northern tribes. As was the case with Isaac and Rebekah, Joseph's relationship with Aseneth, despite his prominent position in Egypt, is portrayed as monogamous, in contrast with other relationships in Genesis's patriarchal narratives. Ancient interpreters understood this monogamy as communicating true affection and love between a husband and wife.

The Problem of Intermarriage

For many ancient Jewish interpreters, however, monogamy did not make the marriage between an Egyptian and a patriarch as significant as Joseph any less problematic. While the Torah, and indeed most of the Old Testament, displays a certain level of indifference toward people's ethnic origins, provided they come to worship Israel's God, after the Babylonian exile in Ezra's time intermarriage was seen as highly problematic, regardless of religious conversion. By this later standard, Joseph's mixed marriage would make the father of Ephraim and Manasseh little different from his sons' Samaritan descendants.

Various ancient Jewish sources found ways of working around this perceived difficulty. The Midrash and the Targums, especially Targum Pseudo-Jonathan, crafted an elaborate story to make Aseneth not actually an Egyptian at all. Genesis 34 describes the rape of Dinah, Joseph's sister, by Shechem and the killing of the men of the city. The midrashic interpreters hypothesize a daughter born out of this sexual assault whom Jacob took and abandoned on "the walls of Egypt." This implies that at some point Egypt had a border wall of some sort. Potiphar found the daughter and raised her as his own. While this elaborate explanation would make Aseneth an Israelite, it creates far more problems than it solves. First, of course, the story requires the construction of a bizarre, ahistorical narrative that, if accepted, makes Aseneth herself only half Israelite and half Canaanite. Further, Aseneth would be Joseph's niece, a marriage that is clearly condemned by the Torah and more problematic than marrying a woman of foreign birth who has come to worship Israel's God.

The simplest understanding is also the least problematic from the perspective of the Torah and most later parts of the Old Testament. After joining Joseph's household, Aseneth came to worship the God of Abraham, Isaac, and Jacob, and their children were raised as part of the extended family of Israel. One need only turn a few pages in a Bible from the marriage of Joseph and Aseneth to begin the Book of Exodus, in which an ethnically diverse group forms the nation of Israel around a core group descended from the patriarchs. Many of the prominent members of that Israelite community, such as Miriam, even possess Egyptian names that, like Aseneth, include the names of Egyptian gods. From the perspective of the early traditions that make up the Hebrew Bible and Christian Old Testament, Aseneth's Egyptian heritage is no more innately problematic than the Moabite heritage of Ruth, the great-grandmother of David.

Jewish or Christian Origin?

The proposed date of the text's composition is primarily a function of whether a given scholar believes it to be Jewish or Christian in origin. Most of the arguments that the text is of Christian provenance, rather than a Jewish work with possible later Christian editing, are exceptionally weak. It is clear that the story of Joseph and Aseneth was far more popular in Christian circles than Rabbinic Jewish ones and was preserved in the former and not the latter. This, however, is true of a vast amount of Jewish literature of the Second Temple period that was embraced as part of the Christian tradition and therefore rejected by early Rabbinic Judaism. It is also true that Christian interpreters have tended to see within the romantic relationship between Joseph and Aseneth an allegory of Christ and His Bride, the Church. The same, however, could be said for the Song of Songs, or Song of Solomon, in the Hebrew Bible, since that book traveled a rocky road to inclusion. As the Christian Church emerged from Judaism, she interpreted the canonical Jewish texts within her communities in light of the Person of Jesus of Nazareth, the Messiah. Her rival, Rabbinic Judaism, rejected these interpretations, sometimes leading to Rabbinic Judaism's rejection of the texts themselves.

There is, in fact, a very strong argument in favor of Jewish origin related to the setting of Joseph and Aseneth. While obviously the story is intended to be set, roughly, in Egypt in the early nineteenth century BC, the particular descriptions of the area in Egypt accord not only with the Egypt of the first century BC, but also with the dwelling of a particular prominent Jewish community there at that time. Within the thirteenth nome, or province, of Egypt surrounding Heliopolis was a large Jewish settlement established by Judahite refugees at the time of the Babylonian exile. This community was centered around the city of Leontopolis.

Though it is not well known today, from about 170 BC to AD 73, some 240 years, a functioning Jewish temple stood at Leontopolis. While it is clear from the final form of the Hebrew Bible that sacrifices to Yahweh, the God of Israel, ought to be offered only at the Jerusalem temple, it is likewise clear historically that more than one community in the Second Temple period constructed alternate temples or quasi-temple structures for carrying out temple rituals. Though the temple at Leontopolis was not constructed according to the pattern of the tabernacle or the temples that stood in Jerusalem, it was a place of sacrifice continuously offered according to the same pattern. Most of the differences in layout and furnishings probably stem from the Leontopolis temple having been a renovated temple of Bubastis.

Given its date of construction, we can infer the reasons for the building of this temple. This was a period of war between the Ptolemaic dynasty ruling over Egypt and the Seleucid monarchs over Syria who controlled Judea. In addition to this general strife that made travel from Egypt to Palestine dangerous if not impossible, the construction coincides with the desecration of the Jerusalem temple by Antiochus IV Epiphanes, which led to the Jerusalem temple lying unused for some years until the Maccabean revolt retook it and allowed for its rededication. The end of these hostilities and the eventual annexation of both territories to Rome did not lead to the abandonment of the Leontopolis temple, however. It continued to be used regularly until, in AD 73, the Roman emperor Vespasian ordered the governor of Egypt to destroy it. Vespasian feared that with the destruction of the Jerusalem temple three years earlier, the Leontopolis temple might become a new rallying point for future Jewish revolts.

The relationship of the Egyptian Jewish community to the Leontopolis temple is complex. Despite the political issues that likely brought about its construction, the Leontopolis temple did not functionally replace the Jerusalem temple in the religious lives of Judeans permanently dwelling in Egypt. Rather, the Judeans of Egypt offered sacrifices at the temple in Leontopolis while also honoring what they perceived as obligations to the temple in Jerusalem in the form of pilgrimage, financial support, and the endowment of sacrifices. This was true both of the community dwelling in the immediate vicinity of the temple and throughout Egypt, with Philo of Alexandria as a prominent example. Though little known today, the existence of this temple was well known to ancient writers like Josephus, the Church Fathers, and early Church historians.

The fact that Joseph and his wife and sons had lived in the region provides an obvious reason that traditions surrounding Joseph and Aseneth would propagate in the Jewish community around Leontopolis. Further, the descriptions of the area show a close affinity to the reality of the first century BC. The temple overtones and themes in the text are more likely a function of the presence of the Jewish temple than a function merely of the identity of Joseph's father-in-law. These and other factors make the explanation most plausible that the text of Joseph and Aseneth emerged originally, in Greek, from the Jewish community in the area surrounding Leontopolis in the early part of the first century BC. This does not rule out the possibility that certain elements of the text may be the product of later Christian copyists. It does, however, argue that any additions would most reasonably take the form of interpretations and applications rather than outright changes in the text.

Contents

The text of Joseph and Aseneth can be divided roughly into two sections. The first section constitutes the main body of the work, consisting of the first twenty-one chapters. The second section then comprises chapters 22–29. The second portion does not seem to be able to function independently, making it unlikely that it represents a second, separate source document that has been incorporated into the first section. The first section, however, can function independently, meaning that the current state of the text represents either an original first section as a separate document onto which other material has been appended, or a single text incorporating a variety of Joseph and Aseneth traditions.

SECTION 1: CHAPTERS 1–21

The first chapter of Joseph and Aseneth lays the groundwork for the second portion of the text, describing Aseneth as the most beautiful and wonderful young woman of Egypt and also telling of the intent of Pharaoh's son to marry her. However, Pharaoh tells his son that he will marry the daughter of another king—a more suitable mate for a future Pharaoh. The text then describes Aseneth both as hating all men and as never having encountered one, as she has been confined to her father's palatial tower for her entire life. In fact, she badmouths Joseph in particular. Joseph, however, intends to court and marry her, and he approaches her father to arrange to do so. Once her father agrees, Joseph blesses Aseneth, praying that God Most High will grant her a rebirth as one of His elect.

Joseph's blessing begins a process of repentance and rebirth for Aseneth, who cries out her confession of sin to the Most High God, the God of Joseph and his family. In response to her prayer of confession and repentance, she sees the morning star rise; then the heavens rip open and a "man from heaven" emerges. The "man from heaven" language is familiar from the Book of Daniel as a descriptor of the second Person of Yahweh, the God of Israel. The heavenly man tells her that her repentance will bring about purification and ongoing transformation. At the conclusion of this process He offers Aseneth a miraculously produced honeycomb, the food of Paradise, to eat. The main story then culminates in the marriage of Joseph and Aseneth, officiated by Pharaoh himself.

SECTION 2: CHAPTERS 22–29

A turn happens at the beginning of chapter 22. As the seven years of plenty end and the seven years of famine predicted by Joseph begin (Gen. 41:1–36), Pharaoh's son, seized by jealousy, seeks to kill Joseph. The crown prince first approaches Simeon and Levi, Joseph's elder brothers, to see if he can persuade them to betray Joseph once again. Their response is to remind Pharaoh's son of the fate of the men of Shechem, who violated their sister. Nevertheless, the son of Pharaoh is tormented by the fact that he cannot have the woman he wants for a wife.

Pharaoh's son then hears that Dan and Gad, two of Joseph's other brothers, are jealous of Joseph and might be more willing to betray him. Jacob had prophesied the tribes of Dan and Gad to have rather dark futures (Genesis 49). For the author of Joseph and Aseneth, this was a matter of history. Dan was seen as treacherous from the beginning, to the point that in the New Testament and in some other Second Temple listings of the twelve tribes of Israel, the tribe of Dan is replaced by Manasseh—not coincidentally, a son of Joseph. While Gad is less clearly treacherous in the biblical text, it is one of the tribes that chooses to settle in the Transjordan rather than enter into the land promised to them by the God of Israel. Commentators of the Second Temple era widely interpreted this choice as representing a certain kind of greed that wanted to seize good land close at hand rather than trust in the promises of God. Gad was also one of the first tribes to be destroyed by the Assyrians. Outside of the biblical narrative proper, Gad and Dan appear to be the two tribes that were not directly ethnically related to Abraham and the other patriarchs.

Dan and Gad prove more willing to betray Joseph and set out to kill him, but two other brothers, Benjamin and Levi, defend Joseph. Benjamin, Joseph's younger brother, is the other son of Joseph's mother, Rachel. In later history, both during the Israelite civil war described in the latter chapters of Judges and in what unfolds in the line of Saul, the tribe of Benjamin appears as a group of particularly bloodthirsty fighters. Benjamin's character in Joseph and Aseneth reflects this. He attacks and nearly kills the Pharaoh's son, but Levi, the future head of the priestly line, stops him from delivering the final blow. Levi instead ministers to and heals the crown prince and returns him to his father. Nevertheless, the son dies, and soon after so does Pharaoh, leaving Joseph as the Pharaoh of Egypt.

Significance to the Church

This final ending to the text is likely not intended as any kind of historical claim. Rather, this slight exaggeration of Joseph's situation in Egypt seems aimed at messianic foreshadowing. Israel, delivered from near destruction, displaces the oppressing rulers and reigns in their stead. Viewing the courtship of the early portion of the text as an extension of the common biblical metaphor of Israel as the bride of God then seems natural. It likewise seems natural that early Christian communities would process these themes in light of the identification of Jesus of Nazareth as the Christ, the Messiah. Christian communities understood the handing over of Joseph to death in Genesis and his eventual reign as an image of Christ, so the narrative of Joseph and Aseneth is a natural fit. In the same way, the Christian understanding of the Church as Christ's Bride, taken from among the

Gentiles and redeemed from sin through repentance, continues the themes the text would have borne in a pre-Christian Jewish context.

PART II

New Testament and Apostolic Fathers

CHAPTER NINE

The Edge of the New Testament Canon

THE APOCALYPSE OF PETER,
THE EPISTLE OF BARNABAS,
AND THE GOSPEL OF THE HEBREWS

The Special Case of the Apocalypse of St. John

A S NOTED EARLIER, widespread agreement on most of the content of the New Testament was reached very early in the life of the Church. By AD 150, the Christian community in every major city of the Roman Empire had accepted the four Gospels. Saint Paul's epistles, including Hebrews, had been collected together and were circulating through the churches by AD 100. The authority of these texts was established so early that Marcion, in the early second century, could be widely accused of having altered them in the texts he used. While agreement on the general epistles took longer, by the end of the second century Clement of Alexandria was able to write a commentary on them as a unit.

However, the Apocalypse of St. John, or the Book of

Revelation, is something of a special case. Though accepted and widely promoted by early Fathers who came from the Johannine school[32] (such as Ss. Irenaeus and Justin the Philosopher), the text became associated with chiliasm,[33] which led many Christian communities not already familiar with it to reject it. Only in the fifth century in the West, through the efforts of St. Jerome, and the sixth century in the East, through the efforts of St. Andrew of Caesarea, did more widespread acceptance begin. But in the ninth century, St. Nikephoros listed the book as one about which different local churches had differing opinions.

Three Texts, Three Genres

In this same category of books—those read publicly in some churches but not in others—St. Nikephoros lists three other works under the heading of "New Testament" writings. Before his time, several other texts discussed in this book also could have been included in this category. But the continued public usage of these three particular texts for such a long time indicates their importance to Christian thought and worship. Ultimately, however, they fell out of public usage, even in those churches that read them liturgically in the ninth century. The disagreement among the churches was not about whether these works were heretical; the question was about their proper use—public or private.

The three texts in question are the Apocalypse of Peter, the

---

32 Fathers who studied either under St. John the Evangelist directly or under those who had.
33 Chiliasm was the belief in an earthly paradise of plenty to be enjoyed by faithful Christians before the Last Judgment.

Epistle of Barnabas, and the Gospel of the Hebrews. Each is from a different genre. The Epistle of Barnabas is now generally included as part of the works of the Apostolic Fathers. Though not publicly read by any local church, it has been read and discussed throughout the history of the Christian Church around the world. The Apocalypse of Peter is still preserved but is far less well known. It represents a Christian entry into the genre of Jewish apocalyptic literature and seems to have been favored by communities that, for various reasons, did not accept the Apocalypse of St. John. The Church's ongoing embrace of the Apocalypse of St. John seems to have reduced St. Peter's Apocalypse to a lesser-known footnote. The Gospel of the Hebrews suffered an even worse fate over the last millennium, with most of the text being lost. It appears to have been a gospel written in Aramaic that contained a handful of sayings and miracles of Christ not recorded elsewhere. Though it was read publicly only in parts of greater Syria, the Church Fathers often cited it for various purposes.

Dante's Divine Comedy, *Enochic Literature, and Views of Hell*

The Apocalypse of Peter is a window into early Christian conceptions of the afterlife. Popular conceptions of heaven and hell in the modern world have been deeply shaped by Dante's *Divine Comedy*. Specifically, our ideas of hell have been formed by the *Inferno*, which has enjoyed a far wider readership and fascination than the *Divine Comedy's* sections on purgatory and Paradise. In fact, Dante's vision of hell has had so profound an impact on the West that modern debates over universalism tend to take for granted that anyone who accepts historic Christian teaching on eternal condemnation believes in some variation of Dante's hell. Perhaps no other work of literature has so transformed Western Christianity's popular understanding than Dante's, with the possible exception of Milton's. Both of these authors, however, were composing works of literature, not of dogmatic theology, and their depictions ought not to be confused with the historic teaching of Christianity. The Church's teaching, of course, is foundational to the Orthodox Christian Faith. Literary works are not, no matter how inspiring or noteworthy they may be. To affirm Dante's and other similar depictions of hell as fictional is not to overturn what the Church has historically taught regarding eschatology.

Dante's literary efforts, however, stand in a line of inheritance that stretches all the way back to the Second Temple period in apocalyptic literature. Much of this literature—both within the Scriptures in Daniel, Zechariah, and the Apocalypse of St. John, and adjacent to them in the Enochic literature, the Apocalypse of Abraham, and others—describes a journey through the invisible creation, or the spiritual world. This journey includes, in many cases, travels through the heavens and the underworld, with emphasis on the eschatological fate of both spiritual and human beings. One does not have to accept 1 Enoch as a historical account of Enoch's vision in order to understand its value as a preserver of spiritual experience and knowledge from the Second Temple period. Readers who desire to understand how the faithful of that era understood the fate of humans after their physical death, at the Day of the Lord, and afterward can draw on the rich, available literature and derive coherent teaching from it. While nascent Rabbinic Judaism placed a ban on writing in the wake of the rise of Christianity, Christians continued to write. Thus the literature from the early Christian period reveals how the advent of Christ maintained and transformed this understanding.

THE APOCALYPSE OF PETER

Textual History and Reception by the Early Church

A critically important text for understanding early Christian teaching regarding the afterlife is the Apocalypse of Peter. Its composition dates to around AD 135, and it forms a part of the Petrine literature of the early Church. Saint Peter himself did not, of course, write it. Rather, along with the Gospel of Peter, this Apocalypse enjoyed early popularity in the Egyptian Church. Both books there were understood to reflect St. Peter's teaching, as does the Gospel of St. Mark, who founded the Alexandrian church. So well regarded was the Apocalypse of Peter that some considered it to be a book to be read in the churches—what we would today call "canonical." Even those otherwise inclined, like Eusebius of Caesarea and St. Nikephoros, list it as a text considered authoritative by some and not others. In Eusebius's case, this means that the Apocalypse is ranked together with 2 Peter. The Muratorian Canon[34] states that the churches accept "only the Apocalypses of John and Peter, but some do not want the latter read in the church." While St. Clement of Alexandria quotes the Apocalypse of Peter as Scripture,

---

34 The Muratorian Canon is a manuscript fragment from the late second century AD. It is one of the earliest attempts to make a list of authoritative Christian texts that would eventually become the New Testament.

St. Macarius the Great, in debating a pagan who was citing the text against him, rejects its authority as not deriving from Peter. Though the Church ultimately did not regard it as part of the New Testament, the Apocalypse of Peter continued to be cited authoritatively, in a manner similar to the way in which the early Fathers were cited, into the fifth and sixth centuries AD. In this regard, it is not unlike its fellow early Christian apocalypse the Shepherd of Hermas.

An Entirely Christian Document

The text of the Apocalypse of Peter is an early second-century summation of preceding religious experience and the literature that recorded it. Its content depends heavily on the apocalypse of 4 Ezra. One of the most important manuscripts of the text was found with a version of 1 Enoch that contained added Christian material. The Apocalypse of Peter, however, is an entirely Christian document. In fact, in its second chapter, it seems to allude to then-recent events in Palestine, the Bar Kochva rebellion, in a way that clearly distinguishes Christian and non-Christian Jewish communities. Its chief aim is to portray the blessedness of the saints and the state of condemnation in Hades. It therefore presents this portrait in light of the death and Resurrection of Christ, His defeat of death, the harrowing of Hades, and the transformation that these events wrought in the world. The Apocalypse builds on earlier apocalyptic traditions and visions that portrayed the origin and fate of rebellious spirits and humans before the advent of Christ.

Two-Stage Eschatology

The Apocalypse of Peter reflects the two-stage eschatology that has been the teaching of Christianity since the beginning. The first stage, this life, is the arena of repentance. Material life in mortal flesh is God's gift to humanity to allow for repentance and an escape from the fate of the demons. The Apocalypse of Peter affirms that humanity is the entire creation's purpose—specifically, human destiny in Christ. Therefore, unlike the fate of the angels who rebelled, God gave the humans who joined in their rebellions a life in this world ending in death, and death is an opportunity. At the end of mortal life, as commonly understood throughout the Second Temple period, the soul of the departed comes before the throne of God and then proceeds either to Paradise or to Hades. There the souls experience a preliminary blessedness or condemnation until the end of this age. But this first stage is not eternal. Christian teaching has never spoken of an eternal heaven and an eternal hell as permanent destinations at death. This first, intermediate state is a part of this age.

The second stage begins at the end of this age, at Christ's glorious appearing as He comes to judge the living and the dead. The Apocalypse of Peter describes the events that then take place, drawing on the Scriptures: Christ appears to judge, along with the saints and angels of the divine council who will share in His act of judging the living and the dead (Matt. 16:27; 25:31; Mark 8:38; 2 Thess. 1:7). The earth and Hades give up their dead, whose flesh is restored in the general, bodily resurrection of every person who has ever lived (Dan. 12:2; John 5:28–29; Rom. 2:6–16; 2 Thess. 1:6–10). The Apocalypse of Peter also describes the gathering up of the various rebellious spirits for judgment, "the spirits of those sinful ones who perished in the flood, and of all those who dwell in all the idols, in every metallic image, in every passion and in paintings, and of those that dwell on all the high places and in stone waymarkers whom men call gods" (Apoc. 6).

All risen humanity and the demons themselves are immersed in the river of fire, which purifies or torments them according to their deeds in the life of this age. This is explicitly the river of fire that Daniel saw in his vision. Many subsequent Fathers use the imagery of the river of fire coming from the throne of Christ at the judgment in precisely this way, following the interpretation taken by the Apocalypse of Peter. This river is also depicted in Christian iconography of the Last Judgment. Those who have refused to repent in this life and to follow Christ share the fate of the rebellious spiritual powers they have followed. This would have been the fate of all humanity had it not been for the exile from Paradise into this world and the saving work of Christ.

The Final Judgment is not extrinsic and judicial, based on whether individuals broke certain rules of behavior and then are sentenced to various punishments; rather, it is revelatory. A person's inner life and character stand revealed to all, and each receives the direct consequences of their choices in life. Consequences, however, are not necessarily punishments. A lifetime of tobacco smoking may produce lung cancer as a consequence, but this is not the same as God giving someone lung cancer as a punishment for breaking a rule against smoking. All that is hidden is revealed, and all are judged by the Truth (Matt. 10:26; Mark 4:22; Luke 8:17).

The Apocalypse of Peter gives vivid, grotesque descriptions

of the torments that people who have committed grievous sins experience in the state of eternal condemnation. These will seem quite familiar to any reader of Dante. Blasphemers are hanged by the tongue. The wealthy who took no care for the poor are dressed in filthy rags and impaled on a pillar of fire. A key point of the apocalypse, however, is that the sins themselves torment those experiencing eternal condemnation: the sins they have clung to, refusing to be set free, now hold them captive permanently. For this reason, even they must admit that their fate is utterly just and deserved. Yet amid these horrid descriptions, the Apocalypse of Peter is capable of moments of great beauty and tenderness. For example, it describes the souls of infants who had been aborted or exposed by their parents being carried to Paradise by angels, who feed them, care for them, and raise them to adulthood in the Kingdom.

Universalism, Purgatory, and Prayers for the Departed
After the Last Judgment, the fate of all angels and humans is fixed and eternal. Our oldest fragment of the Apocalypse of Peter, however, adds an important element connected to the practice of the Church from the very beginning: specifically, the prayers of the saints, both in Paradise and on earth, grant mercy before the Judgment Seat of Christ for those in Hades.[35] The souls of those who find this forgiveness actually receive bap-

---

35 When St. Augustine addresses the Apocalypse of Peter in his *City of God*, he focuses on this element and its misinterpretation, though he ultimately misinterprets it himself (*Civ. Dei* 21.17–27). Augustine correctly explains that this is not teaching universalism, i.e., not all will be saved through the prayers of the saints. He errs, however, by inserting the concept of purgatory into this description.

tism within a lake in Hades and thence depart purified. Within the Apocalypse, this is carefully worded in order not to suggest universalism, but rather to reflect the Second Temple and later Christian practice of prayers for the departed. Earlier literature attests to these prayers, but the text here demonstrates that they have been a part of Christian worship practice from at least the early part of the second century AD. According to the teaching of the Church, prayer for the departed is both a part of the role of the saints in the Last Judgment (Matt. 19:28; Luke 22:30; 1 Cor. 6:3) and also an aspect of the power committed to the Church to bind and to loose in forgiving sins (Matt. 18:15–20). This intercession is possible up to the Last Judgment. Afterward, both the righteous and the rebellious are confirmed in eternal life or condemnation. This second phase of Christian eschatology is eternal.

Both universalism and the teaching of purgatory misunderstand this data in similar ways. Throughout the Second Temple period, apostolic Christianity, and the ante-Nicene Church, the emphasis in the discussion of eschatology is almost entirely on the glorious appearance of Christ on the earth to judge the living and the dead. Very little attention is devoted to the intermediate state of departed souls beyond the most basic affirmations, as can be seen in both the Old and the New Testament. The culmination of the gospel proclamation itself is that individuals must prepare to stand before the Judgment Seat of Christ at His *parousia*, His "glorious appearing" or "return." Particularly in the Western Church, over time the pendulum has swung to the other side. In most Christian contexts, very little attention is paid to Christ's Return, to the point that many Christians talk about the departed as being "gone" to heaven or hell as a permanent state. Yet certain sectarian groups, reacting against this general trend, move so far in the other direction that Christ's imminent Return becomes the sole topic of preaching and public witness.

Without the proper emphasis and understanding of the resurrection of the body and the life of the world to come, the transition between the two stages of Christian eschatology disappears—it becomes an immaterial shift from one place to another. In many universalist frameworks, this is a shift for the temporarily condemned to share in the blessedness of the saints. In traditional Roman Catholic teaching, the saved experience two stages, proceeding from a state of purgation to a state of blessedness, while the condemned remain eternally condemned. Not only do these understandings distort Christian eschatology, but they are also at odds with the mission of the faithful to intercede for the departed, including the departed wicked. The prayers for the departed in the Divine Liturgy, in the memorial and funeral services, are not for the psychological assistance of the living faithful. They are offered as intercession for the salvation of those who have fallen asleep. The rituals associated with Soul Saturdays are no more "memorials" in the bare sense than the Eucharist is. The Church ever intercedes, as a royal priesthood, for the life of the world and for its salvation, including the whole of humanity and the whole of creation.

Significance to the Modern Church
After St. Peter and the apostles have received their eschatological vision in the Apocalypse of Peter, the text culminates in a

particular event in the life of Christ—not, as one might expect, in Christ's Crucifixion or Resurrection. Nor does this vision come in the context of one of Christ's post-Resurrection appearances to His disciples and apostles, followed by His Ascension. Rather, the climax of the Apocalypse is Christ's Transfiguration atop the holy mountain. Christian eschatology has never focused on bodiless states of reward and punishment. Rather, it has always focused on the redemption and transfiguration of the entire creation in Christ, including our shared humanity. The Christian hope concerns not primarily our individual souls, but our bodies and this world, which the glory of God will permeate and deliver from corruption. And this Christian hope is not one to cherish as we sit back in an armchair. We are not commanded to hope that all may be saved, much less to stomp our feet and demand it of God. We are commanded to work and to pray, and in so doing to cooperate with Christ in bringing about the fulfillment of all creation.

THE EPISTLE OF BARNABAS

Textual History

The Epistle of Barnabas has been attributed to St. Barnabas the Apostle of the Seventy, the companion of St. Paul, since the earliest surviving references to the text from Clement of Alexandria and Origen at the end of the second and beginning of the third centuries AD. Origen introduces it as the General Epistle of Barnabas, placing it in the company of the Epistles of St. James, St. Peter, St. John, and St. Jude. Eusebius of Caesarea likewise categorizes the Epistle of Barnabas with these books as works that were read publicly in worship in some

Christian communities but not in others. The earliest known extant Christian Bible, Codex Sinaiticus, includes the Epistle of Barnabas and the Shepherd of Hermas at the end of its New Testament. The Jerusalem Codex, an eleventh-century Christian Bible in Greek found at Jerusalem, includes the Epistle of Barnabas, First and Second Clement, and the letters of St. Ignatius at the end of its text. Though the public reading of the Epistle of Barnabas as Scripture appears to have faded away relatively quickly in the life of the Church, its inclusion with these other texts attests to its continued importance.

Interestingly, there is little discussion among the Fathers and other early Christian writers regarding the authorship of the epistle. Both those who show the text great reverence and those who see it as holding secondary authority merely refer to it as the work of St. Barnabas. Well into late antiquity, the argument was made, based on similarities in the Greek, that St. Barnabas also was the author of the canonical Epistle to the Hebrews. This argument presupposes that St. Barnabas in fact wrote the epistle, but it is made by people who do not hold the Epistle of Barnabas to be Scripture. This serves as a further example that the Fathers did not consider apostolic authorship to be in any way decisive in adopting a text for public reading.

As a matter of course, modern scholars tend to assume that a work was likely composed at or near the location where we first have record of its citation. This assumption can be incorrect for several reasons; we have only a fragmentary record of these references, so our first known one may not be the actual first reference. In the case of the Epistle of Barnabas, however, composition within Alexandria's large Jewish community is likely, whether or not the author is actually St. Barnabas. There are clear parallels between other Alexandrian literature of the Second Temple period and the style of the Epistle of Barnabas. Further, the text includes a quotation from the Greek version of 1 Enoch, which was in wide circulation in and around Alexandria.

The text also makes clear the window of time in which it was written. On one hand, Barnabas makes direct reference to the destruction of the temple in Jerusalem in AD 70 (16:1–5). This event is identified as the fulfillment of certain prophecies made by Christ (i.e., Matt. 24—25; Mark 13; Luke 21). At the same time, the entire text of Barnabas has the character of internal debate. It is an argument over the correct interpretation of the Hebrew Bible: whether it is telling a story that culminates in the Person of Jesus Christ or whether the Scriptures, and the Torah in particular, represent an end in themselves. The expulsion of Christians from the synagogues following the Bar Kochva rebellion ended this particular form of debate in the middle part of the second century AD. After this point, Christianity and Rabbinic Judaism continued to interact, but as separate traditions—no longer as factions within a single tradition, as the Epistle of Barnabas casts it. With reasonable certainty, then, the writing of the Epistle of Barnabas can be narrowed down to the late first or early second century.

Content

The Epistle of Barnabas argues that the entire Old Testament speaks of Jesus the Messiah. For Barnabas, the Christians within the Jewish community are the ones who are keeping the true tradition of the Torah and the rest of the Scriptures. Jewish communities that have rejected Jesus as the Messiah have done so because they have taken the literal words of the commandments as an end in themselves, not as pointing to Christ. Likewise, they have mistaken the building in Jerusalem for the true temple of God. By making a text or a building identical with the embodiment of God, they have made these things into idols and worshipped them. Not knowing God because of this idolatry, they have failed to recognize Him in the Person of Jesus Christ.

The argument of Barnabas moves across a variety of "works of the law"—commandments particularly related to Israel that distinguish them from the nations, such as circumcision, dietary laws, and the sabbath. Barnabas also spends a significant amount of time on sacrificial ritual in general and the Day of Atonement in particular. The essential argument is twofold: First, Barnabas seeks to demonstrate that these practices point beyond themselves to a greater reality. For example, Israelites were circumcised, but so were Syrians and Arabs and even pagan Egyptian priests (9:5). Clearly then, circumcision in and of itself is not of any particular spiritual benefit. Second, Barnabas argues that all these ritual practices and commandments of the Torah actually refer to the Person of Jesus Christ; they were aimed at communion with God in Christ.

The Epistle of Barnabas does not argue, then, that the Torah and its commands are to be set aside now that Christ has come and the faithful have received this communion. Rather, these commandments continue to function but in a transformed way. For example, though the physical temple has been done away with, Barnabas affirms that there is a temple of God not built with human hands, which is being built in and by the Church (16:7–10). For Barnabas, Christ does not abolish the Torah but rather fulfills and transforms it by His fullness.

One charge against the Epistle of Barnabas, by those who say it ought to be completely disregarded, is the allegation of anti-Semitism. Critics pass over in silence the nuances of the argument about Christ fulfilling the Torah and frame the text as merely a Christian's series of criticisms of Jewish practice. This accusation, of course, reeks of presentism. When the Epistle of Barnabas was composed, two separate religions called "Judaism" and "Christianity" did not exist. There was no concept of Jewish ethnicity or race. No history had yet come to pass of a Christian majority oppressing a Jewish minority. Reading this ancient text against the background of all these later developments will therefore lead to a fundamental misunderstanding and distortion of its message and historical import.

Significance to the Church

The Epistle of Barnabas is the product of an internal struggle between various Jewish groups of the Second Temple period. Before the Birth of Jesus Christ, countless scattered Jewish groups already subscribed to diverse practices, beliefs, and texts they considered to be authoritative. In the wake of the death and Resurrection of Christ, one portion of these communities embraced Jesus of Nazareth as the Messiah and transformed their belief and practice in light of His fulfillment of their received traditions. These Christians began to produce their own writings, including the texts of the New Testament and works like the Epistle of Barnabas. Another major section of the

Second Temple Jewish world rejected the claim that Jesus was the Messiah, and in the wake of the destruction of the temple and then Jerusalem, they consolidated their practices into Rabbinic Judaism. In the Epistle of Barnabas, we see a pronounced example of the friction between these segments of Judaism and the nuanced way in which early Christians interpreted and applied the Torah.

THE GOSPEL OF THE HEBREWS

A Tale of Three Texts

The Gospel According to the Hebrews, or the Gospel of the Hebrews, is commonly believed to be the same text as the Gospel According to the Nazoreans, simply because no full text of either document still exists. The book called the Gospel of the Ebionites was used, possibly exclusively, by the Ebionites, a group of Semitic Christians who did not fully embrace the deity of Christ, and it is commonly supposed that this is also the same text. There are, however, several problems with attempting to match up these three texts as a single book.

First and foremost, the only preserved portions of the Gospel of the Hebrews are in quotations from Church Fathers and early Christian writers. In broad strokes, most authors tend to cite the Gospel of the Hebrews and the Gospel of the Nazoreans positively, or at least ambivalently, while they cite the Gospel of the Ebionites by means of disagreement with and refutation of Ebionite beliefs. Often, the Gospel of the Ebionites is asserted to be a corruption of one of the canonical Gospels, usually that of St. Matthew. This differentiation strongly implies that those who had access to the complete texts saw them as different works.

On the other hand, the Gospel of the Hebrews is not read authoritatively in the Church, meaning that those who thought it valuable or who cited it did not fully embrace its every theological nuance. For example, St. Cyril of Jerusalem made use of an extensive summary of the flow of the gospel as a whole. Included in this summary is the idea that the Theotokos is an incarnation of the Archangel Michael, that Christ was born after seven months rather than nine, and that the people of Judea, consumed with jealousy, handed Christ over to Pilate to be crucified. Within the context of his *Discourse* and his other writings, we can certainly say that St. Cyril embraced the third of these points— that Christ was handed over to the Roman governor by His own people for crucifixion. He notes the seven-month pregnancy for symbolic purposes, as it references a Second Temple tradition that certain prophetic figures, including Isaac and Moses, were born after seven months, with seven as a sign of perfection. Equally clear, however, is the fact that St. Cyril rejects the idea that the Theotokos is anything other than a human woman chosen by God to be the mother of Christ.

However, St. Cyril and other Fathers and early Christian writers were able to deal with these texts in complex and nuanced ways. There are a thousand options between total unquestioning acceptance and equally total rejection. The same Father could use a portion of a text as confirmation of a truth, find another portion to be interesting, and condemn a third part of the same text as a heretical falsehood. It is therefore not impossible that these are three labels for one text, and that calling it "the Gospel of the Ebionites" is a pejorative mode of introducing it. Moreover, all the quotations from the Gospel of the

Ebionites come from St. Epiphanius in his *Against Heresies*. It is entirely possible that he simply had a less nuanced evaluation of the text than the other Fathers and writers who cite it. Nevertheless, St. Epiphanius used the text in order to cite it against the Ebionites.

Another argument against identifying these three as the same text is the perceived difficulty in reconciling the various fragments together into one narrative. However, this is a difficult argument to make convincingly. The extant fragments are rather scanty, and many Fathers and writers reference the same handful of citations. If someone were to take a dozen out-of-context quotations from the Gospel of St. John, a person unfamiliar with the source text might have an equal amount of difficulty in piecing them together to fit within an overarching whole.

Textual History

All discussion of the Gospel of the Hebrews is further confused by the fact that it was not originally written in Greek. The book is universally recognized as originally written in Aramaic and only later translated into Greek, from which the majority of the citations are taken. Saint Jerome, while living in Bethlehem, translated the text into Latin from the Aramaic with reference to the Greek. If the texts are understood to be identical, and if the original Aramaic found its primary circulation in Ebionite circles, it is difficult to know who might have been responsible for the Greek translation and what their theological biases might have been.

The Gospel of the Hebrews is believed to have been composed in the early second century AD, with its earliest citations in Clement of Alexandria and Origen. Origen had a knowledge of Hebrew and Aramaic, making it entirely possible that he, or someone else in the catechetical circles of Alexandria, performed the translation. If this is the case, it is worth noting that Origen appears to share several of the more troubling aspects of the teaching of the Gospel of the Hebrews, such as the preexistence of souls and a sub-Nicene understanding of the Holy Trinity.

The Words of Christ in the Text

By a wide margin, the words of the Gospel of the Hebrews most commonly quoted by a number of Fathers and early Christian writers are Christ's reference to the Holy Spirit as His mother: "After this my mother, the Holy Spirit, took me by one of my hairs and carried me further to the great mountain Tabor." Various authors quote this for different purposes, often in commentary to explain feminine language and imagery applied to God in different portions of the Scriptures. At one point, St. Jerome went as far as explaining this quotation in more detail by pointing out that the word "Spirit" is feminine in Hebrew and Aramaic, unlike in Latin. Interestingly, the longer form of this quotation carries the earliest known identification of the mount of Christ's Transfiguration as Mount Tabor.

The Fathers often introduce these quotations from the Gospel of the Hebrews with the words in that text, "the Lord said." This form of citation is notable because it is neither "it is written" nor "the Scriptures say." As a quotation it does seem to carry some form of authority, or else it makes little sense to quote it positively. The pattern of how the Gospel of the Hebrews is cited is, therefore, a prime example of the way in which a text in the "middle" category of books to be read in the home functions within the Fathers' thought and interpretation.

Most of the quotations from the Gospel of the Hebrews take the form of modified or elaborated versions of Jesus' stories or sayings in the canonical Gospels. Appropriately, given its composition in Aramaic, the text appears to have functioned in a manner similar to the Targums of the Hebrew Bible. As mentioned in the discussion of the Book of Jubilees, the Targums translated the Hebrew words of Old Testament books into Aramaic and also offered commentary on the "correct" understanding of the text. They incorporated various traditions—sometimes very well-developed ones—into the literature, shedding light on very early modes of interpreting, understanding, and applying a text.

Put simply, writers cite the Gospel of the Hebrews in order to help explain or interpret the text of Scripture, and they considered it to be a venerable interpretation. The Fathers quote it along with the earlier Fathers and ecclesial writers who came before them. This means that quoting this work, including purported words of Christ that are not contained in the canonical Gospels, does not represent a claim that He historically spoke those words. Rather, the Gospel of the Hebrews is treated as itself an interpretation of Christ and His words at a very early phase. Because it is written in the language most often spoken by Jesus, the book can shed light on His words in the canonical Gospels and in the rest of the Scriptures.

So, for example, St. Jerome refers to Isaiah 11:2: "Then the Spirit of Yahweh will rest on Him; the Spirit of wisdom and understanding, the Spirit of counsel and strength, the Spirit of knowledge and of the fear of Yahweh." In his commentary he cites two sections of the Gospel of the Hebrews that refer to Jesus' Baptism and appear to be elaborations on St. John's account of it. In the first, St. John, before the Baptism, identifies Jesus as the one upon whom the "whole fountain of the Holy Spirit" will come to rest. The second citation is of the Baptism itself, where this same wording is used to describe the descent of the Holy Spirit upon Christ. This connection between imagery of a fountain of water and the Spirit is already present within St. John's Gospel, such as the "rivers of living water" in John 7:38. The Gospel of the Hebrews makes this connection explicit and thereby assists St. Jerome's interpretation in connecting the water imagery of the Prophet Isaiah to the Holy Spirit.

Another example comes from the Latin text of Origen, who cites Jesus' interaction with the rich young ruler as recorded in the Gospel of the Hebrews. Origen explicitly states that the testimony of this text is not authoritative, but it sheds light on the story in his commentary on St. Matthew's version (19:16–22). The insertion into the story, which otherwise generally matches St. Matthew's Gospel, is a statement by Christ that makes clear the implicit teaching in His interaction with the man:

Then the Lord said to him, "How do you say, 'I have kept the law and the prophets'? For it is written in the Torah, 'You will love your neighbor as yourself.' See, many of your brothers, sons of Abraham, are attired in filth, dying of hunger, but your house is filled with many good things, and none of it goes out to them."

The rich young ruler has not kept the Law in that many of his fellow Judeans are living in poverty, want, and degradation, while he has wealth but has not helped them. It is only after this explicit saying that Jesus states the difficulty of a rich man entering the Kingdom of heaven. Origen does not imply that Jesus actually spoke those words, but he points to the saying as an early application of His words to those who have been blessed with material wealth and their responsibility to their brothers and sisters.

Saint Epiphanius of Salamis, however, took a more negative approach. His citations take place within his repudiation of various doctrines of the Ebionites, who had taken to using this text authoritatively. That said, Epiphanius is not attacking the text directly, but only insofar as the Ebionites use it in certain errant beliefs and practices. Specifically, Epiphanius at several key points compares the text of the Gospel of the Hebrews to the text of St. Matthew, using the latter as a corrective to certain points under consideration in his dispute. His argument, therefore, is essentially that wherever the Gospel of the Hebrews contradicts the canonical Gospel, it is to be set aside in favor of St. Matthew. This is precisely the approach that one would expect from the saint if he considered the text to be of some subsidiary interest or authority but not properly authoritative.

The Gospel of the Hebrews and the Gospel of St. Matthew

Saint Epiphanius does not compare the Gospel of the Hebrews and St. Matthew's Gospel by coincidence. There was, in the early centuries of the Church, a strong tradition that St. Matthew's Gospel was originally composed in Aramaic and then translated into the present Greek. That said, no fragments, citations, or examples of that Aramaic original survive to this day in any form, including in the writings of the Fathers and others who transmitted this tradition. This absence of evidence has led modern scholars to speculate that the Gospel of the Hebrews might itself be that Aramaic original, or, more conservatively, that certain segments of the early Church might have held it to be. The difficulties with such an identification are twofold.

First, what we do have of the Gospel of the Hebrews contains elaborations that are found neither in St. Matthew's Gospel nor in the other Gospels—including those written later than Matthew's, according to the same Fathers who record these traditions. These Fathers, unlike modern scholars, had the full text of the Gospel of the Hebrews available and would have been in a better position to make or verify such an identification. Second, the Fathers, such as Tatian in his *Diatessaron*, treat this text not as a variant or translation of one or several of the four canonical Gospels, but as a separate document of subsidiary authority to them. The authority of these four texts in their Greek version was uncontested by the time the Gospel of the Hebrews begins to be cited. It is hypothetically possible that if an Aramaic Matthew existed, the Gospel of the Hebrews is an expanded version of it with additional material brought in from elsewhere. Even if this theory were true, however, it would mean that no trace of that original Matthew remains untouched, and the Gospel of the Hebrews, by the time we are able to encounter its remaining fragments, has become a completely different textual tradition.

Significance to the Early Church

In the third through fifth centuries, the Fathers of the Church and other writers made extensive use of the Gospel of the Hebrews, despite its use by certain heretical sects. Their use of it was not authoritative but comparative, and they saw it as shedding light on certain elements of the early hearing and interpretation of various canonical Gospel texts. Even in the time of St. Nikephoros in the ninth century, it found a place in his list of books that were read not in public but privately by Christians. Though the full text has not survived to this day, it serves as a prime example of the use the Fathers made of a book written in a biblical style that remained outside the canonical lists of texts read publicly in worship.

CHAPTER TEN

Noncanonical Gospels

THE GOSPELS OF THOMAS, PETER, AND NICODEMUS

Gnostic Texts and the Historical Jesus

AT THE APEX OF THE ERA of historical Jesus research, a mode of inquiry now fallen into disfavor and resigned to the last century, much was made of noncanonical gospel texts. Eighteenth- and nineteenth-century biblical scholars, having rejected miracles and the supernatural, distinguished between the "Jesus of history" and the "Christ of faith." They then made a series of attempts to describe the historical Jesus of Nazareth while leaving aside all Christian material as suspect.

Scholars involved in this research treated any and all ancient texts that identified themselves as gospels, canonical or not, as equally valid witnesses to Jesus, regardless of date of composition. The majority of these texts are of Gnostic[36] provenance,

---

36 Gnostic communities predate Christianity and generally represent a combination of traditional Greco-Roman religion with various Eastern religious practices. The Eastern practices adopted by Gnostic sects

many of them found as part of the Nag Hammadi trove, which preserved the full manuscripts of a number of Gnostic texts that had been lost for centuries.

Central to these discussions of early noncanonical gospels was the Gospel of Thomas. The complete version of the text found at Nag Hammadi is in Coptic and very clearly Gnostic. This reality may make absolutely shocking the inclusion of the Gospel of Thomas in St. Nikephoros's list of texts to be read in the home. But several factors about the Gospel of Thomas must be taken into account. Most importantly, we have fragments of a Greek text composed earlier than the one found at Nag Hammadi. These language versions, even from the extant fragments, show a great range of variations. Saint Nikephoros undoubtedly was reading and speaking of the Greek text, not the Coptic, in the ninth century. In this chapter we will discuss these textual variations as well as other factors in the oddly ambivalent relationship of the Church Fathers to a particular version of the Gospel of Thomas.

Largely through the research of those involved in the quests for the historical Jesus, a handful of other ancient texts and fragments have been found that also constitute noncanonical gospels. Here we will discuss the Gospel of Peter and certain fragments found at Oxyrhynchus, Egypt, that do not manifest as clearly a Gnostic bent as, for example, the Nag Hammadi texts. Finally, we will discuss the Gospel of Nicodemus, a product of late antique Christian reflection upon the harrowing of hell, as an example of the kind of writing that was still taking place even centuries into the Christian era.

---

included forms of Judaism and Christianity, albeit paganized versions.

THE GOSPEL OF THOMAS

Background

Those familiar with the Gospel of Thomas would probably think it unlikely to be listed in St. Nikephoros's recounting of the New Testament books to be read at home. One need not look far to find a plethora of quotations from the Church Fathers and other early and medieval Christian writers denouncing the Gospel of Thomas, ascribing its composition to a disciple of Mani and the Manichean sect, and anathematizing it. At the same time, many Church Fathers and other writers cite sayings of Christ from the Gospel of Thomas as authentic. In several cases, we find the same Father doing both.

The Gospel of Thomas is a "sayings gospel" consisting of recorded sayings of Jesus without any context or significant narrative elements linking them together. Thomas does not tell us stories about Jesus or narrate His life; the book is merely a collection of supposed quotations. Twentieth-century scholars, more so than today, see such texts as evidence for the existence of Q, or the Q source, a hypothesized collection of quotations employed by Ss. Matthew and Luke. In attempting to understand the relationship between the synoptic Gospels—Matthew, Mark, and Luke—researchers noted that Matthew and Luke generally follow the structure and outline of St. Mark's Gospel. Saint Matthew and St. Luke, however, also incorporate a large number of direct quotations, even entire homilies, spoken by Jesus. Much of this quoted material is common to both Matthew and Luke, leading to the suggestion of another, since lost, document containing these and other quotations; thus Ss. Matthew and Luke are supposed to have used St. Mark's Gospel and this Q source to compose their own.

Beyond this hypothesis, however, there is no material evidence of the existence of Q. Various published "critical editions" of Q from the twentieth century are pure theoretical reconstructions. This lack of evidence has led many scholars away from the Q hypothesis and toward hypotheses that focus on more complicated relationships between the preserved texts themselves. But in the era when the Q hypothesis was wildly popular, its conjectural existence was used as an argument for the antiquity of the Gospel of Thomas. There is no evidence of the book's written existence before the mid-second century AD, but if Q existed in the first century, then one could argue that sayings gospels were written first and represent an earlier stage of development than narrative gospels. From this supposition, one could argue that the Gospel of Thomas might predate the canonical Gospels. Clearly, this is a house of cards built on thin air. Each step of the argument is built on a series of "what-ifs" with no supporting evidence.

Textual History

Confining ourselves to the actual evidence, based on references to the work in other ancient literature, the Gospel of Thomas was written in Greek sometime in the mid-second century. This does not mean that none of its traditions predate the written text. When Fathers cite elements of the book as dating back to Christ Himself, they presuppose their existence as independent traditions apart from this written form. Today, we possess only three fragments of the original Greek text, found in Oxyrhynchus.

The whole text is available only in Coptic, in a manuscript found at Nag Hammadi in a cache of Gnostic literature.

While the Greek text is quite fragmentary, the fragments can be compared to the Coptic. A few tendencies in the translation imply at least some small editing. Direct references to God appear to have been removed by the Coptic translator so that, for example, "the kingdom of God" becomes simply "the kingdom" (GTh 27). In one fragment, the Coptic drops a reference to "raising up," though scholars contest whether the Greek is referring to resurrection and therefore the reference was omitted due to antipathy to the idea of bodily resurrection (GTh 5). The saying recorded in the Greek of Gospel of Thomas 36 is very similar to Matthew 6:25–34 and Luke 12:22–32, where Jesus admonishes his followers not to worry about food, drink, and clothing. In the Coptic translation this section has been heavily edited, and major portions have been omitted. It may not be coincidental that this text refers to provision for bodily needs, which the Gnostics rejected as worldliness. Lastly, the Coptic text appears to have rearranged the order of a number of the sayings. What effect this would have on the reading and meaning of the text as a whole is difficult to discern, because the Gospel of Thomas as a whole seems to be deliberately ambiguous, and we possess only fragments of the Greek ordering.

Views of the Church Fathers and St. Nikephoros

As already mentioned, the Fathers and St. Nikephoros would have been familiar with a version of the Gospel of Thomas that was undoubtedly in Greek. That said, the Greek Gospel of Thomas contained enough problematic elements for it to be actively rejected by every Father who mentions it, and not only through guilt by association. Many of the Fathers who reject it write of having read it. It remains, then, to explain how a rejected Gnostic text can still be cited and also appear on St. Nikephoros's list in the ninth century.

In the first place, the Gospel of Thomas contains many of the sayings that are immediately apparent as the words of Christ included in the biblical Gospels. Some examples include:

"You see the sliver in your friend's eye, but you do not see the log in your own eye. When you take the log out of your own eye, then you will see clearly to remove the sliver from your friend's eye." (GTh 26)

"One can't enter a strong man's house and take it by force without binding his hands. Then he can rob his house." (GTh 35)

"If a blind man leads a blind man, both of them will fall into a ditch." (GTh 34)

"Often you have desires to hear these sayings that I am speaking to you. And you have no one else from whom to hear them. The days will come when you will seek me but you will not find me." (GTh 38)

Interestingly, several sayings roughly parallel those from both the synoptics and the Gospel of St. John, as with the last of these examples. But other sayings do not directly parallel the canonical Gospels and instead point toward certain Gnostic tenets. For example, "If the flesh came into being because of spirit, that is a wonder. If the spirit came into being because of the body, that is a wonder of wonders. Nonetheless, I wonder at how this great wealth has come to dwell in poverty" (GTh 29). Here the physical elements of humanity, whether termed *body* or *flesh*, are regarded as an impoverished form of being compared to that of immaterial spirit. Another verse states, "He who has come to know the world has discovered a carcass. And he who has discovered a carcass, of him the world is not worthy" (GTh 80). Here again, the material world is seen as a dead body from which the spiritual must escape. Other sayings are suggestive but more deliberately ambiguous, such as, "Be passersby" (GTh 42). As the references show, these two types of sayings are found intermingled.

There is, however, a small third category of sayings: those from the Gospel of Thomas that do not parallel sayings in the canonical Gospels but which are quoted by Church Fathers and other Christian writers as authentic sayings of Christ. It is likely going too far to say that the Fathers are quoting the Gospel of Thomas, given what they say about the text as a whole. More likely, they are citing these sayings from the same traditions that were sources for the Gospel of Thomas. Writers as early as St. Irenaeus of Lyons use references and allusions to sayings within the Gospel of Thomas that don't necessarily spring from its written text.

Of the sayings of Jesus quoted directly by Fathers and other authors, the most common is likely Gospel of Thomas 82, which reads, "He who is near me is near the fire, and he who is far from me is far from the kingdom." Origen quotes this saying twice; St. Didymus the Blind and St. Ephraim the Syrian quote it; and it is alluded to elsewhere. While in one of Origen's citations he frames the quotation as something he read somewhere, in other places he confidently cites these words as Christ's own. At the same time, St. Didymus describes the Gospel of Thomas elsewhere as a rejected book. The consistent testimony of the Fathers is that the Gospel of Thomas, particularly the version used by the Manicheans, is heretical and rejected.

The particulars of St. Didymus's words likely contain the answer to this apparent contradiction. In his *Commentary on Ecclesiastes* 8, he states one primary reason why the apocrypha are not to be read publicly in the churches, using the Gospel of Thomas and the Gospel of Peter as examples: the average person in the Church is not able to distinguish "what has been combined in them by heretics." Books designated apocrypha, useful for only private reading, are designated so because they contain within them both valid and important traditions on one hand, and heterodox or outright heretical ideas on the other. A private reader, by virtue of being literate, was thought in the ancient Church to be sufficiently able to sift the wheat from the chaff in these texts. Any given person who heard them read publicly, on the other hand, might not be so equipped.

Significance to the Church

The earliest Fathers of the Church had access to people who directly knew the apostles. They therefore received second- or thirdhand knowledge about Christ that was not preserved in the writings of the New Testament. Some of these traditions found their way into the writings of these Fathers and of others, and some of these writings have made their way down to us today. While more texts were available to St. Nikephoros in the ninth century than to us today, the same situation was true for his day, many centuries after the lives of the apostles. Then as now, sifting through authors and texts to find which are and are not reliable, and to what extent, requires wisdom and study. One of the texts that contains some of these traditions, albeit mixed with dross, is the Gospel of Thomas.

THE GOSPEL OF PETER

Textual History

The vast majority of the extant text of the Gospel of Peter comes from a single manuscript found at Akhmim, Egypt, in 1886. It dates to the late eighth or early ninth century AD, meaning its copying is roughly contemporaneous with the life of St. Nikephoros. This date also reveals that the text was still being copied at that time. Further, the fragment is in Greek, rather than Coptic, and was found in the grave of an Orthodox monk. By then the Gospel of Peter had been clearly numbered among the apocrypha, but the traditions contained within it were still seen as worthy of preservation and study by Orthodox Christians.

In addition to this manuscript, which contains the Passion narrative, additional fragments of the Gospel of Peter were discovered later at Oxyrhynchus, Egypt, that date to the late second or early third century. These fragments are from earlier portions of the narrative of Christ's life but are likewise told from the first-person perspective of St. Peter. The fact that all these fragments were found in Egypt is less a function of their place of origin and more the result of Egypt's arid climate—ideal for the preservation of papyrus and parchment manuscripts. It is generally agreed, based on the dating of these fragments, that the whole text was written sometime in the mid-second century AD.

Content

The text itself seems to take the form of a written tradition that had previously been passed on orally. "Oral tradition" is a category that is often bandied about and used loosely to mean whatever a given author needs for a theory. In this case, however, "oral tradition" means something very specific. Within the fragments we currently possess, there are many general parallels to the canonical Gospels but no particular ones. In other words, the Gospel of Peter generally follows the narrative of the canonical Gospels, with additional brief stories and details added here and there. However, when comparing the canonical Gospels, particularly Matthew, Mark, and Luke, whole sections within them are worded identically or virtually identically. This includes not only the wording of the sayings of Christ but the wording of narrative sections describing events. In the case of the Gospel of Peter, however, no such direct verbal parallels are present. This may indicate that the author is a person who has heard the content of the Gospels but is not working directly with the texts in front of him. He is remembering what he has heard and recording it—not revising, reworking, or commenting upon written literature.

Usage in the Early Church

Our first knowledge of the Gospel of Peter comes from St. Serapion of Antioch, who served as bishop of that city from AD 191 to 211. Saint Serapion was, in his day, a renowned theologian, but his corpus of theological works vanished rather quickly. By the time of Eusebius of Caesarea in the fourth century, only three of his works were still extant, and all three have since vanished.

During the period in which he served as bishop, the church in the city of Rhossus on the Syrian coast, a Christian community under St. Serapion's canonical authority, was reading the Gospel of Peter in its liturgies. At one point, the church had received St. Serapion's blessing to do this, as it had been read publicly for at least a generation before his consecration as bishop. The early date of its usage likely indicates that the text was written originally in Syria. This permitted usage of a text not read publicly in other cities also serves to point out the descriptive, rather than prescriptive, character of canonicity in the ancient Church.

Later, however, St. Serapion received a report that the Gospel of Peter contained elements of Docetism, the heretical view that Christ was not truly incarnate but only appeared in human form. The bishop requested and received a copy of the book, and upon examination, he found that most of the Gospel of Peter was consonant with the four Gospels; however, he did detect certain elements that at least lent themselves to docetic interpretation. Based on this, St. Serapion retracted his permission for the church at Rhossus to use the Gospel of Peter liturgically.

The Gospel of Peter never became well known in the West. When later Western authors refer to it, they generally appear to be citing Eusebius's record of the events described above rather than indicating that they read the text themselves. Authors particularly in Syria and Egypt refer to it through the centuries from time to time, generally listing it among gospels not actually written by the apostles whose name they bear, or gospels not read in the churches, but with little other information. Nonetheless, the date of our most complete manuscript serves to indicate that in some of these regions the text was still copied and studied privately for its early witness to certain traditions surrounding St. Peter.

Significance to the Modern Church

The Gospel of Peter survives only in fragmentary form to this day, though the fragments include a significant portion—specifically, the narrative of Christ's Passion. While the Gospel of Peter was never widely used in churches throughout the world, it became widely known. Early commentators such as Eusebius of Caesarea group it not with heretical books but with other Petrine books not widely accepted as canonical. For Eusebius, this means that he grouped the Gospel of Peter with the Acts of Peter, the Apocalypse of Peter, and the eventually universally recognized 2 Peter. The Gospel of Peter is not a part of St. Nikephoros's list. It is included in this book, however, as an early noncanonical gospel whose interesting history within the Church reveals certain realities about the understanding of canonicity.

THE GOSPEL OF NICODEMUS

Textual History

The text now known as the Gospel of Nicodemus was earlier known by the title "The Acts of Pilate"—a title possibly chosen as a way to insert the text backward into history. Saint Justin Martyr, for example, refers the readers of his *First Apology* to the Acts of Pilate, which he believes is still held at Rome, to verify the truth of at least the broad strokes of the events of Jesus' Crucifixion. Later, a pagan document called "The Acts of Pilate" was put together and circulated against the Christians, purporting to be Pilate's account of what really happened, contradicting the Gospels. The Acts of Pilate mentioned by Justin Martyr, then, was intended to replace the pagan, anti-Christian Acts of Pilate for the inquirer.

The Gospel of Nicodemus was compiled rather than written. The main body of the text was put together in its current form sometime in the late fourth or early fifth century, around AD 400. This version, however, was cobbled together from preexisting written material that varies in style. Those previous pieces of written tradition, of course, recorded earlier oral tradition, and scholars broadly agree that significant elements of the Gospel of Nicodemus originated in a written form in the second century. However, this compilation did not cease once the main body of the book was compiled. Differing versions of the text in various languages include additional material, such as letters from Pilate placed as cover letters or additional supporting documents, and individual, inserted story elements.

Contents

The unifying factor between the various versions of the Gospel of Nicodemus is that each serves as a compilation of local traditions surrounding the understanding of the death and Resurrection of Christ. This understanding is primarily framed around Christ's harrowing of Hades on the sabbath, during which He rested in the Tomb. Some Latin versions, therefore, add the story of St. Veronica wiping the face of Christ with a cloth on His way to crucifixion and receiving back an icon not made with human hands. Other versions include the names of St. Longinus, the centurion who testified to Christ's divine identity; St. Dismas, the wise thief; and Gestas, the other thief who perished at the Crucifixion. These names and the veneration of these saints preceded the compilation of Nicodemus.

The earliest forms of this compilation are generally believed to have come together in Greek. However, extant forms of the text in Latin, Syriac, Coptic, Georgian, Slavonic, and various medieval and modern languages attest to the incredible popularity of the Gospel of Nicodemus. As already mentioned, each of these language traditions freely appended or inserted elements of their own local tradition into the original Greek compilation. These changes included, for example, the Anglo-Saxon version of the text updating Hades to Hel. Despite its popularity, all parties appear to have recognized the character of this work: there is never any question about canonicity or other liturgical usage, nor about authorship or theological value. The text merely functions as a gathering point for various elements of Church tradition.

Unlike the Gospel of Peter, the Gospel of Nicodemus spends relatively little time on the Crucifixion and death of Christ. Rather, the first part of the text, as one might expect of an Acts of Pilate, narrates Jesus' trial before Pontius Pilate and His condemnation to crucifixion. The second part of the text, focused on the harrowing of Hades, presents itself as the testimony of Leucios and Charinos, two of the saints of old who were raised in Jerusalem at the time of Christ's Crucifixion and who emerged from the tombs at His Resurrection (Matt. 27:52–53). These two were called before the Sanhedrin, and they describe the events in the underworld that unfolded prior to Christ's Resurrection. This description is essentially a dramatization built around prophetic texts from the Old Testament that Christ's conquering of death and Hades fulfilled.

Significance to the Church

While Christ's invasion of Hades, the binding of the devil, the resurrection of the fathers of old, and their conveyance to Paradise are all traditions within the New Testament documents themselves, the dramatization of these events in the Gospel of Nicodemus proved overwhelmingly influential. Nicodemus does in narrative form what paschal homilies from the Church Fathers did in rhetoric and paschal liturgies do in ritual. The Gospel of Nicodemus seeks to bring the reader into the place of the dead in Hades, awaiting the freedom that will come with the Messiah. The text then narrates that deliverance through the Old Testament Scriptures, bringing the reader over into light and new life. As a treasure house, it preserves these and related traditions in very early forms.

CHAPTER ELEVEN

The Shepherd of Hermas

Background

THE SHEPHERD OF HERMAS is a unique text both as part of the collected writings of the Apostolic Fathers and as a work sometimes included in New Testament manuscripts. Its uniqueness is mainly a question of its genre: The Shepherd of Hermas is, for all intents and purposes, a prophetic book written in the Christian era. While it contains accounts of a series of visions the author received, the genre of the whole text does not match other Christian apocalypses such as St. John's canonical Revelation and the apocryphal Apocalypse of Peter.

The Shepherd of Hermas is also unique in that it seems to have been the subject of very little debate. Despite its inclusion in several prominent early New Testament codices, our earliest, nearly contemporary comment on the canonical status of the text is that it occupies a secondary position, to be read privately but not in the public worship of the Church. Christian Fathers and other writers maintained this categorization from the second through fifth centuries AD with near total consistency. The Shepherd of Hermas, therefore, represents a prime example of such a book and of the existence of this "middle" category—holding authority without being reckoned among the Christian Scriptures.

The Shepherd of Hermas is written primarily in the first person, and its protagonist and author is the Hermas of the title. He is a former Roman slave who has since been emancipated and gone on to start a family of his own. He receives a series of visions near the city of Cumae, an already ancient Greek colonial city in Italy, near Naples, at the time of the composition of the book. The shepherd of the title instructs Hermas to pass on the content of these visions to the presbyters at Cumae, implying that a Christian community was relatively well established already at the time.

Textual History

The time of writing of the Shepherd of Hermas can also be established with relative confidence in that several ancient sources, and potentially a few that are no longer extant, give further details about the author. The earliest of these witnesses, the Muratorian Canon—a list of canonical and noncanonical texts written around AD 170—is also our earliest witness to the list of the twenty-seven books of the New Testament. Concerning the Shepherd of Hermas, the Muratorian Canon indicates that it was written very near that time in Rome by a certain Hermas, the brother of Pius, the bishop of Rome, now known to history as Pope Pius I. It goes on to say that the book ought to be read, but not in the churches because though it is prophecy, the number of the Old Testament prophets is complete; additionally, it was written after the time of the apostles, so it is not a part of the

New Testament. This would place the composition of the text and the recorded events in the 140s. Several later sources confirm the identity of Hermas and his time period, which fits with the earliest citations of the text in the second half of the second century AD.

Modern Controversies

While there was relatively little debate about the Shepherd of Hermas in antiquity, it became the cause of much debate and conjecture within modern scholarship. This controversy is largely due to the fact that the text fails to fit in well with various modern scholarly theories regarding the early Church, the process of the canonization of the Scriptures, and the development of Christian doctrine. The book clearly describes a way in which the Torah, or Law, continued to function within the Christian Church, which is problematic from the perspective of most Protestant denominations. Likewise, the Shepherd of Hermas emphasizes the necessity of leading a Christian life to avoid exclusion from salvation. This emphasis runs counter to the Protestant understanding of salvation by faith alone, which is sometimes projected back onto the early Church.

Likely the largest area of discussion and debate surrounding the theology of the Shepherd of Hermas has been its Christology. Modern scholars, exemplified by Adolf von Harnack and his treatment of the text within his *History of Dogma*, attempt to place the text along a proposed schema in which the first Christians saw Jesus Christ as a sort of special human, and only several centuries later did Christians come to teach that Christ was God Himself. The Shepherd of Hermas at one point refers to a son of God who became so by being filled with the preexistent Holy Spirit, that is, by adoption. It therefore became common to argue that the Shepherd of Hermas is one example of what has been called "adoptionist Christology," common in the second century AD, in which Christ Himself "becomes" the Son of God at some point in His earthly life, usually at His Baptism.

In contrast, more recently, Fr. Bogdan Bucur has argued persuasively against this interpretation. One seemingly obvious and fundamental problem with the theory that the Christology of the Shepherd of Hermas represents a well-known second-century heresy is that Christian writers continued to cite the text with a sense of authority for several centuries. Additionally, the wholly Orthodox Fathers citing it never make the sort of disclaimers one might expect if quoting a text with known heretical elements. Other condemned ancient texts, regardless of how well revered in the past, rather quickly cease to be cited. Bucur demonstrates that the text of the Shepherd of Hermas can be understood to be describing not Christology per se, but rather the adoption of Christians as sons of God through Christ's presence in their midst and through the power of the Holy Spirit. This explanation offers a plausible way for Orthodox Fathers to have read the Shepherd of Hermas on an ongoing basis, though it fails to accord with developmental theories of Christian doctrine. The Shepherd of Hermas therefore provides one more reason why such theories ought to be set aside.

Contents

As previously mentioned, the Shepherd of Hermas is a prophetic work. Because a significant portion of the Old Testament and most of its saints are given the title "the Prophets," readers often assume that prophecy as a phenomenon ceased to exist in the apostolic era. The New Testament, however, reveals that this is not the case. Within the Acts of the Apostles, the Prophet Agabus twice appears to utter prophetic words and perform prophetic actions (11:27–28; 21:10–12). Saint Paul also mentions prophecy as a gift of the Spirit and a role within the Christian Church in 1 Corinthians 12:10 and 14:1–22. Indeed, throughout the history of the Church, according to the will of God, certain Christians have received the vision of Christ in His uncreated glory—the same vision that the prophets of old received. Likewise, they have experienced visions and encounters with angelic spirits and the saints. As with the prophets before them, these Christians have come away from these experiences with a mission directed toward the rest of the Church. The Shepherd of Hermas, then, is an early example of this phenomenon, not exceptional or strange.

Structure and Themes

The text of the Shepherd of Hermas can be divided reasonably into three sections according to its own internal structure. The first section is a series of five visions that Hermas experiences while on the road. After the visions, an angelic being called "the shepherd" entrusts him with a series of twelve commandments. This angel of repentance then delivers and explains ten parables to Hermas. He is called to pass on these prophetic communications to the leadership of the local church, who are to meditate upon them and derive wisdom.

The central theme of the Shepherd of Hermas is the necessity of repentance and obedience to the commandments of Christ in the Christian life. This instruction includes a number of passages that speak of the severity of sin after baptism and the need for fasting and prayer. Maintaining purity of thoughts and actions is also a major emphasis. While these themes have often led scholars to argue that the Shepherd represents some kind of rigorist position or "works righteousness," such characterizations tend to come from those who hold the Protestant presupposition that works are irrelevant to salvation. In actuality, the Shepherd of Hermas consistently mirrors language about the Christian life that is used throughout the Scriptures (e.g., Heb. 10:26–31).

The opening series of visions focuses on the nature of the Church. The Church appears to Hermas as a woman, at first old and weak. Through the visions, Hermas comes to see that the Church is built up by her members. As Christians repent, become holy, and are conformed to the image of Christ, Hermas beholds her strengthened, rejuvenated, and ultimately transformed into a beautiful bride. These visions combine two sets of imagery found in the Scriptures. The first is the idea of the Church being built as a temple from believers, who function as stones or bricks (1 Cor. 3:16; Eph. 2:20; 1 Pet. 2:5). This symbolism is blended into the image of the Church as the Bride of Christ (2 Cor. 11:2; Eph. 5:21–27; Rev. 19:7–8).

Several themes within the Shepherd of Hermas become commonplace in the writings of later Fathers of the Church. Within the sixth commandment in the text, the shepherd tells Hermas that he has two angels assigned to him, one good and the other wicked. The good angel, Hermas's guardian angel, seeks to lead him gently toward the path to life. The other angel, the wicked one, enters into him in the form of the passions, which lead him into sin. The language here explains the preceding fifth commandment, which contrasted the Holy Spirit entering a person with the spirit of anger entering. In the text, sin is the product of the influence of evil spirits who inspire passions, leading humans to actualize the works of the devil. The devil himself is seen as having no power, but his works, when a human brings them into being, have the power to lead the person away from God.

In the explanation of parable 6, the shepherd describes to Hermas a compatriot of his, another angel. This angel is described as the "angel of punishment" as contrasted with the shepherd as agent of repentance. Both are good angels and, contrary to possible assumptions based on the Western understanding of guilt and punishment, the angel of punishment is not associated with the afterlife or the judgment of God. Rather, he works hand in hand with the angel of repentance. But many refuse the ministration of the angel of repentance, and they will not follow his guidance into a life of contrition and reconciliation with God.

Those who refuse the angel of repentance are then turned over to the angel of punishment, who brings into their lives sicknesses, failures, and difficulties of all kinds. The word "punishment" here may still mislead, as this chastisement is not an end in itself. Rather, all these hardships befall humans in order to bring them to penitence, at which point they are returned to the ministrations of the angel of repentance. Both of these angels, then, aim at bringing men and women to God through applying various medicines as needed for each person. This activity continues biblical themes from the Old Testament and St. Paul's discussions of excommunication—themes that we have also seen in the Book of Jubilees and elsewhere, that the sufferings of this life offer the potential to aid us in finding repentance and renewal.

The Shepherd of Hermas and the Church Fathers

The later Fathers develop many themes and ideas from the Shepherd of Hermas in their writings, and many Fathers and other early Christian writers cite it directly. Saint Irenaeus, Clement of Alexandria, and Origen all cite the Shepherd as carrying some authority, though the latter two acknowledge its secondary rank. When the text was cited against Tertullian, he pointed out that it was highly regarded in some churches and not others and was generally less popular, from his perspective, than the Epistle of Barnabas. Both St. Athanasius and Eusebius recommended it as a work for the education of catechumens in the Christian way of life. By the fifth century, though St. Jerome was familiar with the text, he states that the Shepherd of Hermas was no longer of much interest to most people. On the other hand, his contemporary St. John Cassian cited it repeatedly as an authority. Even in the early ninth century, St. Nikephoros lists the Shepherd of Hermas as one of the texts to be read privately rather than in the Church.

Significance to the Church

The Shepherd of Hermas, though not part of the New Testament, is an important text in the life of the early Church. It reveals the ongoing existence of prophecy and visionary experiences within Christian communities after the apostolic era—experiences of the kind that would continue throughout the history of the Orthodox Church. The main emphasis of the text, however, and the purpose for which it was primarily used and cited, is explaining the way of life of a Christian in shunning evil and choosing the good. From the New Testament, and the Johannine literature in particular, the text continues the emphasis on sin as the product of demonic influence, as humans cooperate with the demons' work in the world. The Shepherd of Hermas presents the Christian life as one that ever pursues virtue and enacts repentance, taking every thought captive.

CHAPTER TWELVE

The Protoevangelium of James

Who Was St. James?

THE PROTOEVANGELIUM OF JAMES, sometimes also
known as the Protevangelion or Gospel of James, is one
of several texts circulating in the earliest centuries of the life of
the Church that were attributed to St. James, the brother of the
Lord. These traditions can be grouped, but not neatly, into two
categories. Some of them, like the Protoevangelium, are written records of preexisting, orally preserved information about
St. James himself, St. Joseph the Betrothed, and the Theotokos.
Some of this literature, on the other hand, is clearly aimed at
appropriating St. James's authority in the apostolic Church, particularly in and around Jerusalem, and using that authority to
endorse the author's ideas. None of these texts fit purely in one
or the other category.

The depiction of St. James, the Lord's brother, as a figure
within the New Testament invites a number of questions.
Much of his story happens "off-camera," as it were, and external sources such as Josephus communicate more detailed information on his way of life and the manner of his death than the

Scriptures do. Beyond being named as among the brothers and sisters of Jesus, the first substantive thing we learn of St. James in the Gospels is that he did not believe that his brother was, in fact, the Messiah (John 7:5). Nevertheless, James becomes a major figure in the Acts of the Apostles and is identified as the central leader of the mother Church at Jerusalem (e.g., Acts 12:17; 15:13; 21:18; Gal. 1:19; 2:9, 12). The only clue within the text of the New Testament as to how this transformation occurred is St. Paul's passing reference to an appearance of the risen Christ to St. James in particular (1 Cor. 15:7). This appearance is nowhere narrated in the canonical Scriptures.

Even St. James's precise relationship to Christ invites a series of questions. Given the clear presentation within the Gospels of Christ's Virgin Birth, is St. James to be understood as a half brother whose parents are Ss. Joseph and Mary? Is he a stepbrother, a son of Joseph from a previous marriage? Is he, as St. Jerome would suggest centuries later, a cousin? The text of Scripture in isolation answers none of these questions. An assumption exists—largely the product of a particular understanding of sola scriptura—that anything not spelled out in the text of the New Testament concerning anyone who appears there is pure conjecture and fable.

This assumption, however, is not necessary—or even particularly sensible—for two reasons. First, the truth is out there. This seems both obvious and vague, but we must admit to some actual familial relationship between St. James and Jesus Christ. An event unfolded when the risen Christ appeared to James. Even if we were to conclude that the answers found in ancient sources are conjectures or incorrect, this does not change the fact that a reality existed that does indeed provide the correct answer to each question. Secondly, the idea that all the answers to these questions are conjecture assumes that the questions only arose sometime later, after all those who knew the truth had died, and their memory had been lost. Rather, the opposite would have occurred with these gaps in the written text: they would have triggered the preservation and communication of the actual, correct answers to these questions. Eventually, those answers would be written down in various textual sources.

Saint James was clearly a public figure. Not only was he the overseer or bishop of the Christian community in Jerusalem, the first such community that exercised a status as mother Church, but he was known to be such a leader even at the periphery of the evangelized world, as evidenced by St. Paul's references to James in his Epistle to the Galatians. Josephus, a non-Christian Pharisee, devotes a fair amount of time to St. James, recording his reputation as a holy man of prayer. It is Josephus who recorded the details of his murder within the Jerusalem temple complex by an angry mob. Despite not being a member of the party of the Christians, Josephus considered St. James's murder to be a great crime against a man of piety.

The idea, then, that the earliest Christians did not feel any need to retain information about St. James, his relationship to Christ, the Lord's Mother and her life, and other such details is strange. It can be motivated only by presuppositions external to the historical evidence. When we find such information in early Christian texts, especially when the same information appears in diverse places, we should consider it reliable. The Protoevangelium of James is one such early record. But we must distinguish the fact that the Protoevangelium contains extra-biblical details from the idea that it is the *source* of these details. Readers rarely make this distinction in casual conversation; for example, the names of the parents of the Theotokos, Ss. Joachim and Anna, are often said to "come from" the Protoevangelium. The Protoevangelium of James is the earliest extant text that contains their names, but, assuming the information is accurate, its source is history—not the text itself.

Textual History

The Protoevangelium is universally accepted and demonstrable as a very early text. It is referenced, and therefore was already in somewhat wide circulation, by about AD 150. It is exceedingly likely that it was written about AD 125 at the latest. It is likewise clear that the Protoevangelium of James was originally written in Greek. Literally hundreds of Greek manuscript copies have survived to the present day, as have translations into Syriac, Ethiopic, Coptic, Georgian, Slavonic, Armenian, and Arabic. Though direct dependence is unclear, many parallel traditions exist between the Arabic translation of the Protoevangelium and information regarding the mother of the Lord contained in the Quran. On one hand, the Protoevangelium contains a number of apparent geographical and small cultural errors regarding first-century Palestine. On the other hand, elements such as the names of the parents of the Theotokos do match names common in the period, adding confidence to the veracity of those traditional elements.

The Protoevangelium of James was formally rejected in the West by the Gelasian Decree of AD 500, which referred to a

Latin translation that is no longer extant, likely because of the decree. This rejection took place because of certain details of Christ's Birth and the midwife's subsequent anatomical examination of the Theotokos that, possibly more so in the Latin text, were seen to smack of Docetism, making Jesus less than fully human. Possibly relatedly, the Protoevangelium of James does not appear at all on St. Nikephoros's list, though the end of that list has been lost by a fragmentation of the manuscript. It is possible that the Protoevangelium was once included. In any case, the text was widely preserved throughout the Orthodox world down through the centuries, with more extent copies than nearly any other work covered in this book.

Content

The text of the Protoevangelium is written from the perspective of St. James. The first seventeen chapters are a narration of the life of the Theotokos, containing the story of her miraculous birth to the elderly Ss. Joachim and Anna, their bringing her to the temple to be raised, and angels feeding her there. The same elements found here are also present in the liturgical texts of the feasts of the Nativity and the Entrance of the Theotokos, and in related Orthodox iconography: At the age of twelve, the Theotokos must leave the temple so that her menstruation will not render it ceremonially unclean. She is therefore betrothed to St. Joseph, an elderly widower with several children, who will serve as her protector until foreseeably, much later in her life, she might return again to temple service. She conceives Christ following the Annunciation, and when St. Joseph discovers her pregnancy, they both undergo the test of the bitter waters described in Numbers 5:11–31. This test publicly proves that St. Mary has not committed adultery, nor has St. Joseph been with her before marriage.

Chapters 18–20 describe Christ's Birth in Bethlehem in a way that mostly conforms to the accounts of Ss. Matthew and Luke. This section includes details of a midwife's anatomical investigation of Mary's virginity before and after her giving birth, as well as certain details that were later considered problematic, even by those who accepted her ever-virginity. Because of the rise of various forms of Docetism in the early Church, Christian writers constantly emphasized the real humanity of Christ. Thus in discussions of His Birth, they must maintain a careful balance between the miraculous nature of Christ's Nativity and any suggestion that it was something other than a human birth. The final four chapters, then, describe the visit of the Magi, which triggers the death of the innocents. The Protoevangelium of James also narrates the murder in the temple of Zacharias, the father of St. John the Forerunner, and the appointment of St. Symeon the God-Receiver as priest in his place.

Significance to the Life of the Church

The Protoevangelium of James is not a text that itself holds a position of authority in the life of the Church. Indeed, the West formally rejected it well before the Great Schism. Nevertheless, the Church preserved the text through centuries of copying and recopying. It stands as the earliest written witness to the antiquity of a number of important traditions related to the New Testament Scriptures regarding the lives of the Theotokos, St. James, and their family. The Protoevangelium of James did

not originate these traditions, nor does it provide their authority. Their authoritative form exists in the liturgical life of the
Church, in hymnography and iconography. The Protoevangelium reveals and confirms the great antiquity of these liturgical
traditions, dating them back to the early part of the second century—mere decades after the falling asleep of the Theotokos. In
contrast to Protestant polemics, the information regarding St.
Joseph, the Theotokos, and St. James is not a series of medieval
developments based around some form of imported, pagan goddess worship. Rather, these traditions are the living memory of
the Church regarding the life of the Theotokos.

CHAPTER THIRTEEN

The Acts of Various Apostles

Background

THE ACTS OF THE APOSTLES is a pivotal book in the New Testament. It continues the narrative of St. Luke's Gospel while also introducing St. Paul and describing his early missionary journeys. Acts functions as a pivot point between the Gospels and the Pauline Epistles. It begins with a focus on St. Peter and the other apostles in Jerusalem following the Ascension of Christ. After the martyrdom of St. Stephen, it shifts its focus to Saul of Tarsus and describes his transformation into St. Paul. This latter portion of the text focuses almost solely on Paul, so much so that even the apostles who were the focus of the earlier chapters drop out of view. Many of the apostles are not even mentioned by name in the text.

Nevertheless, the apostles did journey throughout the known world, and the Christian communities that they helped found remembered the events of their lives. The broad strokes of their journeys have been, in many cases, verified historically. Saint Thomas's journey to India, for example, as one of the journeys most extreme in distance, was for some time the subject of skepticism before recent archaeological finds confirmed the memories of the local churches. These memories included not only general itineraries, but also traditional stories handed down from generation to generation regarding events in the apostles' respective careers.

Over the early Christian centuries, many stories about the apostles were written down in various documents in various places, and many of those that have been preserved to this day follow the pattern of the canonical Acts of the Apostles. Of these texts, St. Nikephoros identifies several as books to be read privately: the Acts of Paul, the Acts of Peter, the Acts of John, and the Acts of Thomas. In addition to these accounts of the acts of the apostles, another text, the Didache, identifies itself as "The Lord's Teaching through the Twelve Apostles." The Didache dates from the beginning of the second century AD and represents the earliest known church order. It is often included with the works of the Apostolic Fathers, and St. Nikephoros lists it as another text worthy to be read in the home.

I. THE ACTS OF PAUL

AMONG EXTRACANONICAL ACTS of various apostles, the Acts of Paul enjoys a certain pride of place. Saint Hippolytus of Rome considered its traditions to be reliable, if not canonical. By the fourth century, Eusebius of Caesarea describes the Acts of Paul as a text that is treated as canonical by some Christian communities and not by others. The first major denunciation of the text comes from Tertullian and is based purely on the authority St. Thekla exercises in the narrative, which he finds offensive due to her gender. But aside from Tertullian's concern about gender roles, the book is very clearly a deliberately anti-heretical, anti-Gnostic text.

Textual History

The Acts of Paul is a composite document but was written as a single whole. Both ancient writers and modern scholars generally agree that it was written in Asia Minor, now Turkey, in the first half of the second century AD. Ancient writers identify the author as an unnamed priest. The text is a written record of a series of traditions surrounding St. Paul, his later missionary journeys, and particularly the end of his life. These traditions were likely native to western Asia Minor, the region that was the focus of much of Paul's missionary activity. Once these traditions were compiled into a single work, there is good evidence that elements of it circulated or were translated separately. Some fragmentary evidence also exists that certain manuscripts of the text later had other Pauline traditions appended to them.

The Acts of Paul contains four major stable elements, consisting of two epistles sandwiched between narrative passages. The text opens with the Acts of Paul and Thekla. Next is an epistle addressed to St. Paul from the church at Corinth regarding the proto-Gnostic teachings of two teachers who had recently arrived in the community. Paul's epistle to Corinth, sometimes labeled his Third Epistle to the Corinthians, follows to answer their questions and condemn the false teachers. Finally, a narrative portion describing the martyrdom of St. Paul concludes the work. This last portion details Paul's final journey to Rome and his beheading under Nero.

The first section, the Acts of Paul and Thekla, became

particularly popular in independent circulation. Manuscripts that contain only this portion of the book begin very abruptly since the introduction to the larger work has been removed, as has the later material. The Acts of Paul and Thekla is the earliest extant textual source concerning St. Thekla and represents the most definitive evidence for an early date of composition. Saint Thekla was well known not only in Syria, where many of the events of her life transpired, but also in Asia Minor and even in Rome, where she inspired the ministry of St. Eugenia around AD 185. While her memory was certainly carried in oral tradition, knowledge of details of her life extended throughout the known world, suggesting some form of textual transmission.

Noteworthy Elements

The focus in this portion of the text is most certainly on St. Thekla rather than St. Paul. It is worth noting that Tertullian's objections to St. Thekla's preaching and baptizing were likely shared by certain Latin, Ethiopic, and Coptic translators, who omitted those elements. The description of St. Thekla in the Acts of Paul and Thekla fits quite neatly within St. Paul's ministry in the Acts of the Apostles and his canonical epistles. She is presented as a convert at Iconium during his first missionary journey, and she continues to accompany him even in his later imprisonment. At several points, Thekla faces persecution and execution, generally related to her desire to maintain her virginity. Her trials here represent a cultural watershed: The idea that a Christian woman had the responsibility and the right to maintain her virginity, and therefore not submit to marriage, was a new one in the Roman world, in which marriages were arranged entirely by men. The narrative surrounding the life of St. Thekla is the beginning of what would ultimately produce the modern concept of sexual consent.

The Acts of Paul and Thekla also contains our earliest narrative description of St. Paul's physical appearance. This description is entirely consonant with his appearance in Christian iconography, though the antiquity of certain iconographic elements suggests that the images may not be directly based on this text. Readers should note once again that this work dates to within roughly fifty years of St. Paul's death, adding weight to the veracity of his description in living memory. Paul is portrayed as being of average height; balding, with little hair remaining on the top of his head; bandy-legged with protruding knees; and with large eyes, a long nose, and eyebrows meeting in the middle. Adding to the reliability of this description is the fact that these are not the features of an impressive or imposing figure by either Jewish or Roman standards.

PART 1: ST. THEKLA'S STORY

After her conversion, St. Thekla accompanies St. Paul on his journeys and is the frequent object of persecution. God rescues her from being burned to death by sending rains. She is protected from being eaten by wild beasts by a friendly lioness, by other miracles, and then by the unified front of the women of Pisidian Antioch. Finally, a group of soldiers bent on rape pursues her, and she is saved by rocks that open before her, allowing entrance to a cave, where a miraculous spring preserves her. An Orthodox monastery at this site in Maaloula stands to this day.

The Acts of Paul then includes what seems to be a

Christianized version of the story of Androcles and the lion. Interestingly, that story in its original Roman form dates to the first century AD. In the version told within the Acts of Paul, St. Paul encounters a wounded lion whom he not only helps and heals but baptizes. Roman persecutors throw Paul to the beasts, only to find that the lion who is to eat him is his old friend, who preserves him from harm. This incorporation of a Roman folktale reveals an understanding in the second-century Church that the redemption of Christ goes beyond humanity to the rest of the creation, including animals. This belief connects an otherwise quaint story to the overarching anti-Gnostic themes of the later portions of the text. Against the Gnostics, the Acts of Paul clearly sees the goodness of the material, created world.

PARTS 2 AND 3: A LETTER TO ST. PAUL FROM THE CHRISTIANS OF CORINTH AND HIS RESPONSE

The Acts of Paul then segues to a letter St. Paul received from Corinth. The Corinthian Christian community describes the teaching of two itinerant priests, or presbyters, who had recently arrived, and they ask Paul if they should receive this teaching. As very briefly described, the priests' teachings bear notable affinities with Marcionism and other early forms of Gnosticism. They teach that the cosmos is evil, having been created by lower angelic beings rather than by God, and they deny that Christ was actually incarnate in the flesh through the Theotokos. Saint Paul, as one might expect, refutes all these positions with the apostolic teaching of the goodness of creation and Christ's Incarnation.

PART 4: THE MARTYRDOM OF ST. PAUL

The final portion of the book describes the end of St. Paul's life, specifically his final visit to the city of Rome. A certain Patroclus, likely named after the figure from the *Iliad*, serves as the cupbearer for the emperor Nero. Patroclus falls from a great height and dies, only to be raised from the dead by St. Paul. Rather than greeting this miracle with wonder, Nero is terrified that the Christians will use their powers to overthrow his empire and so begins a massive persecution. This persecution also sweeps up St. Paul, who is beheaded. At the point of his decapitation, milk rather than blood miraculously pours from his neck. After the execution, St. Paul appears to Nero to pronounce his immanent doom.

Significance to the Church

The Acts of Paul is our earliest witness to a number of important traditions concerning St. Paul and his later life after the close of the Acts of the Apostles. Further, it is our earliest source for the veneration of St. Thekla, which would become a major feature of the Church in Syria and beyond. Though not Scripture and therefore not to be treated as such, this important text attests to the antiquity—and therefore the veracity—of the Church's memory of St. Paul and his martyrdom.

II. THE ACTS OF PETER

Structure

The Acts of Peter is in several ways similar to the Acts of Paul. This similarity likely represents at least part of the reason St. Photios believed they were the work of the same author. The book has three major parts: The first part, the introduction, describes the arrival of St. Peter and his family in Rome. The second portion narrates a contest there between Peter and Simon Magus, which ends rather badly for Simon. Finally, the third part describes the martyrdom of St. Peter in Rome under Nero. The text was originally written in Greek, somewhat later than the Acts of Paul, toward the end of the second century AD. Copies have survived in Latin, Coptic, Slavonic, Syriac, Arabic, Armenian, Ethiopic, and the original Greek.

Like the Acts of Paul, the Acts of Peter is clearly a composite document—once again, not in the sense of being composed of several preexisting texts. Rather, the book records a series of traditions regarding St. Peter's later life, after the close of the canonical Acts of the Apostles. Simon Magus is here depicted as the founder of Gnosticism in all its later forms. The Acts of Peter therefore, like the Acts of Paul, also carries a strong anti-Gnostic sentiment. The work even draws a parallel between the preservation of St. Thekla's virginity and that of Peter's daughter.

Contents

In 1 Corinthians 9:5, St. Paul notes, albeit obliquely, that St. Peter traveled with his family. Peter's mother-in-law even makes an appearance in the Gospel of Luke when Christ heals her (4:38–40). Nevertheless, the Acts of Peter is the first place in which we meet any members of Peter's family—in this case primarily his daughter, whose virginity is preserved, ultimately, by paralysis. To prevent a Roman man from taking her for marriage at the age of ten, Peter prays that she would become paralyzed, leading to the man's rejection of her. While this seems bizarre to modern ears, a Roman man could claim any Jewish non-Roman citizen for a concubine, regardless of her age. Once the danger has passed, Peter miraculously heals his daughter of her paralysis.

In the city of Rome, while St. Peter works legitimate miracles in the power of the Holy Spirit, Simon Magus is also in the city, gaining converts to a form of Gnosticism through the use of a combination of sorcery and sleight of hand. Simon had had a previous run-in with the apostles when he sought to buy from them the power to work miracles, cementing the impression of him as a charlatan (Acts 8:9–24). Peter confronts him, and they engage in a sort of duel that culminates in Simon Magus flying over the city. Peter prays, causing Simon to crash to the ground. Despite the care of Roman physicians, he dies.

Saint Peter then becomes aware that Nero's persecution is imminent, and, fearing for his life, he prepares to flee the city. As he departs Rome on the road, he encounters Christ Himself, carrying His Cross, on His way into the city. Peter asks him, in Latin, "*Quo vadis?*" or "Where are you going?" Christ responds that He is going to Rome to be crucified again. Upon hearing this, Peter realizes that by attempting to flee persecution and martyrdom, he is once again denying Christ. He then returns to Rome, where he is seized to be crucified. At the place of his martyrdom, he requests that he be crucified upside-down, as he is not worthy to die in the same manner as the Lord. This request is honored. Other Fathers and writers from the third century, writing in ways that do not appear to be dependent on the text of the Acts of Peter, also testify that St. Peter was crucified on an inverted cross.[37]

---

37   Saint Peter's ministry and death in Rome are attested to by St.

Significance to the Church

Like the Acts of Paul, the Acts of Peter gives early witness to the antiquity and veracity of the Church's shared memory of the end of the life of the apostle. In recent years, the traditional burial sites of both St. Peter and St. Paul have been at least partially confirmed by archaeological and scientific investigation of their remains. Though apocryphal, the Acts of Paul and the Acts of Peter constitute a repository of firsthand knowledge from those who knew the apostles and were the beneficiaries of their ministry.

III. THE ACTS OF JOHN

THE ACTS OF JOHN is in many ways similar to the other apocryphal books of acts, but its history is tied up with the struggle in the Church against iconoclasm. Like the Acts of Paul and the Acts of Peter, the Acts of John is a composite document collecting various traditions about St. John the Evangelist. But unlike those other two, it is more truly composite, with a large and quite problematic central section inserted at some later point, possibly in a Manichean context. The original portions of the text, however, contain the earliest witness to certain Johannine traditions that are likewise preserved in the liturgical life of the Orthodox Church.

Clement, St. Ignatius of Antioch, St. Irenaeus of Lyons, Tertullian, and Eusebius of Caesarea, and in many other places in late antiquity.

The Problematic Middle Section

In its present critical edition, the Acts of John is divided into 115 chapters. The section labeled chapters 87–105 is the later insertion. It is written in a different style that does not match the rest of the work, shows signs of having originated centuries later, and gives evidence of a different theological viewpoint. The earlier and later portions of the text consist primarily of stories from the life of St. John after the close of the Acts of the Apostles. The portion added later is a lengthy discourse, supposedly by St. John, about the nature of Christ. As one example, in chapter 92 he states that when he tried to touch Christ, sometimes he would make contact and sometimes his hand would pass right through Him. The connections here to Gnostic denials and revisions of Christ's Incarnation are obvious. This portion of the text also retells the story of Christ's Transfiguration, removing the Prophets Moses and Elijah from it—likely out of antipathy toward the Old Testament.

The earlier and later portions of the Acts of John, surrounding the added material, appear in every way to date to somewhere in the second century AD, alongside the other books of acts discussed in this chapter. The narrative picks up as St. John travels to Ephesus, arrives, and ministers in the city. If one accepts its traditional ascription to St. John the Apostle, the Johannine corpus within the New Testament reveals Ephesus as his eventual base of operations, as does the direct testimony of the second-century Fathers who were his spiritual grandchildren in that region. The portion after the addition describes St. John's eventual death of old age; he is the only apostle who was not directly martyred.

Contents

The Acts of John begins in media res, and scholars generally believe that the original opening is lost. The numbering of the chapters takes into account this omission, so the book begins with chapter 18. As St. John is traveling to Ephesus, the wife of the ruler of the city, Lycomedes, dies. Lycomedes receives a vision telling him that St. John is coming and that John's God will raise Lycomedes's wife, Cleopatra, from the dead. Despite the vision, Lycomedes falls into despair and dies from his overwhelming grief. When the entire city has gathered to mourn their ruling couple, St. John raises both of them from the dead in front of the crowds as the beginning of his ministry in Ephesus.

In gratitude, Lycomedes summons the greatest portrait painter in his domain, who paints a portrait on wood of St. John. Lycomedes shows the finished product to John and states that though he worships only God, he also venerates as gods on earth those who are benefactors, so he will keep the portrait to maintain the apostle's memory. Saint John responds by chiding Lycomedes for having produced "a dead likeness of a dead man" (AJohn 29). He says that what Christ wants is for Lycomedes to paint a portrait with his life, using faithfulness, knowledge, kindness, goodness, love, purity, and the like as colors. In its original context, this story was likely focused on John's humility and on the idea that true worship of God and veneration of His saints is to live a life of virtue in imitation of those saints, not merely to honor them outwardly.

After the incident with the portrait, Lycomedes arranges for St. John to speak at the Ephesian amphitheater, where, after proclaiming the gospel, he heals all those who come to him.

Shortly thereafter, a feast honoring the Ephesian Artemis—a major cult of the Roman world—ensues. Saint John goes to the central temple, one of the seven wonders of the ancient world, but declines to wear the required festal garb. When threatened by the priests, he challenges them to a showdown reminiscent of that between Elijah and the prophets of Baal on Mount Carmel. John suggests that they should pray and ask Artemis to strike John dead, while he prays to his God that they be struck dead; then they can all see what happens. The priests, aware of the miracles St. John worked, are terrified at this prospect and decline to participate. John points out that their fear means they are following the wrong god. He then prays against the temple, which partially collapses, killing one of the chief pagan priests. Saint John then raises him back to life.

The next tradition related regarding St. John's ministry at Ephesus is an example of extreme repentance. It is also extreme in several other ways. A dream guides St. John to travel three miles outside Ephesus, where he finds a young man running, carrying a sickle. John catches up to him, and the panicked man drops the weapon. Upon interrogation, the young man admits that he had been having an affair with another man's wife. His father ordered him to end the illicit relationship, at which point the young man flew into a rage and beat and kicked his father to death. Realizing what he had done, he took the sickle and was on his way to kill his lover, her husband, and then himself. Saint John asks the young man if he will repent and mend his ways if John can restore his father's life. When he indicates that he will, St. John raises the father and then directs the young man to consider the person he once was to be dead, and to begin a new life in

Christ. The young man, however, still not in his right mind, again seizes the sickle and uses it to remove his own genitals, which he takes and hurls at his former mistress, blaming his own body for his sins and crimes. John tells him that his self-mutilation is just as much a sin as murder or adultery, and that they all have the same source. He needs to learn to control his thoughts, and if he repents and seeks to do so, God will help him.

Saint John then travels to Smyrna to perform more healings, and on the way back he dispels bedbugs infesting an inn. In the final story of the early portion, back at Ephesus, a dark story of sexual obsession unfolds. A leading man of the city, Callimachus, is obsessed with Drusiana, a Christian woman married to a Christian man, Andronicus. Callimachus's attempts to seduce Drusiana, combined with stress and anxiety, lead to her sickness and death. Still obsessed, Callimachus bribes a household servant in an attempt to gain access to her and molest her body. A snake kills this servant, Fortunatus, as well as Callimachus, but not before a vision of Christ tells Callimachus to die so that he may live. Saint John arrives and raises first Drusiana, then Callimachus, who is now repentant. Feeling compassion, Drusiana raises Fortunatus from the dead, but the servant refuses to repent and therefore dies again from the snake venom still in his system. Like the previous story, this one concerns St. John bringing someone who is deeply lost in sin back from the brink to repentance, with repentance portrayed as the death of the old person and the beginning of a new life.

In the numbering of the chapters, this is the point of insertion of the later material concerning St. John's reminiscences of Christ. But the Acts of John survives in a number of different language versions, both ancient and medieval, usually in fragmentary form; in many of these recensions, the added material falls in other places. The fact that this portion of text has no stable position in the overall narrative is an important part of the evidence that it is a later addition. As already described, there are several Gnostic emphases within this portion of the text, and the Manichees are known to have used a version of the Acts of John. The center of this added portion is called "The Hymn of Jesus," which presents itself as a song sung by Jesus while He and His disciples perform an elaborate circle dance (AJohn 94–96). The origins of this section may be as simple as its existence as a Manichean ritual text describing dance and antiphonal chant.

In all cases, the Acts of John ends with the final, ancient portion describing the death of St. John the Theologian. In great old age, St. John is made aware that the time has come for him to leave this life. He orders his disciples to dig a long trench that will serve as his grave. Once it is complete, John climbs into it and says a long, final prayer giving thanks to Christ for his life—both its joys and its sufferings—sealing himself for the world to come. He then lies down in the grave, and his disciples cover him with earth. Various versions of the text contain additional traditions: Some forms describe the earth under which he is buried as moving and shifting, implying that St. John is not dead but sleeping. Other versions describe his disciples returning the next day and finding only his sandals, his body having been taken up to heaven. At least one manuscript contains both, paradoxically. The Falling Asleep of St. John the Theologian is celebrated in the Orthodox Church, including the reading from the Synaxarion of a version of the tradition of John's burial and the disappearance of his body, on September 26.

Significance to the Church

In the latter half of the eighth century, the iconoclastic controversy raged in the churches of the East, and the Orthodox faction pressed the iconoclasts to produce some proof in written form of the antiquity of their iconoclastic traditions. In response, at the Second Council of Nicea—the Seventh Ecumenical Council—the iconoclasts produced the Acts of John, and the story of the portrait painter in particular, as a part of their case. Within the debate, opposing sides produced various quotations. Reading the story of St. John's rebuke as an authoritative apostolic condemnation of iconography is difficult, at best. Added to the difficulty are the rather clear heretical overtones to the Christology of the central portion of the text compilation at that time, as well as the Manichean use of it.[38] All these issues led to the council's express condemnation of the Acts of John and its consignment to be burned.

While the statement of the council seems clear, the burning was, in fact, never carried out. Saint Nikephoros still maintains the Acts of John on his list of books to be read privately, even

---

38 Among their other divergent beliefs, the Manicheans held that Jesus Christ is an overlap of three different beings. They believed in a divine Jesus, a sort of demigod who led humans, starting with Adam, down a path to help them shed their material forms and return to God. They also believed in a human prophet, Jesus of Nazareth, who is related in mysterious ways to this being. Finally, the being of God, dispersed throughout the world, forms a sort of universal, invisible "suffering Christ" who is in a mysterious way related to the human Christ on the Cross.

though he had received the title "Confessor" for the sufferings he endured at the hands of the iconoclasts. He was no friend of their arguments or the texts they used to support them. A few decades later, St. Photios the Great maintained the Acts of John in the library of Constantinople and was likewise familiar with it, arguing that it was written by one of St. John's immediate disciples. The iconoclasts' attempt to make such authoritative use of the Acts of John in the late eighth century says much about the view at that time of the authority of these ancient extrabiblical texts. The Acts of John was clearly understood to be written evidence of ancient traditions. This view makes it less surprising that men like St. Nikephoros and St. Photios would consider themselves able in private study to weigh out the valid and invalid among its traditions.

IV. THE ACTS OF THOMAS

The Question of Gnosticism

The Acts of Thomas is again of similar provenance and type to the other apocryphal books of acts. Because it concerns St. Thomas, Gnostic use of him as a figure, as in the Gospel of Thomas, has caused many scholars to read the Acts of Thomas as a similar Gnostic text. It is certainly possible to give this book, especially the poetic portions, a Gnostic reading. However, readers should not forget that the Gnostics also had their own readings of St. Paul, St. Luke, St. John, and other Scriptures. The possibility of a Gnostic reading is not the same as a text in and of itself endorsing Gnosticism.

A good example of this tendency to default to a Gnostic approach is the issue of St. Thomas's "twinhood." Saint John's

Gospel informs us that Thomas was called Didymus, or "the Twin." Most of the extra-biblical Thomas literature identifies this "twinship" not as a reference to his having a biological twin per se but as Thomas being, in some sense, the twin of Christ. Some texts, such as the Book of Thomas the Contender, a third-century Gnostic text, very clearly mean this in a Gnostic sense—that St. Thomas represented the material, physical, or human element of Christ. Tracking with the emphases of the Acts of Thomas, however, it seems clear that Thomas is Christ's twin in the sense of leading a Christlike life. To see St. Thomas and his deeds is to see Christ. This does not necessarily entail any Gnostic teaching.

At the beginning of the Acts of Thomas, the apostles in Jerusalem divide the world and allot its various regions among themselves to spread the gospel. This parallels the ancient tradition of a most high God allotting the various nations to the gods, with the apostles now taking their places. When St. Thomas eventually arrives in the place allotted to him, India, much of his ministry will consist of a contest between Christ, acting through him, and the demons who hold that land captive.

Saint Thomas in India

The stories within the Acts of Thomas primarily preserve the traditions surrounding the beginnings of the Christian Church in India. Multiple contemporaneous sources testify that by AD 200 Christian churches were established across western India, including what is now Pakistan, Baluchistan, and parts of Afghanistan. These churches had bishops and fully realized internal structures and were active parts of the synod at Edessa, participating in Mesopotamian church affairs. They used a Syriac dialect of Aramaic liturgically. The present-day Indian Orthodox Church of the Malabar coast in the Kerala province is the direct historical descendant of these early churches.

These Indian churches also claimed, again verifiably from at least around AD 200, to be the product of the missionary activity of the apostle Thomas, whose relics they claim to possess. While biblical scholars and most historians maintain an attitude of knee-jerk skepticism to this kind of claim, no matter how ancient, recent archaeological finds have served to help confirm the possibility, if not probability, of the truth of these traditions. The Acts of Thomas contains the name of the king under whom St. Thomas began his ministry in India, Guandaphur. For centuries, this name was found nowhere in the historical record and therefore was considered to be evidence for the falsehood of the Thomas traditions. More recently, however, the finding of certain inscriptions in Pakistan and a treasury of coins bearing the name "Gondophares" have led to reconsideration. A regional king by that name in fact reigned in northwest India from about AD 20 to 46. That this foreign king's name was preserved in a written text composed at the beginning of the third century AD in Syria, in Syriac, is strong evidence for its historical veracity.

For the Indian churches to be established by the end of the second century, missionary activity must have begun in the first. It is not only plausible but likely that an apostle was able to travel eastward and evangelize the Indio-Parthian kingdom of Gondophares. Coins minted by Gondophares reveal that his kingdom served as a bridge between India and points west.

These coins bear the images not only of the king, but of gods as diverse as Zeus and Shiva on the reverse side. It is even relatively clear how an apostle would have gotten there. The island of Socotra, currently a possession of Yemen, stood along the relevant trade route, and a Christian community existed there in the first century AD. While it will never be possible to prove to a skeptic that the St. Thomas of the New Testament Gospels traveled to India, the assertion seems entirely secure that someone identified locally and in Syria as "Thomas" brought Christianity to India in the mid-first century.

Contents

The Acts of Thomas casts the apostolic ministry of St. Thomas in India very much in the mold of the ministry of the Old Testament prophets. Thomas not only preaches and works miracles as they did, but also engages in prophetic actions in order to convey important ideas to the Indian communities where he lives. This prophetic cast to his ministry starts from the beginning of the Acts of Thomas, when, like Jonah before him, he at first declines to go to India and asks instead to be sent anywhere else. In response to his refusal, Christ Himself appears to an official sent by King Guandaphur to acquire a slave with trade skills in Jerusalem, and He sells St. Thomas to him. Acquiescing to the fact that he is the slave of Christ, Thomas then dutifully travels back to Guandaphur.

Upon arriving in India, St. Thomas encounters the wedding party of the king's son. In the book, St. Thomas shows a general antipathy toward sexuality even within marriage, and this is generally taken by scholars as further evidence of Gnosticism.

This antipathy is somewhat downplayed, though not entirely, in versions of the text that circulated in Orthodox circles as opposed to those that circulated among the Manichees. On the other hand, these scholars generally fail to take into account the reality that this wedding would normally be consummated with sexual rites related to the pagan gods. Every aspect of life was related to the worship of pagan gods, whom the Acts of Thomas identifies as demons. An apostle coming into this wholly pagan environment would respond from a Christian perspective to issues surrounding sexuality, eating meat, and the like. In these circumstances, chastity is not solely the province of the unmarried, and the Acts of Thomas does not entail a rejection of married sexuality in toto.

Saint Thomas disrupts the royal wedding, and King Guandaphur becomes enraged, accusing Thomas of being a sorcerer based on the reports of miracles he has performed. Nevertheless, the apostle arrived as the workman the king had requested, and the king tasks Thomas with building him a palace. Saint Thomas misleads the king concerning how the work is going, despite repeatedly receiving further funds for the project. The king eventually discovers that in actuality, St. Thomas has built nothing but instead has been distributing all the money to the poor and proclaiming the gospel.

When he discovers this, the king has the apostle thrown into prison to await execution. Saint Thomas offers as his only defense that he has, indeed, built the palace for the king, who does not need the money he was given in this world because he will receive a king's reward in the next. That night, the king's brother dies and is taken to the heavens, where he sees a magnificent palace. When he inquires about it, he is told that that is the palace built for his brother the king by St. Thomas through his acts of mercy. The king's brother asks to return to this world to bring the news to his brother, and the request is granted. Guandaphur's brother is raised from the dead, and after the king hears his brother's report, he immediately frees St. Thomas, embraces Christianity, and becomes the sponsor of St. Thomas's mission in India.

Spiritual Warfare

The narrative of the Acts of Thomas then moves to a series of his adventures that have the character of spiritual warfare. Saint Thomas engages in contests with a series of creatures or outright demons connected to the gods of India at the time and also connected directly in the text to Satan and other demonic beings. The first of these is a giant serpent, possibly a representation of a *naga*,[39] associated with the devil. This serpent claims to be the serpent in the Garden, the being who enticed the angels to lie with human women and produce the giants before the Flood, and the spirit that entered into Judas at the time of his betrayal of Christ. It had recently slain a young man guilty of fornication, and St. Thomas forces the serpent being to suck its own venom out of the man, restoring him to life and causing the serpent to explode. This young man becomes an early convert of St. Thomas.

After this event, a talking donkey who claims to be descended from Balaam's donkey takes St. Thomas back to the city. Upon

---

39　*Naga* are part serpentine, part humanoid divine beings in Southeast Asian traditions.

arriving, Thomas begins a series of exorcisms—a constant feature of his ministry in pagan India, which is deeply infested with demonic beings. A demon-afflicted woman who approaches him is the first, but far from the last, woman he encounters who is tormented by incubi. These demons are distinguished by the fact that they engage sexually with human women in their dreams as a way of violating and corrupting them. In some cases later in the Acts of Thomas, this corruption includes driving the women to commit lewd acts in public. In every case, St. Thomas wields authority over the unclean spirits, who address him as an apostle of the Most High and a twin of Christ.

Saint Thomas begins a second phase of his ministry when he moves deeper into India, into the kingdom of a certain Misdaeus. Through preaching, the working of miracles, and exorcisms, Thomas's profile and number of converts to Christianity grow. The Acts of Thomas constantly maintains a sacramental outlook by presenting St. Thomas's exorcisms and healings as being followed by baptisms and the reception of the Eucharist. As was the case in much of the early Church, a large portion of his converts are women, including the wife of the king and the wives of many of his chief advisers. Many of these wives make the decision to live a chaste life, and they no longer engage sexually with their husbands. This commitment seems to represent both an extension to women of the right of consent, as seen in the Acts of Paul and Thekla, and the related desire to be released from ritualized sexual intercourse, particularly in the case of royal wives.

Logically enough, the wives' abstinence creates great consternation for King Misdaeus and his second in command,

Charisius, so St. Thomas suffers repeated imprisonment. Two of his close disciples, Siphor and Iuzanes, are named in the text and will later hold ordained office as the second-generation leaders of the Indian Church. Despite working miracles and saving the kingdom from flood at the king's request, St. Thomas is ultimately condemned to death and run through with spears. He appears to his disciples to inform them that he is now in Paradise and has received his reward. They bury his body, and eventually his relics are translated to Mesopotamia. Before his death, King Misdaeus himself converts to Christianity.

Poetic Hymns

One noteworthy feature of the Acts of Thomas is repeated instances of poetry. This poetry is generally presented as hymns sung by St. Thomas, and these interludes pepper the course of the Acts of Thomas. They are very clearly Syriac compositions, as evidenced by the nature of the poetry, yet they are not found in all the extant manuscripts, implying that they may have been a later addition. The most famous of these is "The Hymn of the Pearl" found in Acts of Thomas 9 in one Syriac and one Greek manuscript. Despite this scanty manuscript evidence, Orthodox and Manichean writers alike comment on this hymn.

"The Hymn of the Pearl" is an extended parable telling the story of a young man, the son of the great king, who is sent on a mission to go to Egypt and retrieve an incredibly valuable pearl. While he is away in that foreign land, Egyptian women and the gods of Egypt seduce him, and he forgets all about his father and the mission. His father then sends him a letter, reminding him of who he is and of his mission, and he then finds the pearl and returns to his father with it in hand.

Most modern interpreters, presuming a Gnostic Thomas tradition, read this in the way in which the Manichean interpreters of the text likely read it. They understand this to be the story of the human soul falling into matter and being concerned with the things of this world, then receiving gnosis from above, which frees the soul to return to its original state. This is certainly a possible reading of the text. However, this hymn could also be interpreted as a melding together of the Parable of the Pearl of Great Price (Matt. 13:45–46) and the Parable of the Prodigal Son (Luke 15:11–32) from the canonical Gospels. Particularly because the location of the son's exile is in Egypt, this hymn follows the historical pattern of the Exodus as a return to the Promised Land, signifying Paradise. The letter could equally represent the proclamation of the gospel as some form of esoteric gnosis.

Significance to the Church

The Acts of Thomas, despite its guilt by association among modern scholars for being part of Thomas traditions and among ancient writers due to its use by the Manichees, provides important traditions regarding the beginnings of the churches of India. Archaeological finds throughout the region have confirmed the verisimilitude of these traditions. Additionally, an understanding of the pagan milieu into which St. Thomas would have brought the gospel of Jesus Christ does much to defuse the accusations of Gnosticism. Like the Acts of Peter, Paul, and John, the Acts of Thomas is a repository of ancient tradition and insight regarding the later lives of the apostles that are not recorded in the New Testament. The Acts of Thomas is also an important record of the understanding of evangelism and apostolic ministry within the early Church.

V. THE DIDACHE

Textual History and Genre

The word *didache* is simply the word for "teaching" in Greek; thus "the Didache" is a shortening of the full title: The Lord's Teaching through the Twelve Apostles to the Nations. The Didache is a text of a different genre from the apocryphal books of acts discussed in the rest of this chapter. It is, however, ascribed to the apostles and therefore is likewise a tradition associated with their collective ministry rather than with an individual apostle. The Didache is essentially a community rule—a set of standards that govern the life of a community. Before the discovery of the Dead Sea Scrolls in the mid-twentieth century, the Didache was treated primarily as the first church order or catechetical manual. This approach saw the Didache as a novum, a new form of literature for a new institution, the Church.

The Dead Sea Scrolls, however, contained works of numerous categories. The most talked-about texts are the early manuscripts of the books that make up the Hebrew Bible and the Christian Old Testament. Found at Qumran were also texts, many of which were discussed in part I of this book, that fall on the periphery of the Old Testament and Hebrew canons. A third category of literature, generally identified as sectarian, was specific to the community at Qumran and its practices and way of life. Within this latter category is the Manual of Discipline, which describes the duties and responsibilities of a new community member in much the same way that the Didache addresses new Christians. It is very probable that other local Judaisms of the Second Temple period likewise produced such works for the training and guidance of initiates.

The Didache, then, is a Christian entry into an existing genre of literature rather than an innovation. Many scholars now hypothesize that it may be a Christian edit and adaptation of a preexisting Jewish catechetical text. The Didache appears to have been composed in something like its present form at the end of the first or beginning of the second century AD. Many features of the text itself tend to push toward a later first-century date. This means that the distinction between a Jewish and a Christian text at the time was a fine one. It would be another generation or two before Christianity became something other than a form of Judaism.

Saint Nikephoros lists the Didache as a text to be read privately. A generation before him, St. John of Damascus cited the Didache as authentic apostolic tradition. The Apostolic Constitutions (circa AD 375), in Canon 85, accept it as an early layer of the canons governing the Church. The Didache is considered part of the New Testament within the Ethiopian Church; it is appended at its end. In genre, the Didache resembles no other book of the Christian Scriptures, making it an unlikely candidate for inclusion, regardless of antiquity. It fits most comfortably in the place it has occupied in recent memory, among the writings of the Apostolic Fathers.

Despite significant references in ancient works, the whole text of the Didache was lost until relatively recently, although citations from it were significant enough that much of the text had been reconstructed. In 1873, Metropolitan Philotheos Bryennios of Nicomedia discovered a codex at Constantinople that has since been named the Jerusalem Codex. It is dated by its copyist, a certain Leo, to the year 1056. It includes not only the complete text of the Didache in Greek but also the Epistle of Barnabas, 1 and 2 Clement, and the letters of St. Ignatius of Antioch. Metropolitan Philotheos made the codex available for Western critical editions, and the quality of the copy was quickly established by comparing citations in ancient writers. Additionally, fragments of the text of the Didache were discovered at Oxyrhynchus, Egypt, from the early centuries of the Church, providing further validation.

Contents

The teaching of the Didache shows very close affinities with the teaching of Christ in the Gospel of St. Matthew, including direct quotations. The opening section sets out a theme common in Jewish literature from Proverbs: that two ways, or roads, lead to life and death respectively. From there on, the chapter is primarily composed of a mass of quotations from the Sermon on the Mount. These teachings regarding love for enemies and persecutors are presented as the first commandment. The second commandment in the second chapter is based on the prohibitions of the Torah, specifically those against murder, lying, theft, and sexual immorality. It is worth noting that the work expressly prohibits abortion, which is described as the murder of a child.

The sins and vices condemned in the early chapters of the Didache generally parallel similar lists found in the Epistles of

St. Paul (e.g., 1 Cor. 6:9–10; Gal. 5:19–21; 1 Tim. 1:9–11). One notable difference is that the Didache particularly singles out the Greek and Roman institution of pederasty. In the Roman world of the first century AD, male sexuality was seen as a bodily function not inherently different from the need to eat or use the restroom. Outside of reproduction, male Romans treated others sexually more as receptacles than as partners, and no concept of consent existed. It was socially acceptable for adult men to use children—especially enslaved children—below ten years of age for this purpose. Rome had inherited the term *pederast*, which literally means "lover of children," from the Greeks. Early Christians not only found this practice vile but refused to use that term. Early Christians instead used the word found in the Didache and the Epistle of Barnabas, *pedophthoreseis*, or "defiler of children," to abominate the practice.

The middle portion of the Didache deals with the ritual life of the Christian community. It describes the means of baptism, preferably by triple immersion in running water, such as a river, with the Trinitarian formula. While this form is ideal, if running water is not available, then still water may be used. If enough water is not available in a given situation, water may be poured over the head three times. The Didache moves the fasting days for Christians from Tuesday and Thursday, when the hypocrites—in this case the Pharisees—fasted, to Wednesday and Friday. It then prescribes the Lord's Prayer be said three times a day and provides its text, including the dismissal commonly said by the priest or bishop in the Orthodox Church today. Finally, the Didache gives very basic prayers to be said when celebrating the Eucharist. We know from the second-century Fathers that the prayers that accompanied the offering of the Eucharist, surrounding the words of institution, varied from place to place and from bishop to bishop, until the forms attributed to Ss. Basil the Great, John Chrysostom, and others became popular and found widespread use in the Church.

The final portion of the Didache deals with issues regarding church membership and leadership. At this early point, Christian communities were still sharing a common life, so all Christians are to be welcomed and given food and lodging on their journeys. Those who wish to move into a Christian community are likewise welcome to do so, provided they contribute their work to the common livelihood. Though the Didache calls for bishops and deacons to be appointed over each community, it was written at a stage in the life of the Church in which prophets and apostles were still at large in the world, so the text also discusses their welcome and treatment. The end of the first century AD represented a transitional period in this respect. The Didache redirects the Torah's commandments for tithing to the Levitical priesthood to the religious leadership of the Christian community, and these leaders are identified as holding a priesthood. The eucharistic gathering on the Lord's Day is likewise designated a sacrifice.

The Didache concludes with a final exhortation regarding the imminent glorious appearing of Christ. Citing several texts from Matthew 24, Christians are called to vigilance and to preparation, faithfulness, and patience in suffering. The work makes direct reference to the final Antichrist, who will appear and bring about a fiery trial. Afterward, those who endure to the end will be saved as the Lord returns upon the clouds of heaven with His holy ones (see 2 Thess. 2:3–12).

Significance to the Church

The Didache gives a snapshot of the early Church at the close of the apostolic era as she transitioned to a new phase of her existence. Within the short text's description of Christian life, readers can see the direct continuity of these early Christian communities with preceding forms of Second Temple Judaism. At the same time, one sees the familiar shape of the Orthodox Christian Church budding into flower.

The teaching method of the "two ways," one leading to life and one to death, is a Christian adaptation of Old Testament and later Jewish wisdom traditions. The identity of Christ is expressed as the "vine of David" (9). At the same time, the forbidding of food offered to idols and of seeking omens indicates that the Christian way of life, though deeply grounded in Judaism, is being practiced now also by Gentiles. The teaching of the Didache regarding both the sacraments and morality are in continuity with Orthodox Christian practice to this very day. Although the author of the text will never be known, its content is exactly what one would expect to find in an early summary of apostolic teaching that conforms to the first-century world.

CHAPTER FOURTEEN

Clementine Literature

WITHIN ST. NIKEPHOROS'S LIST of works to be read privately, he refers to thirty-two books attributed to St. Clement of Rome. But there is no internal basis in the list itself for determining the precise texts Nikephoros is indicating. Contextually, however, in regard to literature that was available at Constantinople in the ninth century and is still accessible today, we can determine with a very high degree of certainty the identity of twenty-six of these. These are not, however, twenty-six separate, independent books. Saint Nikephoros's reference should be understood in the way we might refer to the collected or complete works of an author.

Who Is Saint Clement?

Saint Clement of Rome served as the third bishop or overseer—the ranking presbyter—of the church of Rome after the apostles. Traditionally, he served from AD 88 to 99, then was martyred. Before his consecration, he was a disciple of Ss. Peter and Paul; Paul mentions him in Philippians 4:3. The Shepherd of Hermas also refers to him as the one in the church of Rome who was in charge of communication with other churches. Saint Clement, St. Ignatius, and St. Polycarp are considered to be the central Apostolic Fathers, the earliest Christian writers after— or in St. Clement's case, perhaps during—the composition of the texts that would come to make up the New Testament.

Texts Attributed to Saint Clement

The first and likely best-known Clementine text, 1 Clement, is widely accepted to have been written by St. Clement himself near the end of the first century AD. First Clement is a letter that the church at Rome sent to the church in Corinth, and it addresses difficulties not unfamiliar to readers of St. Paul's Corinthian epistles, centering on the need for Christians to separate from their former, pagan way of life. While debates about canonicity did not actually occur then, many early New Testament codices contain 1 Clement, among other books numbered with the Apostolic Fathers, at their conclusion. The expense involved in producing such a codex likely incentivized the inclusion of all valuable works possible.

Second Clement, despite the name, is widely agreed to be written by a different author. Further, 2 Clement is not an epistle as such but rather a homily recorded and prepared for circulation. The preacher urges his hearers to repentance and diligence in the Christian life despite persecution. Scholars generally agree that this text is the product of an unknown homilist at Rome in the first half of the second century AD. Based purely on its slightly shorter length and ascription to St. Clement, it received the title 2 Clement, or even the Second Epistle of St. Clement to the Corinthians.

The other known group of Clementine texts that St. Nikeph-oros would have accessed is called the Clementine Homilies and consists of twenty books. Additionally, a series of letters purportedly exchanged between St. James of Jerusalem, St. Peter, and St. Clement, along with a general introduction, came to circulate along with the Clementine Homilies and served as an introduction and attestation to the importance of the text. The elements combined into this text were written much later, based on internal references and the date when it began to be recognized and quoted, likely around AD 330. Neverthe-less, in the time of St. Nikephoros, the Clementine Homilies were universally ascribed to St. Clement of Rome. At the same time, despite the affixed letters purporting to be from authors of canonical New Testament epistles, no real credence was given to any attempt to treat them as canonical. This implies a wide understanding that the ascriptions of the letters were not valid.

Several other texts were, in the past, widely attributed to St. Clement, but either St. Nikephoros did not reference them, or for various other reasons they will not be treated here. Specif-ically, two treatises concerning virginity were widely consid-ered to be the work of St. Clement. These could, indeed, have been two of the books that Nikephoros identified. These, how-ever, have long since been discovered not to be the work of St. Clement and are now often attributed to St. Athanasius, mak-ing them eligible subjects for books in patristics. There is also a group of texts called the Pseudo-Decretals, which claim to be decrees and legislation from ante-Nicene bishops of Rome and Western local church councils. But these works were long ago shown to be fabrications of the Frankish court in the ninth century, meaning that St. Nikephoros would not have known of their existence. Here we will consider only texts that could reasonably have been counted by St. Nikephoros among the works of St. Clement.

1 CLEMENT

Church Structure and Apostolic Authority

First Clement is one of the earliest extant Christian documents, outside of the New Testament texts themselves. It is a short letter that St. Clement wrote on behalf of the Christian community in Rome to the Christian community in Corinth. At this point in history, the Roman church did not have a strong, central bishop but rather a number of presbyters, some of them carrying a sort of senior status that allowed them to represent the entire community to others. From roughly AD 88 to 99, St. Clement was that leader. His title as "Bishop of Rome" is retroactive, based on the structures that solidified there in the mid-second century.

The fact that the magisterial episcopacy developed from the mid-first to the mid-second century, at different rates in different parts of the Church, is in no way a critique of its validity. A bishop was a successor to the apostles upon their departure from this life. We see, within the pages of the Scriptures, St. Paul making St. Timothy such a bishop for Crete by sending him there and enjoining him to ordain presbyters and deacons. At the same time, when Paul stops in Ephesus on his way to Jerusalem, a group of presbyters governs the church there. Ephesus still enjoyed the active ministry of an apostle: not only St. Paul but also St. John the Theologian, as well as the Theotokos and St. Mary Magdalene in the second half of the first century. Rome, as the capital of the empire, was in a similar situation. It is for this reason that St. Clement seems in his epistle to use the terms "bishop" and "presbyter" interchangeably; different Christian communities at that point had somewhat different structures.

Saint Clement writes to the church at Corinth not from the perspective of a leader in that far distant community, nor from the perspective of having a special office that entitles him to do so. He writes the letter from the Roman church to the Corinthian church as a brother. Clement appeals again and again not to his own authority, or even the authority of Rome, but rather to the authority of the apostles, in particular St. Paul. He reminds the members of the church at Corinth of the letters that St. Paul wrote to them (Clem. 47:1). He quotes again and again from the Epistles of St. Paul, including Hebrews. His approach is therefore as an associate of the apostles, to bring the authority of the apostles to bear. Saint Paul is the apostle of Corinth, who founded the community there and wrote at least four letters to the Corinthian church, and so it is to St. Paul that St. Clement repeatedly and directly appeals.

Saint Clement also represents an early testimony to several events in the latter part of the first century known from sources outside Scripture. First Clement refers directly to the martyrdoms of Ss. Peter and Paul without expressly naming their location as Rome, though he wrote the epistle from there (Clem. 5). Clement presents both martyrdoms as the result of jealousy and envy, and the epistle goes on to record the names of other martyrs in this early period at Rome. In describing the martyrdom of St. Paul in particular, St. Clement refers to Paul as having journeyed to the extreme point of the West—an apparent confirmation of the success of the apostle's intention to voyage to Spain.

Content

The primary issue that St. Clement seeks to address is a recent development in Corinth, where a coup of sorts has taken place. Several presbyters of the church have been removed from office and replaced by others. The major theme of the letter, then, is the importance of humility over envy and jealousy, particularly in relation to offices of leadership in the Church. Saint Clement walks through the Old Testament and St. Paul's epistles in relation to this theme, explaining how the situation within the Church is not substantively different from what it has been throughout human history. He calls the members of the Corinthian church to repentance and reconciliation.

Significance to the Church

Saint Clement speaks a great deal about the resurrection—not only of Christ, but that general resurrection at Christ's glorious appearing. He is the first of several early Fathers to use the phoenix, then believed to be a real bird, as an image of resurrection (Clem. 25). The reality of judgment and the eternal life of the world to come is, for St. Clement, a sufficient motivator for the Christian to live a life of faithfulness and humility. Though short, this epistle reveals the continuity between Old and New Testaments as understood by early Christians, as well as the continuity of ministry between the apostles and their immediate successors.

2 CLEMENT

AS ALREADY DISCUSSED, 2 Clement is not a second letter from St. Clement to Corinth or anywhere else. Not only is the text not written by St. Clement, or at least not the same St. Clement; it is not, properly speaking, a letter. Second Clement is a recorded homily, very likely of Roman provenance, from the first half of the second century AD. This is the likely origin of the identification with Clement, due to his prominence in Rome and in literature of the period. Within the ancient world, 2 Clement was far less widely circulated than 1 Clement. By the time of Eusebius of Caesarea in the fourth century, large portions of the Church were completely unfamiliar with a "second" Book of Clement.

Audience

When interpreting a homily, the first questions that scholars ask are related to the intended audience. This is especially true when dealing with a homily preached by an unknown author. Clues within the text of 2 Clement point to the original audience, whether those to whom the homily was first preached or the original recipients of the written text. There are several references to a past that included idolatrous worship, implying that the hearers are converts from paganism. At the same time, the text includes frequent quotations from the Hebrew Scriptures, albeit in Greek translation.

The material in 2 Clement dates to the period before the final separation of Jewish and Christian communities. Many of the early pagan converts to Christianity from St. Paul's missionary journeys onward came from a category of people known as "God-fearers" (e.g., Acts 13:50; 17:4, 17; 18:7). These were pagans who had an interest in the Jewish communities near them. Many Gentile benefactors endowed Jewish synagogues in the first century BC and the first century AD. Learned pagans found the Hebrew Scriptures and religion fascinating due to their antiquity, much as they did the religion of Egypt and its rites. As a result, communities of Christian converts to paganism who were deeply steeped in the Judaisms of the day were not uncommon, including in and around Rome.

Content

Second Clement is a fairly typical Christian homily that could be preached, at least in its broad strokes, in any era of the Church. Christians are encouraged to focus on the good things of the world to come, rather than the things of this world, by pursuing virtue and abstaining from vice. Christians who pursue virtue will receive the enmity of the world and must patiently endure suffering in light of the reward that awaits them in the Kingdom. Those who have fallen into sin and vice must repent in light of the coming Day of Judgment.

Second Clement quotes two sayings of Christ not found in the canonical Gospels, though some have parallels in other noncanonical texts. The first of these quotations is Christ saying, "If you are gathered together with Me in My bosom, but you do not do My commandments, I will cast you away and say to you, 'Depart from Me; I do not know you, where you are from, workers of lawlessness'" (2Clem. 4:5). Elements of this wording are similar to sayings of Christ in the Gospel of St. Matthew in particular. A second, similar quote has partial canonical parallels:

For the Lord says, "You will be as lambs in the midst of wolves." Then, answering, Peter said to him, "What if the wolves tear apart the lambs?" Jesus said to Peter, "The lambs should not be afraid of the wolves after they die. And neither should you be afraid of those who kill you and are never able to do anything else to you. But fear the one who, after you die, has the authority to throw your soul and body into the fire of Gehenna." (2Clem. 5:2–4)

This quotation, because of the narrative element, must almost certainly be a quotation from a now unknown text.

Another similar quotation has been connected to extra-canonical Gospel texts. However, it is going too far to say that 2 Clement's use of it represents a quotation of either the Gospel of Peter or the Gospel of Thomas, which both contain some-what different versions of the same saying. It is entirely possible, for example, that 2 Clement is here citing the original form of a tradition that the two Gospels in question later transformed into other contexts with other meanings. Second Clement 12:2 reads, "For the Lord Himself, when He was asked by some-one when His kingdom would come, said, 'When the two will be one, and the outside as the inside, and the masculine with the feminine, neither male nor female.'" This saying has Gnos-tic overtones that the Coptic version of the Gospel of Thomas brings out especially clearly: "Every woman who makes herself male will enter the kingdom of heaven" (114:3). Despite this, while various authors are rather dismissive of 2 Clement—if they are even aware of it—it is not directly and strongly charged with containing the Gnostic heresy.[40]

---

40   For example, Eusebius of Caesarea writes, "It should be noted also that

Significance to the Church

If 2 Clement is included among the Clementine books in St. Nikephoros's list, as seems likely, it is a short work of low prominence. Such a work, even if it contains certain errors or inauthentic traditions, would be a prime candidate for the category of private reading that he had in mind. It provides a window into the homiletical world of the second-century Church—a world in which apostolic traditions were still circulating independently of writings, and various communities were still reaching agreement about which works would come to make up an authoritative New Testament.

CLEMENTINE HOMILIES

Background

The Clementine Homilies is a title for one edited version of a composite piece of literature that contains traditions surrounding St. Peter and St. Clement. Another, somewhat shorter edit also exists by the title the Clementine Recognitions. The Clementine Homilies and the Clementine Recognitions are in different languages, though they appear to have originally been in Greek, from an older source document that was itself a composite. To make the matter somewhat more confusing, a series of letters back and forth between Ss. Peter and James appears to have been appended to the text at some later point. The main text, without the additions, is made up of twenty books. Though

there is said to be a second epistle of Clement. But we do not know that this is received as the first, because we do not find the ancients making any use of it. . . . No mention has been made of [it] by the ancients; because [it] do[es] not even preserve the pure mark of apostolic orthodoxy" (*Ecc. Hist.* 3.38).

St. Nikephoros's reference to thirty-two Clementine books is vague, it is difficult to imagine that number of texts without including the Clementine Homilies.

Textual History

Though ancient authors attributed these texts to their main protagonist, St. Clement, they are of much later composition. There are simply no references to this work before about AD 330. The earliest extant reference come from Eusebius of Caesarea, who, after acknowledging the importance of 1 Clement and the existence of 2 Clement, also mentions other books attributed to Clement that had "arisen recently," although he found no reference to them whatsoever in any ancient author (*Ecc. Hist.* 3.38). Despite the fairly clear evidence that the text behind the Clementine Homilies is a product of the late third or even early fourth century, some scholars continue to argue for a much earlier date. In most cases, these arguments accompany some intent to use the text as proof of the existence of some sort of Jewish Christian group in the second century. But attempting to prove the existence of a second-century community almost entirely through arguing that a much later text really dates to the second century seems an especially flimsy argument—one that is motivated more by ideology than by any actual material evidence.

Content

The text itself is the story of St. Clement meeting and accompanying St. Peter as Peter travels from Palestine to Rome. Along the way, they meet a wide range of people from the Gospels and the Acts of the Apostles, including Ss. Aquila, Barnabas, and Zacchaeus. Saint Clement begins the narrative in Rome, where he hears the announcement of the Birth of the Son of God and travels to Judea to learn more. There he is introduced to St. Peter and begins journeying with him through a series of healings, sermons, and adventures. Along the way, Clement explains to St. Peter the rest of his biography—though, because of the late date, the veracity of any of these otherwise unrecorded details about the life of St. Clement is dubious at best. That said, at least the broad strokes of his family life and his journey to Palestine are included in the Orthodox Church's Synaxarion. These strokes are broad enough, however, that it is difficult to discern whether the Synaxarion's composers used the Clementine Homilies as their source or whether both are referencing the same traditions.

As with the Acts of Peter previously discussed, the Petrine traditions contained in the Clementine Homilies center in large part on an ongoing contest between St. Peter and Simon Magus. Simon has a coterie of disciples, just as St. Peter also has followers. In addition to direct encounters and debates, Simon has gone around slandering St. Peter at Antioch. The Peter of the Clementine Homilies is a trickster who solves problems through cunning. For example, he clears his name at Antioch by using a magic potion to disguise one of his followers as Simon Magus and sending him to Syria to clear Peter's name. The entire work has the character of an ancient romance and gives a modern reader the impression of fan fiction.

The Clementine Homilies ends with a letter from St. Clement to St. James at Jerusalem, intended to give the impression that the entire collected work represents a sort of report to St. James of St. Peter's doings. Certain scholarly interpreters make much of the honorific titles given to St. James in the text, positing that these titles represent some kind of Jewish or Jacobite Christianity as opposed to the Petrine Christianity of the Christian mainstream. But the idea of a particularly Petrine Christianity seems to be an anachronistic reading of much later Roman Catholic understandings of the Church back into the Church's early centuries.

To wit, in the second or fourth centuries the bishop of Rome made no claims to jurisdiction over the city of Aelia Capitolina, which was Jerusalem's new name following the destruction of the city in AD 70 and the Bar Kochva rebellion. When the early ecumenical councils address the status of the bishops of "the Aelia"—the successors of St. James—they grant them high rank in an honorary way, because the de-Judaification project of the Romans following the revolt had removed the local Jewish community and severed any organic connection between the Christian community there and St. James. Any Ebionite or Jewish Christian group that one might imagine using the Clementine Homilies would have no particular reason to exalt the see of St. James in any subsequent century.

Along with this concluding letter, two addenda were later added to the beginning of the text. The first is a letter from St. Peter to St. James; the second is a description of St. James receiving the letter and the books, and his response. Both additions promote the idea that the content of the Clementine Homilies ought not to be given to just anyone, as they could be dangerous in the wrong hands. Saint Peter urges that these homilies not be revealed to those outside the Church or even to those newly baptized, but only to the experienced, whom both St. Peter and St. James identify primarily as the ordained.

Significance to the Church

Once again, certain commentators rush to use this motif—of allowing only mature Christians to read the Clementine Homilies—as evidence that it is a Gnostic text. Immediately, it seems rather strange that commentators would see it as both a Gnostic text and an Ebionite text when the two represent opposite points of view. Possibly more importantly, this warning from St. Peter's alleged letter reflects the general attitude that we have seen throughout the consideration of apocryphal, privately read works. The Church Fathers did not consider these texts to be books that ought to be read in public, in church worship. They are texts that are, rather, repositories for certain valuable elements of Christian tradition from the earliest period of the Church's life and from the Judaisms that preceded Christianity. Those persons advanced in the Church, in leadership roles, are able to read these works profitably and discern what is good and right and important, what testifies to Christ, and what is secondary or even potentially harmful and should be discarded.

The Scriptures within Holy Tradition

The Fullness of Christian Tradition in the Life of Faith

IN THE TWENTY-FIRST CENTURY, Christianity has become a stripped-down affair. It now exists as a "belief system." In this system, what separates Christianity from other religions is that the Christian assents to the truth of certain propositions concerning the nature of God, the nature of Christ, the nature of the Bible, and so on. One of the primary sources of intra-Christian disagreement is not even the beliefs themselves, but which of the beliefs are required for Christian identity. For some the list is nonexistent—merely identifying as a Christian makes one a Christian. For others, it is an expansive and deeply theological list from which a single divergence makes a person not a true Christian. One of these disagreements involves what texts—what "books"—should and shouldn't be considered a part of the Bible.

This view of Christianity, however, is a relatively recent development. It represents a denuded and watered-down version even of the teaching of the Protestant Reformers. For the original Protestants, *sola scriptura* did not mean that any text not included in the Bible ought to be thrown in the nearest garbage receptacle and considered heretical. Our Christian forebears lived their lives as Christians within a long and well-developed tradition. Christianity was not a set of beliefs but a way of being in the world. Even the first generation of Christians, that of the apostles, experienced Christ within the context of Israelite and Jewish traditions that stretched back for centuries before them.

"Tradition" is not a series of secret truths handed down from bishop to bishop behind closed doors. It is not an ambiguous body of interpretations that cannot be located in any precise place in any precise way. Christian tradition includes iconography and art, hymnography and music, the reflections of previous generations of Fathers and Mothers on the Scriptures and on the tradition of their era. Tradition includes the history of the crises our forebears faced and how those conflicts were resolved. It includes the safeguards that were put in place to prevent the recurrence of those self-same problems and the threat they posed to life in Christ within the Christian community. Tradition also includes a wide range of preserved texts that frame the intellectual, moral, and experiential world of Christians. These texts reflect the way of life of Christians in various times and places and are preserved to guide the lives of Christians in others.

Tradition Is the Life of the Spirit within the Church

The writings of the Fathers are not a new development after the writing of the final book of the New Testament—completely aside from the fact that a few of the Apostolic Fathers' writings may antedate St. John's Apocalypse. The texts that we find preserved in the Church by the Fathers are found preserved throughout the Second Temple period in Jewish communities and in the apostolic community as well. Christian monastics copied and preserved these texts alongside the writings of the Fathers. They made no distinction between monastic wisdom and extra-biblical wisdom literature, between apocalyptic texts and the revelations of the spiritual world made to the Desert Fathers, or between meditations on the Scriptures in the form of doctrinal texts and those in the form of narrative.

These texts, as is true for ancient iconography, hymnography, and the rest of Holy Tradition, are not mere historical artifacts that require some deference mandated by their great age and long usage. Holy Tradition is the historical expression of the life of the Holy Spirit in the Church. The Spirit is the vehicle by which our way of being in the world—what we call the life in Christ—moves from generation to generation. Tradition is therefore always alive, always in motion; and a person wishing to be a follower of Christ—a Christian—does so by living symbiotically with the Spirit as part of the community of Christians, the Body of Christ, the Church.

Modern attempts to taxonomize the elements of the Christian religion, to boil down Christianity to merely the "necessary" elements, or to cut away whatever is deemed unnecessary or lesser, are attempts at dissection. A living organism cannot be dissected without killing it in the process. In any given Orthodox parish—any particular community living within a branch of living Holy Tradition—only certain texts are read. But in no parish church, nor any diocese, nor any patriarchate or linguistic tradition of the Orthodox Church have those publicly read books been the only texts with authority in the Christian life. The Spirit has always expressed Himself in tradition in a panoply of ways—in writings, in pastoral guidance, in iconography, in hymnography, in discipline, in pastoral theology. Each and all of these must be given their proper role and be allowed to function in order for the church community to live and thrive and give life to the Christians living within it.

Many of the elements of Holy Tradition named here are part of the immediate experience of Orthodox Christian worship. When attending an Orthodox service, one is surrounded by holy icons. Hymnography resounds within the church building. One hears the lives of the saints and the readings from the Scriptures. But other elements of Holy Tradition require more effort to partake of. Many of the Church Fathers write in a way that is difficult to understand, even in translation. But the central works of important Church Fathers are readily available in translation in church libraries and bookstores, and other books are available to explain and interpret these patristic writings for readers.

The texts discussed in this book represent an important segment of Orthodox tradition that has been too long neglected. Most Christians are unfamiliar with even their titles. Within them, however, is a repository of wisdom. These works present us with important links between Scripture and our Christian practice. Technically, every book in the world other than the Bible is extra-biblical literature. Nevertheless, this important part of our heritage has often been ignored because of a stigma that, in a double standard, is not applied to medieval sagas, popular novels, newspapers, and magazines, which are likewise "not in the Bible."

Every generation of the Church is called to appropriate for itself the tradition passed down from our Fathers and Mothers in the Faith. Becoming familiar with the writings that the apostles read and that their disciples wrote fills an important hole in our knowledge of tradition. Potentially, the understanding of these texts may even fill significant holes in our lives.

The Canonical List of St. Nikephoros the Confessor of Constantinople

NINTH CENTURY AD

BOOKS ACCEPTED BY SOME BUT NOT OTHERS	
OLD TESTAMENT	NEW TESTAMENT
Three Books of the Maccabees	Apocalypse of John
Wisdom of Solomon	Apocalypse of Peter
Wisdom of Sirach	Epistle of Barnabas
Psalms and Odes of Solomon	Gospel of the Hebrews
Esther	
Judith	
Susanna	
Tobit, or Tobias	
BOOKS TO BE READ IN PRIVATE	
Enoch	Acts of Paul
Testaments of the Twelve Patriarchs	Acts of Peter
Prayer of Joseph	Acts of John
Testament of Moses	Acts of Thomas
Assumption of Moses	Gospel of Thomas
Book of Abraham	Didache
Eldad and Modad	32 Books of Clement
Book of Elias	Writings of Ignatius, Polycarp, and Hermas
Book of Zephaniah	
Book of Zacharias	
Books of Baruch, Habakkuk, Ezekiel, and Daniel	

Glossary

Adoptionist Christology: The terms *adoptionism* or *adoptionist Christology* describe a certain set of views about the identity of Jesus Christ. Adoptionist views generally hold that Jesus of Nazareth was born as a human, and then at some point in His life (typically, when He was baptized by St. John the Forerunner), God adopted Him as His Son. The Church has condemned these views as heresy; the Church instead teaches that Christ is eternally the Son of God, the Second Person of the Holy Trinity, who has united our human nature to Himself.

Apkallu/Seven Sages: The *apkallu*, sometimes referred to in English translations as the Seven Sages, are spirits that appear in Babylonian historical chronicles such as the Sumerian Kings List. One of these spirits acted as an adviser for each of the kings before the Great Flood. After the Flood, historical documents describe the subsequent kings as two-thirds apkallu and one-third human. These Babylonian stories are related to the story of the Nephilim in Genesis 6:1–4, and the Enochic literature elaborates on them.

Apocryphon: This is the singular of *apocrypha* and literally means "a hidden thing." Though the adjectives "hidden" or "secret" give apocryphal texts an air of mystery, they actually refer to the venue in which these texts are to be read. Texts we now call "canonical" are those that are to be read publicly in the church in worship. Apocrypha are to be read in private. In a separate usage of the term, the seven books in the Roman Catholic Old Testament canon that don't appear in the Protestant canon are sometimes referred to as "the Apocrypha."

Azazel: Leviticus 16 describes the ritual of the Day of Atonement, in which the high priest sacrifices one of two goats to Yahweh, the God of Israel. The casting of lots designates the other as the goat for Azazel, and this goat is driven out into the wilderness, bearing the sins of the people. Though the word *azazel* can literally mean "the goat that goes away," Leviticus 17:7 references goat spirits in the wilderness that pagans (and formerly, the Israelites) worshipped. Within Enochic literature, Azazel is a devil figure, a demonic power who leads his fellow rebel angels in seducing human women with secret wisdom, thereby producing the giants.

Bar Kochva rebellion: The Bar Kochva rebellion was a Judean revolution against the Roman Empire staged from AD 132 to 136. It is frequently referred to as the Third Jewish Revolt, taking place after the First Revolt (AD 66–73) and the Kitos war (AD 115–17). Judea sought to restore its independence of the Hasmonean era, which had ended when Rome annexed the territory in 63 BC. The First Revolt had resulted in the destruction of the second temple and much of Jerusalem, and the Third Revolt was led by Simon bar Kochva, whose name literally means "son of a star." Many Jewish people, including prominent leaders such as Rabbi Akiva, believed Simon bar Kochva to be the Messiah. During the initial success of the rebellion, coins were minted identifying Jerusalem's brief independence as year one of the messianic era. The Roman response under Emperor Hadrian was swift and brutal. Temples to Roman gods were built on important Jewish and Christian holy sites. A new city—called Aelia Capitolina, from Hadrian's given name—was built over the ruins of Jerusalem, and a prominent statue of Hadrian was erected in the city. Jewish people were banned from the new city on all but one day a year, when they were allowed inside to mourn their fallen temple. Rome then began a massive campaign of de-Judaification throughout Judea and other parts of the empire, in which synagogues and shrines were demolished. The name of the Roman province was changed from Judea to Syria Palestine.

Bogomils: The Bogomils were a heretical Christian group centered in the Balkans from the tenth to the fifteenth century AD. Their beliefs appear to have been a late form of Gnosticism, which held that the material world is evil and that only the spiritual is pure. The Bogomils also held that God and Satan were two opposed gods of good and evil who had equal power. They rejected the traditional doctrine of the Holy Trinity and the authority of both the Orthodox Church and the state.

Chiliasm: *Chiliasm* is a catch-all term from the early centuries of Christianity for various beliefs that included a literal earthly paradise under the rule of Christ for a period of a thousand years, before the Last Judgment and the beginning of the age to come. These beliefs were similar but not identical to modern premillennialism in Protestant circles. Ancient chiliasm lacked the premillennialist emphasis on ethnic Judaism, and it taught the existence of a thousand-year period of feasting and earthly pleasures that modern views do not emphasize. In the second century, some mainstream Christian writers seem to have embraced forms of chiliasm, and it also appeared in the belief systems of several early heretical sects, most notably the Montanists. When the Church condemned these sects, it proscribed chiliasm as an unacceptable set of beliefs.

Dead Sea Scrolls: The Dead Sea Scrolls are a set of ancient texts dating from the third century BC to the first century AD found at Wadi Qumran, near the Dead Sea, beginning in 1946. A Jewish sect that the Romans eventually destroyed produced these texts and hid them inside sealed jars in the caves around the wadi. Included among these scrolls are our earliest copies of the Old Testament texts in Hebrew, Aramaic, and Greek. Also included are a number of other works, including some drawn from Enochic literature and some known as "sectarian texts," which the Qumran community generated and that governed their communal way of life. These sectarian texts are unknown elsewhere.

Divine council: The "divine council" is another way to refer to the council of the gods. The nations of the world outside Israel believed that a god who had assumed or seized power—often the latest in a long chain of high gods—presided over this council. In contrast, the Old Testament describes the divine council as consisting of spirits created by the single, eternal, Most High God, who created all things and who is radically unlike His creatures. The Old Testament also shows that God has chosen to administrate the cosmos through these created spiritual beings.

Docetism: Saint Ignatius of Antioch and other early Church Fathers used the term *Docetism* to describe the school of thought of certain sectarian groups. The term comes from the Greek verb *dokeo*, meaning "to appear" or "to seem." These communities taught that Christ is God but that He only appeared or seemed to be human. Rather than viewing Jesus Christ as a Person who had assumed human nature, they taught that Christ was just another appearance of God, or theophany, like those the Old Testament recorded in various places.

Ebionites: *Ebionites* is one common name for an early Christian sect the Church considered heretical. This group was located in Palestine and Syria, and it appears to have emerged directly from particular Jewish sects rather than having split away from the mainstream Church at some point. The Ebionites considered Jesus of Nazareth to be the final human prophet and the Messiah, but they did not view Him as God in any greater sense. Because relatively little direct information exists regarding the Ebionites and their religious life and practice, they are the subject of a great deal of conjecture. This is especially true in Islamic circles, where they are sometimes treated as proto-Muslims.

Elkasaites: The Elkasaites were a Christian Gnostic sect of the second century through the fourth century AD. They operated in the region of the Transjordan, then a part of the Persian Empire. They are primarily known for practicing repeated baptisms, and we know of them only through the critical descriptions of a few Church Fathers and early Christian writers.

Enochic literature: Strictly speaking, the Enochic literature is a group of ancient texts that feature Enoch as their central character. Genesis 5:21–24 describes Enoch, the seventh figure from Adam in the genealogy of Seth, as having walked with God before God took him into heaven. Most of the Enochic literature is apocalyptic in genre and describes Enoch's journey through the underworld and the earth into the heavens, and it also depicts their respective geographies. The term "Enochic literature" sometimes more broadly includes other ancient texts, such as the Apocalypse of Abraham and the Book of Jubilees, which do not feature Enoch as the central character but deal with similar themes and traditions.

Essenes: In his histories, first-century AD Jewish author Josephus described a number of Jewish sects in various parts of the world. One of these was the Essenes, who had withdrawn from the regular religious and civic life of the Judean people into the wilderness in order to hold to a higher standard of holiness. Many scholars have conjectured that the Qumran community was a subgroup of the Essenes or was part of an "Essene movement." Other scholars have surmised that various figures, including St. John the Forerunner or even Christ Himself, were part of an Essene community. All of these, however, remain at the level of conjecture, as there is currently no evidence conclusively linking any of these communities or persons to the group Josephus discussed.

Ge'ez: Ge'ez is the proper name of the late antique and early medieval form of the Semitic dialect spoken and written in Ethiopia. It is sometimes also referred to as Ethiopic. While Amharic has replaced it in popular use, Ge'ez is still a Christian liturgical language and for centuries was used for official matters in a way similar to Western Europe's use of Latin.

Gilgamesh epic: *The Epic of Gilgamesh* is likely the best-known piece of ancient Mesopotamian literature. It dates back to at least the eighteenth century BC, though only fragments of that early version survive. Most English translations are based on later, more complete versions of the text. *The Epic of Gilgamesh* is a collection of stories and traditions surrounding Gilgamesh, the ancient semidivine king of Uruk. Other pieces of ancient Mesopotamian literature contain additional traditions regarding Gilgamesh. The central movement of *The Epic of Gilgamesh* describes the friendship and heroic feats of Gilgamesh and his friend Enkidu. After Enkidu's death, Gilgamesh becomes obsessed with immortality, which leads him to visit Utnapishtim, the ancient survivor of the Great Flood. This story preserves one version of the Mesopotamian story of the Flood. Gilgamesh's quest for immortality is ultimately unsuccessful.

Gnosticism: Saint Irenaeus of Lyons, along with later Christian authors, used the term *Gnosticism* to group together a set of sects within the Roman world of late antiquity. Gnostic communities predated Christianity and generally represented a combination of traditional Greco-Roman religion with various Eastern religious practices, including paganized forms of Judaism and Christianity. The term "Christian Gnosticism," then, differentiates those Gnostic groups that incorporated Christian elements from those who, for example, saw Moses or Hercules as a redeemer figure.

God-fearers: In the first century AD, before the Jewish revolts, Roman culture had a brief fascination with Judaism. The antiquity and strangeness of the traditions that various Jewish groups practiced enchanted many Romans. Wealthy Roman patrons would express their interest by endowing and donating to local synagogues and other Jewish institutions within the Roman Empire. Some would even attend synagogue events. For the vast majority of these Romans, however, the idea of actually entering into Judaism—being circumcised and forswearing traditional Roman religion—was a bridge too far. They therefore remained respected but fringe members of Jewish communities. The Jewish term for these Gentiles was "God-fearers," as they respected and venerated the God of Israel but were not a part of His people. Most of St. Paul's earliest converts to Christianity appear to have come from this group.

Grigori: Slavonic texts often used the term *Grigori* for the Watchers (*see also* Watchers, *below*). It is a shortened form of the Greek word *egregoroi*, or watchers.

Hasmonean dynasty: The Hasmonean dynasty is the succession of kings who ruled over an independent Judea from 140 to 37 BC. The Maccabean revolt managed to gain Judean independence from the Seleucid Greeks, and the

Hasmonean kings sought to secure that independence through foreign alliances with first Sparta and then Rome. The latter alliance ended Hasmonean rule when Rome annexed Judea in 37 BC.

"Historical Jesus" research: In retrospect, a series of movements in the nineteenth and twentieth centuries among biblical scholars have been labeled as three "quests" for the historical Jesus. Over the eighteenth and nineteenth centuries, the way scholars read the Bible changed, particularly in continental Europe, based on a "scientific" approach to history. In this approach, scholars completely excluded miracles or other supernatural phenomena from historical consideration. This led to a proposed distinction between the "Jesus of history" and the "Christ of faith." Various scholars attempted to construct a portrait of Jesus from history that excluded all elements associated with later Christianity. Nearly all scholars now agree that these attempts utterly failed and that the historical Jesus any given scholar proposed tended to reflect the scholar's own self-concept and values.

Hypostasis: "Hypostasis" is the English transliteration of the Greek word generally translated as "substance." A very literal translation of *hypostasis* would be "what stands beneath": hence the Latin *substantia* and the English "substance." In the ancient world, people commonly believed that gods and spirits existed in multiple local forms, with various bodies and appearances, at the same time. In Christian theology, this term's most important use is within the doctrine of the Holy Trinity. Christians worship the one God, the Holy

Trinity, who exists eternally in three hypostases—the Father, the Son, and the Holy Spirit. In the context of the Holy Trinity, *hypostasis* is often translated as "Person."

Incubus: An incubus (plural, *incubi*) is the masculine version of the feminine demonic succubus. These demonic spirits of the ancient world tempted men and women to lust. Incubi were believed to appear in various forms and engage in sexual activity with humans. A number of Church Fathers make reference to incubi and succubi.

Johannine school: Several of the most significant Fathers of the second-century Church are considered members of the Johannine school. The Johannine school was a school of thought rather than a formal educational institution. Notable Fathers in this school include St. Polycarp, Papias, St. Irenaeus of Lyons, and St. Justin Martyr. These Fathers were taught either directly by St. John the Evangelist or by those whom the apostle taught in western Asia Minor, today's western Turkey.

John Hyrcanus: John Hyrcanus was both the Hasmonean king and the high priest of the Jerusalem temple from 135 BC until his death in 104 BC. In addition to being instrumental in forming foreign alliances for the independent Kingdom of Judea, especially with Rome, Hyrcanus greatly expanded the territory of Judea through warfare. His conquests notably included Samaria, which resulted in the destruction of the Samaritan temple on Mount Gerizim. In the first century AD, many in Judea saw Hyrcanus as a heroic figure and an image of who the coming messianic king might be.

Judaisms: In the ancient world, the religious practice of the

Judean people was even more diverse than it is today. Jacob Neusner, a preeminent Jewish scholar of the twentieth century, famously argued that it was more appropriate to speak of Judaisms, rather than one single belief and practice of all Judean people.

Lord of Spirits: First Enoch and other Enochic literature ascribes the title "Lord of Spirits" to the God of Israel. This title identifies Yahweh as the One who is the Lord of all other spiritual beings, none of whom are in the same category as He is.

Maccabean revolt: The Book of 1 Maccabees describes the history of a popular Jewish revolt against the Seleucid Greek rulers in the mid-second century. After Antiochus IV Epiphanes sacrificed pigs to Zeus on the altar of the Jerusalem temple, Judas Maccabeus (or Judah the Hammer) and his brothers led a revolt. This revolt was successful for a time and established an independent Judean state.

Manicheans: Manichaeism was a religion founded by Mani, a self-proclaimed prophet in the Persian Empire of the third century AD. Mani attempted to synthesize traditional Persian Zoroastrianism, the religion of the Persian Empire, with the Buddhism he encountered from the East and with Christianity. From the direction of Manichean thought, the Christianity Mani utilized was more accurately Christian Gnosticism. The Manicheans taught that the world as a whole, and the human soul as a microcosm, was the arena for the eternal battle between God and the devil, whom they saw as eternal principles of good and evil, respectively. Manichaeism saw the material world as primarily reflecting the influence of evil and so taught rigorous, even brutal ascetic practices. At its height, Manichaeism was a religious force stretching from Tibet in the East to Gaul in the West. The rise of Islam destroyed the center of Manichean thought and life, though isolated groups practicing forms of Manichaeism continued to exist throughout Europe and Asia until the late medieval period. Saint Augustine of Hippo is likely the most famous convert from Manichaeism to Christianity.

Man of perdition/man of Belial: Jewish expectation in the first century AD of the coming of the Messiah is well known. Less well known, but apparent in a large portion of Second Temple literature, is the anticipation that an anti-Messiah figure would come to oppose Him. Two common titles for this figure in Second Temple literature are the "man of perdition" and the "man of Belial." The first title describes eternal punishment or condemnation as his destiny; and Belial, literally "the yokeless one" or "the lawless one," is one of the names for the devil. Jewish traditions regarding this anti-Messiah developed into Christian teaching about the Antichrist. For example, St. Paul explicitly uses the language of "the man of lawlessness" to describe the coming Antichrist (2 Thess. 2:1–12).

Mastema: Mastema is the name of a devil figure in Second Temple Jewish literature. He appears in the Book of Jubilees as one of the spirits of the Nephilim whom the Flood destroyed in the days of Noah. As the spirits of the dead giants are being condemned to the abyss, Mastema strikes a bargain with God by which God would allow him and one-tenth of the unclean spirits to remain in the world until the time of the end. God allowed these spirits to remain to torment the wicked, with the intent that these torments might drive them to repentance.

Merkavah: "Merkavah" is the English transliteration of the Hebrew word for "chariot." Merkavah refers specifically to the chariot throne of Yahweh, the God of Israel, that the Prophet Ezekiel saw in his vision (Ezekiel 1). Over time, there developed within ancient and early medieval Judaism a school of prayer and meditative practice known as Merkavah mysticism, which sought access to the vision of the throne Ezekiel had received. There are a number of areas of continuity between Jewish and early Christian mysticism.

Metatron: Metatron, sometimes "the Metatron," is the name of a high-ranking—sometimes the highest-ranking—angelic being in certain Second Temple and early Rabbinic Jewish literature. He functions in some texts as the voice of God or His representative in creation. The angelic Metatron became the repository in many Jewish circles for earlier traditions regarding a second power in heaven, or a second hypostasis of the God of Israel, in response to Christian applications of these traditions to Jesus Christ.

Midrash: Midrash is a form of Jewish commentary on Scripture. Most midrash incorporates the commentary directly into the text itself. Someone who is unfamiliar with the original text of Scripture may have difficulty separating the two. This mode of interpretation sometimes appears within the New Testament itself, and both Jewish and early Christian authors heavily employed it.

Muratorian Canon: The Muratorian Canon is a manuscript

fragment containing one of the earliest known listings of Christian texts that would become the New Testament. As a fragment, it is preserved in a later, seventh-century Latin manuscript. The Greek original dates to roughly AD 170. The Muratorian Canon lists all the books contained in the New Testament except Hebrews, James, 1 and 2 Peter, and 2 and 3 John. In addition to books contained in the Christian New Testament, it also adds the Apocalypse of Peter and the Wisdom of Solomon; the latter is included in the Orthodox and Roman Catholic Old Testaments. In addition, the fragment recommends the Shepherd of Hermas but identifies it as a book not read publicly. It goes on to condemn a number of early Gnostic writings.

Naga: Nagas are semidivine beings featured in many ancient stories and traditions from Southeast Asia. These stories and traditions depicted nagas as part human and part serpent, similar to many supernatural beings across the ancient Near East who had human-animal hybrid forms. They are believed to be descended from the consort of one of the seven ancient sages.

Nag Hammadi library: The Nag Hammadi library is the name of a collection of ancient Gnostic texts discovered at Nag Hammadi in Egypt in 1945. This collection was uncovered in a monk's burial site and includes non-Christian texts, such as Plato's *Timaeus*, as well as Gnostic works that communities practicing Christian forms of Gnosticism used. A few of the texts were already known; other titles were referenced in the Church Fathers and other works, but the full texts had been previously unavailable. Before the discovery, the largest collection of still-existing Gnostic texts was the Jung Codex, named for its compiler, psychoanalyst C. G. Jung.

Nephilim: *Nephilim* is the Hebrew transliteration of a word meaning "giants." The cognate Aramaic word *nephilin* makes this clear. This word does not merely describe a person as having a large physical size: both it and the Greek word used to translate it in the Old Testament, *gigantes*, also refers to a tyrant, bully, or thug. In English, the term "strongman" for an authoritarian dictator has a similar usage. The Scriptures thereby describe the god-kings of the pagan nations not as heroes but as villains.

Pederasty: Pederasty was an institution of Greek—and later, Roman—life. The term literally refers to an adult male who practices *eros* toward a child, and the children involved were often enslaved people. Roman records reveal that this practice took place with children as young as eight years old. Roman culture found this practice perfectly acceptable, and literature from ancient Greece and Rome romanticized it. Christians immediately ended pederasty in the Roman Empire once they achieved social power.

Pedophthoreseis: *Pedophthoreseis*, or "defilers of children," is the term early Christians used to describe the Greek and Roman institution of pederasty, which they viewed with disgust. The earliest Christian sources, including the Epistle of Barnabas and the Didache, use this term.

Q source: The Gospels of Matthew, Mark, and Luke are called the "synoptic Gospels" because they present the same perspective on Christ. When the three are placed in parallel and compared, there are a number of passages in Matthew and

Luke that contain nearly identical wording. These passages
do not appear in Mark. One way biblical scholars have
sought to explain the identical passages is to hypothesize a
now lost source document. These scholars refer to this hypo-
thetical document as *Quelle*, the German word for "source."
It is often simply abbreviated as Q. Papias, at the end of the
first century, mentions that St. Matthew recorded the *logia* of
Christ before he wrote his Gospel. Many scholars see this as
evidence of the existence of a Q document.

Qumran community: The Qumran community produced the
Dead Sea Scrolls. This dissident community in Judea lived
in Wadi Qumran, a ravine near the Dead Sea. They believed
that all Judean religion, including the Sadducees, Pharisees,
and other groups, had been corrupted. In response to this
widespread apostasy, they went into the desert to preserve
true, pure religion. In their view, the emblem of the Judean
authorities' compromise was their failure to use the Enochic
calendar (the calendar 1 Enoch described), which the Qumran community held to be mathematically perfect.

Recension: A recension is a revised or edited version of a text.
The word *recension* applies to ancient texts in two senses:
First, most ancient traditions originally existed in oral form,
and cultures passed them down without putting them into
writing. Then, when these traditions and stories were first
put into written form, composition took place in different
places, in different dialects, and in slightly different forms.
Going forward, these different forms of a text would often be
compiled or edited together. Any of these particular versions
of the text is, properly speaking, a recension. Second, the

term *recension* also refers to deliberate edits to a text. So, for example, many pre-Christian Jewish texts, over the course of copying and transmission, passed through the hands of Christians. Along the way, Christian scribes sometimes made what they saw as corrections or added explanatory material to the text to show its connection to Christ. Such an emended text would be a Christian recension of the text in question.

Satans: In Hebrew, the word *satan* means "enemy" or "adversary." When it refers to a particular evil spiritual being, it generally occurs in Hebrew with the definite article: that is, "the Satan." The term also sometimes appears in the plural to refer to malign and unclean spirits in general as "satans."

Second Temple Jewish literature: Throughout the Second Temple period, Jewish communities centered in Judea, in Mesopotamia, and in Alexandria, Egypt, produced a vast quantity of literature in a variety of genres. Most of these works are not included in the canonical Scriptures of any Christian church or of Rabbinic Judaism, though Christians in later times found some of this literature important and preserved it. The Old Testament section of this book treats some of this preserved literature.

Second Temple Judaism: "Judaism" is a broad term that describes the religion of the people of Judea: the Jewish people. Judaism has always been diverse, in both ancient and modern times, and Second Temple Judaism refers to the multiple forms of Judaism practiced by Jewish communities in various places during the Second Temple period.

Second Temple period: Solomon built the first temple in

Jerusalem, which Babylonian invaders destroyed circa 587–586 BC when they took Judah into exile. Seventy years later, when the people of Judah were allowed to return to the land, they built a second temple in Jerusalem. They further built up this temple and developed it until the Romans destroyed it in AD 70. The period of time from about 515 BC to AD 70 is therefore referred to as the Second Temple period.

Targum: The Targums are Aramaic versions of various ancient Hebrew texts. They chiefly include the books that came to make up the Hebrew Scriptures, but a wide array of other traditions regarding biblical persons and events are also incorporated directly into the text. Because of these additions, when a Targum was read in the synagogue, that reading was accompanied by a reading of the original Hebrew in order to make the additions and expansions apparent. While the Targums preserve a wide array of pre-Christian and early Rabbinic Jewish traditions, they never enjoyed the authoritative status of the Greek translations of the Hebrew Scriptures during the pre-Christian era.

Targum Pseudo-Jonathan: Targum Pseudo-Jonathan is one of the Aramaic Targums (*see* Targum, *above*). There is considerable debate about the date of the final compilation of the text. Some have dated it as early as the fifth century AD, though it contains material that is clearly medieval and dates from closer to the time of the Crusades. Likely, Targum Pseudo-Jonathan contains some material dating to the early Rabbinic period or even preceding Rabbinic Judaism, but the text took on its final form with some late-stage editing and additions during the Middle Ages. The proper name of this text is Targum Jerusalem, which distinguishes it from Targum Onkelos, compiled in Mesopotamia. Owing to confusion surrounding the first printed edition, the text of Targum Jerusalem was first published as Targum Jonathan Ben Uziel. Once the confusion was revealed, Targum Pseudo-Jonathan became the most common way to refer to the text.

Testament: English translations of the Bible sometimes use the term "testament" as a synonym for "covenant." An example of this is the division of the Scriptures into the Old Testament and the New Testament. A testament is also a genre of literature that was popular in Second Temple Jewish circles. Testaments generally follow the format of Genesis 49, in which Jacob, on his deathbed, blesses his sons and makes certain prophetic statements regarding the future of the tribes that will bear their names.

Tractates (Talmud): The Second Temple period included a massive flowering of Jewish literary activity. Following the Bar Kochva rebellion in the early second century AD, as Judaism regrouped and faced Christianity as a significant rival upon their separation, Rabbinic circles placed a ban on this literary activity. While early Christians continued to produce a wide range of literature, Rabbinic Jewish circles passed down traditions orally for several centuries within rabbinic schools. Then, beginning in the fourth century, a movement within Rabbinic Judaism sought to finally codify the traditions and teachings of the rabbis in the intervening centuries. Jewish communities in various parts of the world recorded these teachings piecemeal in what became known as tractates, with individual names like Tractate Sanhedrin or Tractate Hagigah. These tractates were then brought together into small collections, followed by larger collections, the Mishnah and Gemara. Ultimately these larger collections were themselves collected into what became known as the Talmud. There are two different versions of the Talmud: the Babylonian Talmud, compiled in Mesopotamia; and the Palestinian or Jerusalem Talmud.

Watchers: The Watchers are a group of angelic beings within the spiritual realm that Scripture refers to in the Book of Daniel. The Book of Enoch also uses the term in the first major portion of the Book of the Watchers, where the angels follow Azazel in consorting with human women and falling into sin. As their punishment, these angels were imprisoned in Tartarus. The fallen Watchers, under this and other names, also appear in other Enochic literature.

Further Reading

The texts discussed in this book, as well as a wealth of others, can be found in the following collections:

Charlesworth, James H., ed. *Old Testament Pseudepigrapha*. 2 vols. New York: Doubleday, 1983.

Schneemelcher, Wilhelm, ed. *New Testament Apocrypha*. 2 vols. Louisville, KY: Westminster John Knox, 1991.

Apostolic Fathers. 2 vols. Edited and translated by Bart D. Ehrman. Loeb Classical Library 24. Cambridge, MA: Harvard University Press, 2003.

Index

Note: Books prefixed with a number are alphabetically sorted according to the name of the book. For example, 1, 2, 3, and 4 Maccabees can all be found by searching for Maccabees.

We hope you have enjoyed and benefited from this book. Your financial support makes it possible to continue our non-profit ministry both in print and online. Because the proceeds from our book sales only partially cover the costs of operating **Ancient Faith Publishing** and **Ancient Faith Radio**, we greatly appreciate the generosity of our readers and listeners. Donations are tax deductible and can be made at **www.ancientfaith.com**.

To view our other publications,
please visit our website: **store.ancientfaith.com**

 **ANCIENT FAITH RADIO**

Bringing you Orthodox Christian music, readings,
prayers, teaching, and podcasts 24 hours a day since 2004 at
www.ancientfaith.com

CPSIA information can be obtained
at www.ICGtesting.com
Printed in the USA
LVHW042010020523
745889LV00007B/515